R

P9-BJU-533

Philosophy, and Theory

Is it possible for postmodernism to offer viable accounts of ethics? Can these accounts be coherent and stable? Or are our social and intellectual worlds now too fragmented to provide any broad consensus about the moral life? These issues have emerged in recent decades as some of the most contentious in literary and philosophical studies. In *Renegotiating Ethics in Literature, Philosophy, and Theory*, a distinguished international gathering of philosophers and literary scholars addresses some of the major reconceptualisations involved in this so-called 'turn towards ethics'. An important feature of this 'turn' has been a renewed interest in the literary text as a focus for the exploration of ethical issues. Exponents of this trend include Charles Taylor, Bernard Williams, Iris Murdoch, Cora Diamond, Richard Rorty, and Martha Nussbaum – a contributor and a key figure in this volume. The book tries to assess the significance of this development for ethical and literary theory. *Renegotiating Ethics in Literature, Philosophy, and Theory* also attempts to articulate an alternative postmodern account of ethics which does not rely on earlier appeals to universal truths.

JANE ADAMSON, formerly Senior Lecturer in English at the Australian National University, is the author of *Othello: Some Problems of Judgement and Feeling* and *Troilus and Cressida*.

RICHARD FREADMAN, Professor of English at La Trobe University, is the author of *Eliot, James and the Fictional Self: a Study in Character and Narration*; (with Seamus Miller) *Re-thinking Theory: a Critique of Contemporary Literary Theory and an Alternative Account*, and editor of *Literary Theory and Philosophy: A Cross-Disciplinary Encounter*.

DAVID PARKER, Reader in English, Australian National University, is author of *Ethics, Theory and the Novel*, and editor of *Shame and the Modern Self*.

Literature, Culture, Theory

General editors

ANTHONY CASCARDI, *University of California, Berkeley*
and RICHARD MACKSEY, *The Johns Hopkins University*

Renegotiating Ethics in Literature, Philosophy, and Theory

edited by

JANE ADAMSON, RICHARD FREADMAN,
DAVID PARKER

CAMBRIDGE
UNIVERSITY PRESS

PUBLISHED BY THE PRESS SYNDICATE OF THE UNIVERSITY OF CAMBRIDGE
The Pitt Building, Trumpington Street, Cambridge CB2 1RP, United Kingdom

CAMBRIDGE UNIVERSITY PRESS
The Edinburgh Building, Cambridge CB2 2RU, United Kingdom
40 West 20th Street, New York, NY 10011–4211, USA
10 Stamford Road, Oakleigh, Melbourne 3166, Australia

First published 1998

Printed in the United Kingdom at Biddles Limited, Guildford

Typeset in Palatino 10/12.5 pt   [VN]

A catalogue record for this book is available from the British Library

ISBN 0 521 62079 1 hardback
ISBN 0 521 62938 1 paperback

Contents

vii

Contents

Introduction: the turn to ethics in the 1990s

DAVID PARKER

This volume starts from the perception that in 'advanced' literary circles for most of the 1970s and 1980s, few topics could have been more uninteresting, more dépassé, less likely to attract budding young theorists, than the topic Ethics and Literature. For most of that period, explicit 'ethical criticism', to borrow Wayne Booth's phrase, had 'fallen on hard times'.[1] I will say nothing about what Booth might have regarded as the good times for ethical criticism, the 1950s and 1960s, that period when straw dinosaurs walked the earth – we are perhaps still too close to those times to say anything useful about them. On the other hand, there is reason to think that, at the more humble level of undergraduate pedagogy at least, ethical criticism has continued on among us alive and well. Frederic Jameson, one of the most vehement critics of ethical interests in literature, said fifteen years ago that when most teachers or students of literature ask of a novel or a poem, 'What does it mean?', the predominant 'code' in terms of which an answer is expected is the 'ethical'. 'What does *Lord Jim* mean?', for example, is a coded demand that we talk about the moral conflicts of the hero. Jameson's point is that literature, even the latest novel, always comes to us through what he calls 'sedimented reading habits and categories developed by ... inherited interpretive traditions'.[2] Put simply, when our

---

[1] Wayne Booth, *The Company We Keep: An Ethics of Fiction* (Berkeley, 1988), chapter 2.
[2] Frederic Jameson, *The Political Unconscious: Narrative as a Socially Symbolic Act* (Ithaca, 1981), p. 9.

critical traditions are formed by the likes of Aristotle, Pope, Dr Johnson, Matthew Arnold, Henry James, F. R. Leavis, and Lionel Trilling, it is small wonder that we highly educated Western readers may share a prejudice (in Gadamer's sense) in favour of both ethical interpretation and literature that offers moral insight. Indeed, what we think important enough to call 'literature' in the first place will be partly constituted by the demand that works offer such insight. If this is circular, it is less a vicious circle than an hermeneutical one, and something about which we can be reasonably relaxed.

Despite these traditional presumptions about literature and the ethical, or perhaps because of them, most avant-garde Anglo-American literary theory in recent years has been either more or less silent about ethics or deeply suspicious of it. The oddness of this state of affairs is registered by a number of contributors to this volume: Charles Altieri, Tony Coady and Seumas Miller, Cora Diamond and Simon Haines. In *Love's Knowledge: Essays on Philosophy and Literature* (New York and Oxford, 1990), Martha Nussbaum talks of the strange 'absence of the ethical' in literary theory. She notes that amidst literary theory's deep interests in such areas of philosophy as epistemology, semantics, and ontology, and despite its multitudinous references to figures such as Nietzsche and Heidegger, the work of leading contemporary moral philosophers such as John Rawls, Bernard Williams, and Thomas Nagel is hardly noticed at all. This is especially hard to understand, she says, as it is a time of great ferment in moral philosophy: 'One cannot find for generations – since the time of John Stuart Mill, if not earlier – an era in which there has been so much excellent, adventurous, and varied work on the central ethical and political questions of human life.' Nussbaum goes on to suggest that in view of the importance of this work, literary theory's apparent uninterest in it is itself significant:

it signals a further striking absence: the absence, from literary theory, of the organising questions of moral philosophy, and of moral philosophy's sense of urgency about these questions. The sense that we are social beings puzzling out, in times of great moral difficulty, what might be, for us, the best way to live – this sense of practical importance, which animates contemporary ethical theory and has always animated much of great literature, is absent from the writings of many of our leading literary theorists. (pp. 169–70)

2

The urgency of Nussbaum's own tone shouldn't lead us to over-look the fact that there has been engaged, urgent, practice-oriented literary theory in the past twenty years. Most of it has been political, concerned with issues of race, gender, class, and sexuality. But what Nussbaum calls 'the organising questions of moral philosophy', and specifically the question of how we should live, are rarely if ever explicitly addressed.

But then does this lack of explicitness necessarily mean there has been an 'absence of the ethical', or at least a significant turn away from it, in Anglo-American literary theory and criticism in the seventies and eighties? One answer is surely not: the period has been dominated by forms of political and post-structuralist criticism that are at the very least implicitly ethical. According to this view, ethical criticism has remained the predominant mode of criticism in this period. This is Wayne Booth's argument in *The Company We Keep*. What he calls the 'new overtly ethical and political' feminist, neo-Marxist, and anti-racist movements, as well as the earlier structuralist and deconstructive 'formalism', both 'have an ethical program in mind' (p. 5).

To this extent, I would agree with Booth. These days, even the most linguistically focused recovery of the marginalised Other of a logocentric philosophical or literary text at least implicitly links itself with the defence of those who have been Other to Western imperialism, to patriarchy or to bourgeois interests. As Seyla Benhabib puts it, one of the defining perceptions of this period is that the 'logic of binary oppositions is also a logic of subordination and domination'.[3] It is hard to see how a concern with such evils as 'subordination and domination' is not at least implicitly oriented towards a conception of a good life centring around goods such as freedom, self-expression, and self-realisation. And in practice, some forms of feminism especially have explicitly developed a picture of human flourishing not simply in terms of 'thin' concepts such as social justice and equality but also drawing on 'thicker' conceptions of human character which tend to revalue such goods as connectedness, emotional responsiveness, and care as alternatives to an allegedly masculinist concern with moral autonomy, rationality, and obligation. Of all the various forms of the politics of difference that have emerged strongly in the past

---

[3] Seyla Benhabib, *Situating the Self: Gender, Community and Postmodernism in Contemporary Ethics* (Cambridge, 1992), p. 15.

twenty years, feminism (see Annette Baier's 'Ethics in many different voices', below) has perhaps gone further than the others in recognising the need for explicit debate over such central questions in moral philosophy as the role of traditions, essences, and universals.

At the same time, some forms of feminism and much neo-Marxist criticism and literary theory have been at the very least ambivalent towards the whole sphere of the ethical. For example, Terry Eagleton's influential book, *Literary Theory: An Introduction*, veers between a somewhat reductive view of ethics and a fuller and more adequate one. On the one hand, the moral is restricted to a meiopic concern with 'immediate interpersonal relations', as opposed to the political, which can put such relations into the broader view of 'our whole material conditions of existence'. The assumption is that to see things politically, from a neo-Marxist perspective, is to see them as they are, 'in their full implications' (p. 208). In their chapter, C. A. J. Coady and Seumas Miller ('Literature, power, and the recovery of philosophical ethics') talk in detail about this sort of view, which boils down to the idea that the ethical is ideological, or a form of false consciousness, the true alternative to which is political consciousness. But Eagleton does not quite go that far here and argues that political argument is what he calls '*genuine* moral argument', which implicitly concedes that moral thought might extend well beyond the sphere of 'immediate interpersonal relations'. Here Eagleton goes some way towards a more adequate conception of the ethical, one which recognises that ultimately there is no excluding the question 'How should a human being live?' from political reflection, any more than we can permanently exclude the political from reflection on interpersonal relations. Richard Bernstein, in his book on the 'ethical–political horizons of post-modernity', is surely right when he says that although 'we can distinguish ethics and politics, they are inseparable. For we cannot understand ethics without thinking through our political commitments and responsibilities. And there is no understanding of politics that does not bring us back to ethics.'[4] (In part 3, Martha Nussbaum insists on the same point in her 'Literary imagination in public life'.) To underline this inseparability, Bernstein uses the phrase

---

[4] Richard Bernstein, *The New Constellation: The Ethical–Political Horizons of Modernity/Postmodernity* (Cambridge, 1991), p. 9.

'ethical–political', which is an attractive solution in some ways, and one which reminds us of why Booth was right in calling all the political movements that have dominated literary discourse in recent years forms of ethical criticism.

But the reason why we cannot simply talk of the 'ethical–political' at this stage, and the main reason why Booth's argument is inadequate, is that one dominant vein of political criticism in recent years has been hostile to ethics and has either ignored it or disavowed any connection with it. This is the vein represented in its least compromising form by Frederic Jameson. In his work, Marxism becomes a master-narrative in terms of which ethics must be constantly deconstructed. The essential thrust of Jameson's case against ethics is that it legitimates by universalising into a system of binary moral oppositions the characteristics of one group or class *versus* another, so that 'evil' inevitably denotes imagined characteristics of those who are Other to the hegemonic group. Thus ethics is an ideological mask of the will-to-power of the dominant class, or, as others would put it, race or gender.

It is reasonable to concede that ethics *can* be ideological in this way. Ethics can be unconsciously masculinist or bourgeois, unwittingly privileging a certain sort of gender-biased conception of autonomous rationality or certain class-biased conceptions of social order. Indeed I would want to suggest that one of the permanently valuable legacies of the political literary theory of the seventies and eighties has been precisely to keep reminding us of the historically and culturally contingent basis of formations like ethics and the so-called literary canon, which therefore cannot be unproblematically conceived of as timeless or universal.[5] On the other hand, the characteristic weakness of such theory has been to suggest that that such formations are *nothing but* the masks of ideology. It is this 'nothing but' which is the signal weakness of Jameson's enterprise, a weakness with significant ethical implications.

One important element of Jameson's case is his claim that ethics is inevitably 'judgmental', following a simple binary pattern of me

---

[5] There has, of course, been a great deal of discussion in recent years of precisely this point. See for example, Barbara Herrnstein Smith, *Contingencies of Value: Alternative Perspectives for Critical Theory* (Cambridge, Mass., 1988); Richard Freadman and Seumas Miller, *Re-thinking Theory: A Critique of Contemporary Literary Theory and an Alternative Account* (Cambridge, 1992); David Parker, *Ethics, Theory and the Novel* (Cambridge, 1994).

and my group 'good', the Other and her group 'evil'. Once again, it is reasonable to concede that moral judgments can be like this and often are. Judgmentalism (or 'moralism'– see Coady, below) is a permanent possibility within ethics so long as my focus on the perceived difference between me and the Other is not qualified by a perception of commonality between us. Where Jameson's account is deficient, however, is in not recognising this perception of commonality as a possibility *within ethics*, a possibility which is, after all, central in the Judeo-Christian tradition. The *locus classicus* is the familiar gospel story of the woman taken in adultery: the Pharisees are ready to stone her to death as they are bound by law to do, until they are prompted to look into their consciences and see that none of them is without sin either. That is, they are prompted to recognise an element of commonality with her, at which moment they transcend the self/other binarism of their judgmental attitude. In 'Common understanding and individual voices' (part 3), Raimond Gaita discusses the ethical implications of what he calls 'the "we" of fellowship' as opposed to cultural and other classificatory forms of judgmentalism.

My claim is that, partly constituted as we in Western societies are by the Judeo-Christian tradition, among others, non-judgmentalism is not merely an abstract possibility for us, but one which is part of our cultural milieu and identity. In fact the very term, 'non-judgmental', surely owes its modern connotation to a tradition of spiritual and moral discrimination mediated to us, among other ways, by our literature: by *Measure for Measure* or *The Scarlet Letter* or *Daniel Deronda*, the subject of Lisabeth During's chapter in the first part of this book. And these are only some of the most explicit examples.

Another claim I would make is that judgmentalism, the powerful temptation in us to divide the world self-righteously into simple binaries, is a possibility within any belief system that is oriented towards some conception of the good, be it religious, ethical, or political. Pharisaism is as much a temptation of Marxism or feminism as it is of any theological creed or moral commitment: all can degenerate into dividing the world rigidly into sheep and goats. And all can search out the goats, and all the secret ideological hiding-places of goatism, with puritanical self-righteousness. What begins as a just project for the proper political recognition of difference can easily tip over into a zealous intolerance of it. It is this intolerance that has come to be called 'political correctness'.

One powerful reason why an explicit ethical criticism is needed as well as political criticism, and why Booth is seriously mistaken in simply conflating them, emerges from this example of judgmentalism. The example shows why there is permanent need for a criticism that foregrounds the organising questions of ethics, a need for an ethical vocabulary in which to articulate the humanly destructive impulsions that can lurk precisely in the thirst for righteousness, including political righteousness. My point is that just as ethics can have a political unconscious, so politics can have an ethical unconscious, which expresses itself nowhere more dangerously than when it tries to repress specifically ethical reflection altogether. What follows is that there is also permanent need for a literary discourse that goes further than ideological demystification and puts us back in touch with those most complex and exhaustive forms of ethical inquiry available, classic works of literature.

But then to talk so blandly about literature and ethical inquiry is surely to forget where we are in time, to forget that we do not simply live post-Marx and post-Nietzsche, but post-Saussure and perhaps post-Derrida. Once again, not quite so, according to Booth. When we turn to the more formalist end of the theoretical and critical spectrum of the seventies and eighties, that is, to deconstruction, we discover that, as Booth put it, even this displays 'a belief that a given way of reading ... is what will do us most good'.

There are two important points to be made here. First, there has been significant work in the past few years persuasively arguing precisely Booth's point. For example, Tobin Siebers in his book *The Ethics of Criticism* (Ithaca, 1988) points to the tacit ethics of post-structuralist theory and criticism. As Siebers says: 'Whether we assert a theory of the self or deny it, we remain within the sphere of ethics' (p. 5); in other words, we draw, even if only sketchily, some picture of human character, some vision of human flourishing. But the second thing that needs to be said on this subject is that very recently deconstruction has begun to present its way of reading texts, its rigorous resistance to closure, as an ethical imperative. Viewed in this way, the ethical imperative is a dynamic within language itself to which deconstructive reading is alone properly responsive. This has been something of a sub-theme in the work of Julia Kristeva, Jacques Derrida, and Paul de Man, but it has suddenly become a major theme in the past five or six years with the publication of Barbara Johnson's *A World of Difference* (Baltimore, 1987) and Hillis Miller's *The Ethics of Reading* (New York, 1987). The contemporary importance of this theme is emphasised by two recent books, *The Ethics of Deconstruction: Derrida and Levinas* (Oxford, 1992) by Simon Critchley, and *Getting it Right: Language, Literature and Ethics* (Chicago, 1992), by Geoffrey Galt Harpham. The interest, or cluster of interests, expressed in all these works in the points of intersection between post-structuralism and ethics was hardly visible at all ten years ago. This is important evidence for the claim that there has been a significant and recent turn to the ethical in literary studies.

But then if it seems so clear now that post-structuralism, like political criticism, was always already crypto-ethical if not explicitly so, why was that not so clear ten years ago in literary theory's confident expansive phase? The reason is that, like much political criticism of the period, post-structuralism seemed to be antipathetic in several significant ways to any interest in what would seem the most obvious ethical dimension of literature, that is to say, the narrative or dramatic presentation of moral questions, dilemmas, embodied in characters, imagined agents, lives, selves or subjectivities.

Deconstruction ruled out such moral interest in at least two ways. First, it has insisted that literary meaning is finally undecidable, so the very notion of determinate 'moral questions' or 'dilemmas' is defeated in the end by the instabilities within language itself. Secondly, deconstruction has presented the inner life of moral deliberation, intentionality and choice not as something prior to language but as a mere effect of language. Thus the supposedly autonomous rational subject of Kantian ethics is de-centred into the various different discourses of which he is constituted. In this way, any interest in character or imagined characters, selves or subjects is displaced by a rigorous attention to the differential system of signs in which such 'traces' allegedly have their only being. A number of authors in this volume, including Altieri, Freadman, and Wiltshire, reject such eviscerated accounts of agency and argue that various forms of 'literary' discourse – poetry, autobiography, pathography – reflect complex modes of individual agency and envision new modes that such agency might take.

By a curious twist it is precisely the deconstruction of (humanist) Ethics which has now emerged (along with much new attention to Emmanuel Levinas) as the Ethics of Deconstruction. A key starting point in this enterprise is the following passage from Paul de Man's *Allegories of Reading* (New Haven, 1979):

Allegories are always ethical, the term ethical designating the structural interference of two value systems. In this sense, ethics has nothing to do with the will ... of a subject, nor *a fortiori*, with a relationship between subjects. The ethical category is imperative ... to the extent that it is linguistic and not subjective. Morality is a version of the same language aporia that gave rise to such concepts as 'man' or 'love' or 'self', and not the cause and consequence of such concepts. The passage to an ethical tonality does not result from a transcendental imperative but is the referential (and therefore unreliable) version of a linguistic confusion. Ethics ... is a discursive mode among others.

I find a great deal of interest in this view of the ethical, but believe that anyone embracing it needs to answer the following set of challenges. Does not de Man here fall into the philosophical trap referred to by Richard Bernstein as the 'grand Either/Or'? That is, is he not offering us a set of false alternatives? Either subjectivity is a transcendental signified or it is just an effect of language; either morality is grounded in such metaphysical concepts as 'man', 'love', or 'self' or it is nothing but a 'language aporia'. And in the end, does this not amount to saying that either morality is as conceived by Kant or it is nothing substantive at all?

There is of course an alternative view that de Man may not have been aware of in the late seventies, but which can hardly be missed by anyone reading moral philosophy today. The version of it that seems to me to offer the most serious challenge to deconstruction is Charles Taylor's. In *Human Agency and Language: Philosophical Papers* (Cambridge, 1985), Taylor argues that all the interesting insights in the relations between subjectivity and language lie in the space between two extreme hypotheses, each of which gives one of the terms absolute priority over the other. The first, what post-Saussureans call logocentrism, 'centres everything on the subject, and exalts a quite unreal model of self-clarity and control', which obscures the fact that the 'speaking agent' is enmeshed in larger forms of order (including the linguistic), 'which he can never fully oversee, and can only marginally and punctually refashion'. The opposite extreme hypothesis is post-Saussureanism itself, which posits a view of 'the code as ultimate, dominating the supposedly autonomous agent'. What Taylor calls the 'space between' these extreme hypotheses consists firstly of the idea that we are only moral subjects at all because we are parts of a language community; we are only deliberating agents or selves within what he calls society's 'webs of interlocution'. (See Altieri, below, for his related notion of 'a grammatical vision of social interdependency'.) But at the same time, the practical reason that is the cornerstone of ethics can only begin in what Taylor calls our 'moral intuitions'. These intuitions are indeed partly constituted by language and culture, but it is reductive and in any case *beside the point* to regard them as mere effects of language. To think of them in this way violates what he calls the 'B.A. [best account] Principle'. In *Sources of the Self* (Cambridge, 1989), Taylor spends a great deal of time with the question of why we should regard any 'thin' account of ethics, which includes any naturalistic or sceptical reduction of it, as the best account we can give. He asks the question: 'What ought to trump the language in which I actually live my life?' In doing so, he makes the crucial point that the virtue of this lived 'thick' language is that it expresses our moral intuitions in a way that the 'thin' language does not. His point is that any language that does not allow us to express these is language about something else, a language which is subtly constraining us to talk about another subject.

But if our moral ontology springs from the best account of the human domain we can arrive at, and if this account must be in anthropocentric terms, terms which relate to the meanings things have for us, then the demand to start outside of all such meanings, not to rely on our moral intuitions or on what we find morally moving, is in fact a proposal to change the subject.[6]

When he talks here of the demand to start outside of the 'meanings things have for us', Taylor's principal target is that naturalistic reduction of ethics which demands that all conversations begin in a scientific or 'absolute conception' of things. But what he says applies equally to any account of the human domain that would make language itself 'ultimate' and demand that we start from the

---

[6] Taylor's *Sources of the Self*, p. 72.

premise that all 'moral intuitions' and feelings and 'anthropocentric meanings' are mediated by a differential play of linguistic
signs in which meaning is endlessly deferred. A Taylorian reply to
this would bracket the question of whether the post-Saussurean
claims are 'true' or not; it would point out that, insofar as post-
structuralism deflects us from taking certain 'anthropocentric
meanings' seriously, it is simply irrelevant to those meanings.
Demands that we begin with the linguistic sign, or with 'discourse', or with power relations in society, are proposals to
change the subject.

'Moral intuitions', the 'meanings things have for us', 'what we
find morally moving': taking this sort of language seriously, and
the account of practical reason it entails, removes us far from the
discursive worlds of ethical sceptics like J. L. Mackie and Paul de
Man. But it also takes us just as far from the foundationalist
discourse of Kant. Kant's demand that moral thought begin with
normative, universalisable principles is also a demand to start
outside the 'meanings things have for us'. And as has been argued
many times since Hegel, Kant's 'thin' procedural reason is hardly
self-sufficient in establishing moral obligation if it is dis-embed-
ded from a whole range of shared, 'thick' cultural assumptions. As
a Gadamerian would say, what we make of a Kantian deductive
moral argument would depend on fore-understandings rooted in
our traditions and historical moment. I mention Gadamer because
he seems to be an important precursor of the new developments in
Anglo-American moral philosophy summed up by the terms
'anti-foundationalist' and 'neo-pragmatist'. Taylor, rather like
Richard Rorty, implicitly accepts the hermeneutic circularity of
values. In fact what lies behind Taylor's 'we' and 'us' is an account
of moral ontology (a better account than Rorty's) rooted in history
and tradition rather than any meta-ethical theory. For Taylor,
meta-ethical theory promises to provide algorithmic moral validation but ends up narrowing the space of the ethical to that which
can be so validated. Kantianism thus constricts the ethical to the
purely rational, leaving no space for moral feeling (see Nussbaum,
Diamond, and Gaita, below), for 'what we find morally moving',
nor any space for considerations of disposition, virtue or character. If 'moral intuitions' are going to be the starting point of
practical reason, then we are very close to a neo-Aristotelian
account of the virtues. Thus Taylor shows his affinities with the

well-known work of Alasdair MacIntyre, Martha Nussbaum, and Bernard Williams. I have focussed on Taylor because his work, together with that of Rorty and the neo-Aristotelians I have just mentioned, represents a significant way around the impasse, the set of false alternatives, that disables post-structuralist as much as more old-fashioned positivist thought: either we accept a meta-physical foundationalist case for morality or we regard it as a 'language aporia'. In the work of Charles Taylor and the others, the conversation in moral philosophy has moved on.

In this volume, Simon Haines ('Deepening the self: the language of ethics and the language of literature') talks in detail about this recent work in moral philosophy and its implications for literary criticism.

What impact are philosophers such as Taylor, Rorty, Nussbaum, and Bernard Williams having on contemporary literary discourse? Not much probably, if we take 'contemporary literary discourse' in the widest sense. As ever, novels, plays, and poetry continue to be published, and some of these continue to show why literature is rightly esteemed as a highly particularised, complex and richly contextualised mode of ethical reflection – a uniquely valuable mode, according to Nussbaum, Adamson, Diamond, Freadman, Haines, and Wiltshire, because it is able to ponder moral questions in ways unavailable to conventional philosophical discourse. And, as ever, literary criticism has continued throughout this recent period as a highly developed and ever-evolving set of practices that at best have remained finely responsive to, and acutely intelligent about, the ethical implications of literature. Such practices have not depended on the new moral philosophy; nor have they been, with a few exceptions, significantly affected by it. One of the exceptions is S. L. Goldberg's *Agents and Lives: Moral Thinking in Literature* (Cambridge, 1992). But the philosophy *is* going to become increasingly important to these practices, in my view, because a characteristic weakness of literary criticism in the seventies and eighties was its relative unwillingness and/or inability to explain itself in the new *lingua franca* of theory. The importance of Nussbaum, Taylor, Williams, and the others is that they crucially help such criticism to become metadiscursively articulate – in an intellectual climate, partly created by these very philosophers, which has suddenly become favourable to an interest in the ethical.

Introduction: the turn to ethics in the 1990s

What evidence is there that the climate has changed in this way? I can only accumulate what I would interpret as significant pointers, such as an international conference on Literature and Ethics held at the University of Wales, Aberystwyth, in 1996; or a review in the *TLS* by Peter Brooks of Yale, who is better known as a formalist than as a 'humanist' critic. He is discussing the latest work of Hillis Miller:

> the question that lurks somewhere at the heart of Miller's matter – the question of why we have and want fictional persons, the work they do for us. How many children had Lady Macbeth? If we know the question is absurd, the fact that we can ask it all points to something about the puissant illusions that we seek in the novel. To discuss them fully, I believe that one needs to go beyond psychoanalysis as well, and engage the field of ethics. The multiple associations of the word 'character' are no accident, and the ethical implications need to be explored if one is to account for the power of fictional dramatizations of persons negotiating the plots in which they figure. The recent revival of moral philosophy – in the work of such as Bernard Williams, Alasdair MacIntyre, Charles Taylor – may suggest ways in which we can talk about self without reference to discredited notions of 'stable' or 'unitary' beings. Particularly, Taylor's notion of selves as constituted in 'webs of interlocution' suggests that we might turn to novels precisely as the best instances of how the self comes into being, as a dialogic process.[7]

This review was published in November 1992, but if we did not know that (and if we missed the reference to Taylor's *Sources of the Self* (1989)), then I would claim that we could date the article with some confidence as post-1985 simply because of the view Brooks takes of ethics and character. Such a view was extremely rare in advanced Anglo-American literary theory five years ago, and virtually non-existent there ten years ago. Indeed, Brooks's argument about moral philosophy by-passing post-structuralist objections to the concept of 'self' belongs to an extremely recent moment in literary studies, a moment described in 1990 by Martha Nussbaum as a new 'turn toward the ethical'.

In fact, I am taking the liberty of seeing more in Martha Nussbaum's phrase than she originally intended. She was referring to the explicit claims of Derrida and Barbara Johnson for deconstruction to be seen as an ethically and socially relevant procedure. Nussbaum puts these claims down partly to what she

[7] *TLS*, 6 November 1992, p. 25.

calls 'the scandal over the political career of Paul de Man'. However much truth there may be in this, we might also recall that the ethicality of deconstruction was already a theme in de Man's own work.

But the recent 'turn toward the ethical' reaches across a much more varied body of work than this. There has been a profusion of work, especially in the US, that looks very much like the beginnings of a significant resurgence of ethical criticism. That includes the important work of Martha Nussbaum herself, of Cora Diamond, Wayne Booth, Tobin Siebers, Charles Altieri, Richard Eldridge, Paul Seabright, Frederick Olafson, and Murray Krieger, many of whom took part in important symposia on ethics and literature published in the journals *Ethics* and *New Literary History* during the 1980s. More recent examples include the present volume and *Commitment in Reflection: Essays in Literature and Moral Philosophy*, edited by Leona Toker.[8] The resurgence also includes Richard Rorty, Stanley Cavell, and Alasdair MacIntyre, who have all published important books and papers on ethics and literature in the recent past.

One striking thing about these names is that most of them are philosophers by training rather than literary critics, particularly moral philosophers. In other words the 'turn toward the ethical' within literary studies is closely connected to a turn to the literary within ethics. What this suggests is that unlike previous resurgences of ethical criticism associated with literary figures such as Dr Johnson, Matthew Arnold, F. R. Leavis, and Lionel Trilling, this movement (though by no means discontinuous with earlier ones) is fuelled primarily by things going on within philosophy. One significant sign of these developments is Cora Diamond's call (part 1) for philosophers to engage in the 'revolutionary act' of reading novels in appropriately responsive ways. Another is Annette Baier's characterisation (part 3) of ethics as 'a polyphonic art form'. But perhaps the person who has trumpeted these changes most audibly has been Richard Rorty. According to Rorty there is nothing less than a major paradigm shift taking place in our own time in which the culture of positivism is being replaced by the culture of pragmatism:

[8] Leona Toker, ed., *Commitment in Reflection: Essays in Literature and Moral Philosophy* (New York, 1994).

Pragmatism ... does not erect Science as an idol to fill the place once held by God. It views science as one genre of literature – or, put the other way around, literature and the arts as inquiries, on the same footing as scientific inquiries. Thus it sees ethics as neither more 'relative' nor 'subjective' than scientific theory, nor as needing to be made 'scientific'. Physics is a way of trying to cope with various bits of the universe; ethics is a matter of trying to cope with other bits. Mathematics helps physics do its job; literature and the arts help ethics do its.[9]

If Rorty is right about this recent paradigm shift away from the great philosophical questions of metaphyics, ontology, and epistemology, then there seem to be important consequences for ethical criticism. The first is that if ethics and physics are simply different sorts of narrative, then ethics is reinstated as a subject of serious inquiry. The second is that literature and the arts are an integral part of that same inquiry. In other words, the shift from foundationalist to pragmatist, tradition-centred ethics almost inevitably involves a turn to literature and the arts as sites of the culture's deepest moral questioning. Such questioning is apparent in John Wiltshire's account (part 2) of medical narrative, in particular, of pathography – narratives written by patients or those close to them.

There are accumulating signs that ethical criticism, inspired largely by Nussbaum, Diamond, Booth, Rorty, Taylor, and others, is set to become a force in literary studies in the US. The signs are there in reviews, in publishing, in the latest work of formalist critics like Michael Holquist, in the dissertation topics of American Ph.D. students, in new undergraduate courses in literature and ethics. Taken together, these point to the strong possibility that ethics is about to acquire something of the cachet enjoyed by politics ten or fifteen years ago. But it is important not to finish on such a triumphant note because, in the anti-foundationalist form I have pictured as most promising, there are important questions to be raised.

The questions are raised as soon as you move from an ethics based on meta-ethical theory to one based on local practices and traditions, inlcuding literary traditions. The main question is, what if our local practices and traditions are distorted – by the systematic disempowerment of important groups, such as women, homosexuals, and racial minorities? Another is, what if

---

[9] Richard Rorty, *Consequences of Pragmatism* (Hemel Hempstead, 1981) p. xliii.

these traditions systematically promote our own centrality in the scheme of things? This is what Martha Nussbaum calls 'the dark side of the aspiration to community and historical rootedness'. A very powerful case along these lines is made by Susan Moller Okin when she attacks Alasdair MacIntyre in a chapter of *Justice, Gender and the Family* called 'Whose Traditions? Which Understandings?', in which she makes the necessary point that the very moral tales MacIntyre portrays as central in an education in the virtues contain gender stereotypes that are the 'basic building-blocks of male domination'.[10] Nussbaum distances herself from MacIntyre and argues that virtue-based ethics need not be anti-Enlightenment in MacIntyre's way, but then, as Richard Freadman has shown, Nussbaum's own work on Henry James opens her to similar criticisms of ideological bias.[11] One way to make the point implicit here is to say that there is a permanent need for political criticism as an external perspective on the ethnocentric, conservative tendencies of anti-foundationalist ethics. But that raises another question: What sort of 'external' perspective can this be from which 'our' traditions can be seen as 'distorted'?

It seems to me that we can be driven in either of two directions here. Our first alternative is to seek what Seyla Benhabib calls a 'postmetaphysical universalist position', which she finds in 'a communicative concept of rationality' based on the work of Jürgen Habermas.[12] In other words, we can see these questions as a continuation of the Gadamer–Habermas debate of twenty years ago. Our second alternative is to reflect that the universalist, Habermasian leverage in that debate cannot be being applied from some ahistorical, acultural Archimedian foothold either. The universalist desire for human rights and equality across differences of race, culture, nationality, and gender is itself also derived from our Western traditions, as are the concepts ideology, ethnocentrism, and patriarchy. This is Charles Taylor's line: the very Enlightenment ideals of human rights and equality are part of one of the historical strands that constitute what he calls 'the modern identity', our identity. Paradoxically, the ideal of sceptical reason that is so intimately bound up in them makes it hard to see these

---

[10] Susan Moller Okin, *Justice, Gender and the Family* (New York, 1989), p. 45.
[11] 'Disciplinary Relations: Literary Studies and Philosophy', *Border Crossing: Studies in English and Other Disciplines* (La Trobe, 1991), pp. 24–34.
[12] Benhabib, *Situating the Self*, p. 5.

ideals for what they are, goods internal to our tradition, but goods very often in conflict with others also internal to our tradition. This is a fuller tradition-based argument than MacIntyre's because it does not set itself against Enlightenment ideals, but treats them as an integral part of that full range of mutually conflicting goods we actually live by, and need to live by in order to live as well as we can.

PART I

Ethics, literature, and philosophy

1

Deepening the self
The language of ethics and the
language of literature

SIMON HAINES

After twenty-five years of confusion and denial, literary criticism in English is starting to rediscover literature as a distinctive mode of thought about being human, and to regain confidence in itself as a manner of attending to that thought. Valuable support in this process of recovery has come from the diverse group of moral philosophers surveyed in this chapter, who have been critical of the dissociated conceptions of language and the self delivered to us, or imposed on us, by the Enlightenment. Even these philosophers, however, have too seldom seen *that*, and hardly ever shown *how*, it is literature which has actually been the principal mode of thinking about this problem since the seventeenth century.

For thirty or forty years now there has been a steady flow of criticism from a group of English-speaking moral philosophers, directed at what they see as the two dominant and interlocking traditions in modern Western moral philosophy. The first of these traditions, predominantly Anglo-Saxon, empirical and utilitarian, derives from Bacon, Locke, and Bentham. It has been represented this century by G. E. Moore and his various 'intuitionist' and 'emotivist' inheritors, especially H. A. Prichard, David Ross, C. L. Stevenson, and R. M. Hare. The other tradition is principally a Continental European one, deriving from Descartes and Kant, with its own twentieth-century incarnations, especially in existentialism.

The origins of the modern group of moral philosophers critical of these two traditions lie, I believe, in three seminal essays: 'Fallacies in Moral Philosophy', by Stuart Hampshire;[1] 'Vision and Choice in Morality', by Iris Murdoch;[2] and 'Modern Moral Philosophy', by G. E. M. Anscombe.[3] But there are now many philosophers who in their various ways have worked and are still working within a territory first sketched out in the aforementioned essays. A list only of the most eminent would include Bernard Williams, Alasdair MacIntyre, Charles Taylor, Stanley Cavell, Cora Diamond, Annette Baier, Martha Nussbaum, and Raimond Gaita. All, however, express the same frustration at our having been told for nearly a century (Moore's *Principia Ethica* came out in 1903) that in ethics the important things are the ones we cannot speak about; or that to speak about them is simply to say 'boo' or 'hurrah' with rhetorical embellishments; or that the moral questions which really matter are not 'How should one live?' or even 'What should I do?', but 'What kind of thing is a moral judgment?', and 'What kind of concept is "good"?' Between them, these recent thinkers have helped to restore to philosophy this lost and vital language of the self: although many novelists and poets, and some critics, might say that for them it has never been lost at all.

The philosophers we are concerned with argue, first, that philosophy since the Enlightenment has never thought historically enough, and that this failing has been deeply damaging this century, not just to our philosophical moral thinking but to all our moral thinking, and therefore not just to our thinking but to our very lives. Secondly, they believe that modern moral philosophy, and again, therefore, our lives, are partly grounded in an impoverished and blinkered philosophy of language, this century's inheritor of a correspondingly inadequate Enlightenment philosophy of mind. Thirdly, they are saying that these philosophies of mind and language spring from – indeed partly constitute – a certain picture of the human personality or sense of the self; and that this picture or sense is, again, both attenuated and deracinated.

The logician W. V. O. Quine once joked that there are two kinds of philosopher: historians of philosophy, and philosophers. In Iris

---

[1] In *Mind*, 58 (1949), reprinted in *Revisions: Changing Perspectives in Moral Philosophy*, ed. Stanley Hauerwas and Alasdair MacIntyre (Indiana, 1983).
[2] In *Proceedings of the Aristotelian Society*, supplementary volume xxx, (July 1956).
[3] In *Philosophy*, 33.124 (January 1958).

Murdoch's suggestion that 'morality must, to some extent at any rate, be studied historically' ('Vision and Choice in Morality') we can hear the beginnings of a rebuttal of that deep twentieth-century prejudice. G. E. M. Anscombe's paper two years later argued much more fully that when nowadays we speak of 'obligation' and 'duty', or of what is 'morally' right or wrong, or of a 'moral' sense of 'ought', we are relying on 'an earlier conception of ethics which no longer generally survives'. That special modern sense of the word 'moral', implying an implicit compulsion to act in a certain way, depends, Anscombe argues, on the survival of a law conception of ethics, and ultimately a divine law conception, which only made sense within the now-collapsed Judeo-Christian framework. But we go on keeping a flavour of special compulsion – not always a particularly pleasant one – by preserving a foundational concept like 'morally wrong' to explain a supposedly non-foundational concept like 'unjust' or 'unchaste'. The very fact that her second example may already sound quaint to some ears lends weight to Anscombe's contention that our blindness to the history living within moral concepts leads us to truncate them, to reduce all of them to a few elementary common denominators. We have suffered a real 'loss of concepts', in Murdoch's phrase: and therefore a dilution of experience.

Anscombe's paper was important because in it a mainstream philosopher was thinking both historically and critically about philosophical concepts. Major recent works in this vein, such as Charles Taylor's *Sources of the Self* (1989) or Alasdair MacIntyre's *After Virtue* (1981), with their repeated references to 'simulacra of morality' or 'conceptual impoverishment', are likewise both historical and critical: whereas traditional histories of philosophy, including – in this field – Mary Warnock's excellent *Ethics Since 1900* (1960), or even MacIntyre's *Short History of Ethics* (1966), are historical and descriptive. For Anscombe and her fellows, key moral concepts, in general as well as professional contemporary use, can only be fully understood historically. As Taylor would say, history is constitutive of those concepts. They do not have a lightweight lexicographical component of passing antiquarian interest, and then the real, lean and mean, heavyweight, analytical component.

In the words of the American pragmatist Richard Rorty, 'philosophy needs to relive its past in order to answer its questions':

although surely the fuller claim is that philosophy needs to live its past in its present simply to understand its questions. This is precisely what historically minded literary critics have most wanted to say to the more ahistorical literary theorists of the 1970s and 1980s. Just as moral philosophers need to be both historical and critical about the moral thinking they and all of us do, so literary scholars, critics and theorists need to be both historical and critical about the thinking that poets and novelists do, and that they themselves do. They need to stop behaving as if both poetry and criticism were split into lightweight components (lexicography or etymology for some, 'historical context' for others, 'aesthetic qualities' for still others) and heavyweight components (philosophical or political or ethical 'ideas' for some, historical or political 'events' or 'movements' for others). A historical dictionary needs to be recognised and promoted as at least as useful a critical tool as an encyclopedia of poetics. 'Word-utterances are historical occasions', as Murdoch says. This means we have to be alive to the historicity of the word-utterance, as is already being widely recognised once again. But it also means we have to be alive to the history living within, present within, the words uttered.

If, however, literary criticism can profit from these moral philosophers' observations upon the living history present within concepts, the philosophers for their part might more often acknowledge the scale, the intensity, and the kind of warfare which English-speaking poets, novelists, and critics have been waging against the empirico-utilitarian conceptual tradition for the last 200 years: for the first fifty or so (the years of Blake, Hazlitt, Carlyle, and Dickens) without any help or recognition at all from philosophers. Nowadays, of course, there is *some* recognition. Taylor offers his own readings of symbolist poems: MacIntyre, of *Mansfield Park*. But even these most alert and well-intentioned of philosophers still read poems or novels as if they were containers or vehicles with separable concepts inside them, or as if they were examples of re-formulable ideas. Even terms such as 'concepts' and 'ideas' are seen as it were in cross-section, or edge-on, unmetaphorically. It is not enough for a philosopher to respond to such a criticism by saying that to think in this analysing or separating way is just what makes philosophy itself and not another discipline of thought. If moral philosophy wishes to point to a fundamental limitation or distortion of this dissociating kind in its own previous practice, it should beware of reading, or misreading, literature in just the same way.

According to the moral philosophers we are interested in, another field of philosophy, namely epistemology, is both conceptually and chronologically anterior to mainstream modern philosophies of language, whether Continental or Anglo-Saxon. Further, the mainstream assumes that a certain picture of the self, namely its picture, is foundational for *all* philosophy. Modern philosophy of language has been no more resistant to the influence of that picture than any other field: indeed, as several of our philosophers argue, it has been that picture's most powerful twentieth-century manifestation and proselytiser. Richard Rorty argues that it was originally Descartes who 'made possible a discipline in which ... the problems of moral philosophy became problems of metaethics, problems of the justification of moral judgement'.[4] From an epistemology evolved a philosophy of language; but this century it has been the latter which has chiefly forced a certain conception of moral philosophy. As Cora Diamond put it in her essay 'Losing Your Concepts',[5] the 'philosophy of mind which is the source of our inarticulateness in ethics presents to us, as a philosophical necessity, that picture of the human personality which our culture in general has inherited from the Enlightenment'. We describe the world of 'sense' and 'reason' with 'scientific language', and bundle all the rest of ourselves, emotions, desires, will, off into a neglected corner. 'In the moral life of beings conceived in such a way, there is no need for moral concepts other than the most general ones like *good* and *right*, together with straightforwardly applicable descriptive concepts.' There are important connections between these almost spatial criticisms of philosophy of language and Anscombe's historical criticisms of the imperceptiveness of modern moral philosophy. Not only the vast array of moral terms we actually live by (shame, courage, modesty, arrogance, sentimentality, confidence, rudeness, dishonesty, integrity, brutality, honour, etc.) but also the small number of supposed master-concepts like 'good' and 'right' have been obscured as much by the Enlightenment's blinkered philosophies of mind and language as by its historical myopia.

[4] Richard Rorty, *Philosophy and the Mirror of Nature* (Princeton, 1980).
[5] *Ethics*, 98 (January 1988).

'What linguistic analysts mistrust is precisely language', said Murdoch ('Vision and Choice in Morality'). She was actually talking about R. M. Hare's *The Language of Morals* (1952), but her remark is full of significance when one thinks for a moment about Saussure, or indeed Derrida. The diachronic life of words is something poets often recognise more readily than linguists do. It seems that we tried so hard and for so long this century to correct the antiquarian philological biases of the last that we became as obsessed by the synchronic as they were by the diachronic. Be that as it may, Murdoch was asking moral philosophers not to abandon 'the linguistic method' but to take it 'seriously': that is, to 'extend the limits of the language' rather as poets do, enabling it 'to illuminate regions of reality which were formerly dark'. Philosophers, and increasingly the rest of us, have separated language into a scientific and an unscientific component, a clean, perfectly formed part which precisely describes the world of 'sense' and 'reason'; and a messy, shapeless part, much in need of rehabilitation, which imprecisely gestures at everything else. By doing this we have left ourselves in a dilemma over where to put concepts like 'will' and 'desire': in the clean, no-questions-asked scientific part ('I just *want* to'), or in the messy imponderable unscientific part ('I don't know *what* I want')? What we should do, according to Cora Diamond in the essay already mentioned, is pay 'attention to the actual character of language in general and moral language in particular'. The concept of 'a human being' is not the scientific concept of 'Homo Sapiens' plus an imprecise evaluative extra. To grasp it is not a matter of classification; it 'is being able to participate in life-with-the-concept'.

Taking language seriously, in other words, means refusing to think about it as if it were a suspension of grains of sense in an opaque fluid of nonsense, to be separated by the centrifuge of reason. Language is an unseparated medium of life, and to live with it is precisely *not* to centrifuge it, but to use it: to breathe it. Each of the moral philosophers I have mentioned finds his or her own way of saying this. Charles Taylor, for example, comments in *Sources of the Self* that 'with terms like "courage" or "brutality" or "gratitude", we cannot grasp what would hold all their instances together as a class if we prescind from their evaluative point'; whereas to grasp this is to grasp 'how things can go well or badly between people in the society where this term is current'. 'Prescind': do not cut the 'evaluative point' *a priori* off the descriptive shaft. If you do, what you end up with is not a blunt spear, not even a shaft, but just a stick. 'Grasping' 'courage' or 'brutality' is living with that concept, and thus extending your experience. 'Analysing' such a concept must entail some curtailment of life, which is hard for us to accept, as heirs of Socrates and Descartes. Some kinds of thought can actually destroy forms of life. At least, then, let us resist the temptation to separate moral language, as language in general is supposed already to have been separated, into a precise part and a vague part: into a welter of muddy emotional terms and a brief clear terminology of will, desire, and value.

What has happened in modern ethics, according to Bernard Williams in *Ethics and the Limits of Philosophy* (1985), is that G. E. Moore's 'ban on the naturalistic fallacy' has caused 'two classes of expressions' to be set up as all-inclusive: a small, evaluative one containing 'good' and 'right' and a few other terms; and a large, non-evaluative one including statements of fact and mathematical truths. Whether R. M. Hare is claiming that this distinction between the evaluative and the non-evaluative is really one between the prescriptive and the descriptive, or C. L. Stevenson is claiming that it is really one between the emotivist and the descriptivist, or latter-day Humeans are claiming that it is really one between 'ought' and 'is' (Hume's own position was not so simple): all these descendants of Moore think moral words contain, as Iris Murdoch put it, just the 'two elements of recommendation and specification'.[6] And as Anscombe was also implying, it seems that the more neutral, scientific, purged of feeling, the specificatory element is, the more moralistic, condemnatory, judgmental, outraged, politicised, ideologically hysterical the recommendatory one becomes. If you filter out all the distinguishing specificatory characteristics of a moral event (ethical, political: but we should beware of 'either/or' language here) then all the evaluative emotional load gets redistributed down onto the few narrow recommendatory terms left. The result is inevitably highly confrontational: a moral walnut being smashed with an emotivist sledgehammer, bits of shell flying everywhere, broken furniture.

Stuart Hampshire urges us, in the seminal 1949 essay men-

---

[6] Iris Murdoch, 'The Idea of Perfection' (London, 1964), in *The Sovereignty of Good*, (London, 1970).

tioned earlier, to remember Aristotle's dictum: *en te aisthesei he krisis*. The moment of judgment (*krisis*), which is also the moment of recognition, of the sudden feeling of really understanding something, lies literally within (*en*) your sensory, imaginative, and moral apprehension of it (*aisthesis*). How adequately you grasp an event determines how adequately you will judge it. Hampshire points out that the contrary view is of 'an unbridgeable logical gulf' between statements of fact and statements of value. This view, as he also reminds us, has prevailed; and it originated with Kant. 'Fact' and 'value' have for philosophers of Hampshire's persuasion become the two lurking villains, the Rosencrantz and Guildenstern, of modern moral philosophy. Murdoch's 'specification' and 'recommendation' do not have quite the same popular resonance. According to Bernard Williams 'the theorists have brought the fact–value distinction to language rather than finding it revealed there. What they have found are a lot of those "thicker" or more specific ethical notions ... such as treachery and promise and brutality and courage, which seem to express a union of fact and value.'[7] Stanley Cavell had put the point in other terms some years earlier: 'both statements of fact and judgments of value rest upon the same capacities of human nature ... only a creature that *can* judge of value *can* state a fact'.[8] 'Describing' an ethical 'fact' is an activity possible only between consenting valuers. Their presentation of the morally salient is 'always already' evaluative. They must employ what Williams, following Clifford Geertz, and before him Gilbert Ryle, calls '"thicker" or more specific ethical notions', Taylor calls a 'language of qualitative distinction' and Iris Murdoch calls a 'specialised normative' or 'second-order' or simply 'rich' moral vocabulary. In her recent book *Metaphysics as a Guide to Morals* (1992) Murdoch writes that we '*need* a "moral vocabulary"', a detailed value terminology, morally loaded words'. Moral growth is a matter of reflection, of 'deepening the concepts in question'. It is a 'process involving an exercise and refinement of moral vocabulary and sensibility ... We learn moral concepts. Not only "true" and "good", but the *vast numbers of secondary* more specialised moral terms, are for us instruments of discrimination and mentors of desire.' This line of thought was already discernible in the 1956 essay, where Murdoch argued that

---

[7] Bernard Williams, *Ethics and the Limits of Philosophy* (London, 1985).
[8] Stanley Cavell, *The Claim of Reason* (Oxford and New York, 1979).

moral concepts should be 'regarded as deep moral configurations of the world', not 'lines drawn round separable factual areas'.

The argument that moral understanding arises in reflection upon 'rich' moral concepts rather than in an ultimately arbitrary 'choice' made by 'reason' between 'actions' amid a world of 'facts' should remind us (although a poet or a poetically attentive critic would hardly need to be reminded) that an 'undissociated' view of language cannot be disentangled from a corresponding view of the self. Here is an illustrative passage from Raimond Gaita's recent book *Good and Evil: An Absolute Conception* (1991):

> Descriptions of actions and character through which we explore our sense of what we have done and what we are, of what is fine and what is tawdry, of what is shallow and what is deep, of what is noble and what is base, and so on, are not merely descriptions of convenience onto which we project a more formal sense, focused on imperatives, of what it is for something to be of moral concern. (p. 40)

Moral language, in other words, is not divided, as since Kant we have been impelled to assume, into a specificatory, descriptive, scientific, fact-oriented component and a recommendatory, prescriptive, emotional, action-oriented component: the former grounded in physical reality and the latter, as Anscombe reminded us, in the thin dust which is all that remains of a once-fertile metaphysical loam. But more: because of our Kantian preconceptions we are able to recognise actions, which can be classified within the permissible categories of fact, reason and will; but we cannot recognise 'character', which we feel obliged to enclose in inverted commas and classify within the problematic category of value. We can see what people do but not what they mean by what they do, not *how* they do what they do: and certainly not what they *are*. Yet to criticise someone's thought or behaviour by using a word like 'sentimental' (Gaita's example) is not just to claim in a needlessly obscure way that the thought or behaviour are 'simply' false or wrong: it is to 'mark a distinctive way in which' that thought or behaviour 'can fail', can falsify or misprise its object.

If moral philosophy has not taken the language of ordinary life seriously enough, literary theory certainly has not taken the language of literature seriously enough: has not trusted it enough. The language of literature is the 'thickest' of all: here judgment most completely coincides with apprehension. And yet to literary theorists the tug of the scientific model so often seems irresistible. They so often respond to the language of literature by separating it, and therefore of course their own responses, their critical language, into factual and evaluative components. But as Gaita also says, moral speech is more poetic than it is scientific. It is not just that we should treat the language of poetry *as if* it were moral language: it *is* moral language, deployed more thoughtfully than by most philosophy. This is a form of 'serious thought' which is essentially concerned with concept-deepening, not with classifying; with attentive, evaluative reflection, not with the false dichotomy 'fact-or-value'. Murdoch constantly talks about literature as being something between an 'analogy' and a 'case' of moral thought. And reading it, taking it seriously, criticising it, is therefore also a mode of ethical reflection, she says: 'the most educational of all human activities'.

But the best of these philosophers rarely offer attentive and undissociated readings of the language of literature (Martha Nussbaum is a distinguished exception). This is a challenge for criticism, an incentive to re-articulate and recover a practice which has lost both confidence and salience under the prolonged dominion of various theoretical schools displaying their own forms of dissociation, their own divided concepts of language and the self. Even critics and scholars like the Americans Wayne Booth, Charles Altieri, and Tobin Siebers, who have already benefited from this most sympathetic of philosophical conversations, slide in some of their recent work towards the formulaic and programmatic.[9] Siebers is perfectly right to say in his book that the 'danger of ethical criticism is its tendency to think about moral philosophy or about an ideal form of criticism instead of about literature'; but the book itself does not think about literature either. In this metacritical microclimate, so congenial to a conception of poetry as a distinctive mode of moral thought, we need more *critics* actually taking the trouble to *read* it. Meanwhile the wider academic, theoretical, and scholarly climate is still distinctly hostile towards both conception and practice, because so many publishing academics, theorists, and scholars rely on precisely that divided

---

[9] See Wayne Booth's *The Company We Keep* (Berkeley, 1988); Charles Altieri's *Canons and Consequences* (Evanston, 1990); and Siebers's *The Ethics of Criticism* (Ithaca, 1988).

fact–value picture of language, with its implicated picture of the divided self, which 'our' moral philosophers are criticising.

Here is one of the more influential pictures of that picture of the self, again from Iris Murdoch, in her 1967 essay, 'The Sovereignty of Good Over Other Concepts':[10]

We are still living in the age of the Kantian man, or Kantian man-god... How recognisable, how familiar to us, is the man so beautifully portrayed in the *Grundlegung*, who confronted even with Christ turns away to consider the judgment of his own conscience and to hear the voice of his own reason. Stripped of the exiguous metaphysical background which Kant was prepared to allow him, this man is with us still, free, independent, lonely, powerful, rational, responsible, brave, the hero of so many novels and books of moral philosophy ... He is the offspring of the age of science, confidently rational and yet increasingly aware of his alienation from the material universe which his discoveries reveal ... Kant, not Hegel, has provided Western ethics with its dominating image.

All the moral philosophers we have been concerned with are criticising a Kantian picture, or evaluative portrayal, something like this one. In *Sources of the Self*, Charles Taylor finds the origins of the picture in the 'abstracted' or 'punctual' self of Locke, the 'noumenal rational agent' of Rousseau and Kant, the 'instrumentalising' reason of Galileo and finally the 'disengaged' reason, the *cogito*, of Descartes. And, of course, this is also a picture of Miltonic, Faustian, and Byronic man, although the philosophers rarely make enough of the great poetic transmissions, or rather representations, of the picture. Nietzschean, existentialist, economistic, and even Rawlsian accounts or metaphors of will, rational choice, views from nowhere, Archimedean points and veils of ignorance can all be seen as descendants of the Kantian–Cartesian universalising, featureless, dimensionless, rational isolated self. What the philosophers we are considering want to do is to replace this self with one that is both less rational – or rather less rational*istic* – and less isolated. The two undertakings are deeply related, of course; but I shall concentrate here on the first one. As against the Enlightenment tradition, they insist on an *un*divided self, a reintegration, in familiar terms, of reason and emotion, or thought and feeling. This involves a defence of emotion, an attack on a certain conception of 'pure' reason and an attempt to merge the two.

[10] Murdoch, *The Sovereignty of Good*, p. 80.

We are not minds which have bodies but bodies which think, argues Bernard Williams in 'Morality and the Emotions'.[11] It is, for example, hard to separate an emotion from a moral judgment. If you call someone's behaviour or character 'contemptible', how do you distinguish between the emotional and the moral content of your judgment? Williams lists shock, outrage, admiration, and indignation as further examples of modes of judgment that are also modes of emotion. Sometimes, moreover, behaviour or character can only be made sense of in terms of an underlying structure of emotion which is neither amenable nor visible to what is usually termed 'reason'. If reason has any purchase on behaviour or character it may only be through putting the 'facts' of a case in a new light, which is not a matter of overcoming emotion but of schooling, teaching or reforming it (this is an essentially Aristotelean position, of course). Some related questions: would you prefer someone to treat you well on principle, because, she said, 'it was her duty', or to do so out of an emotional response to *you*? Do emotions somehow happen to a separable 'us'? If so, where were they before? And where and what were *we* before? Martha Nussbaum asks similar questions in *The Fragility of Goodness* (1986); but for Nussbaum, a classicist as well as a philosopher, the questions arise out of some fine and powerful readings of Greek tragedy. She concludes, as much as argues, that emotional response is 'a constituent part of the best sort of recognition or knowledge of one's practical situation': suffering, for example, is 'a kind of knowing'. Ethical perception 'is both cognitive and affective at the same time'. And such emotional response, such affective perception, is essential to literature: essential within it, and essential in our reception of it. Nussbaum is right to say all this and right, too, in *how* she says it. Reading her work should remind literary criticism of what it has always known to be its proper process and subject, despite its recent devaluation and marginalisation of both. Poetry and philosophy can both show us these things, and yet they do not do so in the same way. Nussbaum remains properly aware, as Rorty, for example, does not, that philosophy and poetry have different ways of thinking morally. Real mediation between the two is both important and difficult, and this is criticism's peculiar task.

[11] 1965; reprinted in Bernard Williams, *Problems of the Self: Philosophical Papers, 1956–1972* (Cambridge, 1976).

The defence of emotion undertaken in their different ways by Williams and Nussbaum merges imperceptibly into a critique of 'pure' reason (which in a literary context nowadays usually means one of reason's most influential modern avatars, 'theory'). If there is 'an "I" without body, past or character', says Williams, what is there to distinguish it from any other 'I' ('Morality and the Emotions')? And yet this is the dimensionless, featureless 'I' of reason, the Cartesian thinking thing which goes on demanding deeper and deeper 'reasons', but only of the kind it recognises *as* reasons, until no more can be found, at which point, existentially, it declares the world unreasonable. But Williams also argues that "you can't kill that, it's a child" is more convincing as a reason than any reason which might be advanced for its being a reason'.[12] Enlightenment philosophy (and, again, literary theory, as one of its children) is still mesmerised by a *'rationalistic conception of rationality'*, which demands that 'every decision ... be based on grounds that can be discursively explained'.[13] Stanley Cavell believes that modern philosophy has denied and neglected human selfhood or identity by its continuous temptation to scientific, Socratic, Cartesian certainty.[14] Cavell traces our modern sceptical obsession with certainty back to the seventeenth century's failure to substitute a 'presentness achieved by certainty of the senses' for 'the presentness which had been elaborated through our old absorption in the world'.[15] Nussbaum traces the obsession with certainty back to Socrates' promise of a *techne* or method to defend us against *tuche*, contingency or luck. But all these philosophers distrust the belief that 'morality is rational only insofar as it can be formulated in, or grounded on, a system of abstract principles' which can be applied almost computationally so as to govern all rational people.[16] The fact that some people feel they need such principles does not mean there *are* any. Ethical theorists 'wrongly tend to assimilate conflicts in moral belief to theoretical contradiction', as Williams puts it in 'Conflicts of Values'. Perhaps we

---

[12] Bernard Williams, 'Conflicts of Values', 1979, reprinted in *Moral Luck: Philosophical Papers, 1973–1980* (Cambridge, 1981).
[13] Williams, *Ethics and the Limits of Philosophy*, p. 18.
[14] Cavell, *The Claim of Reason*.
[15] Stanley Cavell, 'The Avoidance of Love: A Reading of *King Lear*', 1967, in *Must We Mean What We Say?* (Cambridge, 1976).
[16] Stanley G. Clarke and Evan Simpson, eds., in their introduction to *Anti-Theory in Ethics and Moral Conservatism* (Albany, 1989).

cannot abstract or separate a rational, theorising 'self' from the disposition or desires which it supposes itself to be thinking 'about'. *Can* we ever look at ourselves entirely 'from the outside'? Can we ever make the basis of our relations with others entirely, rationally, theoretically explicit? Perhaps it is a misconception of what thought is to suppose that only something like a theory 'really penetrates the appearances' of morality.[17] Maybe moral thought is more like 'a reflective dialogue between the intuitions and beliefs of the interlocutor ... and a series of complex ethical conceptions, presented for exploration'.[18]

Many of these points, as I have suggested several times, could just as easily be made in the context of modern literary and critical theory as in that of modern moral theory: the misconceptions and ignorings of poetic thought involved in the former are much the same as those of moral thought in the latter. The coincidence becomes even clearer when moral philosophers start calling for a reintegration of emotion and reason in terms of 'dissociation', that once all-powerful concept, invented by T. S. Eliot, which Frank Kermode encouraged us to be sceptical about many years ago, at about the time when this movement in moral philosophy was beginning. I believe we still need the concept. Bernard Williams argues that there is a fundamental error in 'dissociating moral thought and decision from moral feeling'.[19] For Cora Diamond 'dissociation' means an inability even to see the failure in the relation between our experience and our thought. She and others like her direct their writing, she says, at 'those whom the kind of dissociation they discuss is *in* ... someone within whom the dissociations of our culture are well rooted'.[20] If we see the self as a dimensionless, choosing, willing, rational point, then the emotions will seem to rage blindly, savagely, and uncontrollably all around it, threatening all the time to warp judgment and compel wrong action. Even its best decisions will seem arbitrary, unconnected, and absurd. So why dissociate 'reason' and 'emotion', or fact and value, at all? Why appoint 'reason' the moral guide or perceptual centre of the self? Yes, we must have *some* generalisa-

---

17 Raimond Gaita, *Good and Evil: An Absolute Conception* (London, 1991).
18 Martha C. Nussbaum, *The Fragility of Goodness: Luck and Ethics in Greek Tragedy and Philosophy* (Cambridge, 1986).
19 Bernard Williams, 'Utilitarianism and Moral Self-indulgence', 1976, reprinted in Williams, *Moral Luck*.
20 Cora Diamond, 'Losing Your Concepts', *Ethics*, 98 (January 1988), pp. 255–77.

bility, some means of transcending the welter of contingency and the limited or egocentric perspectives of the self. But why respond to this need, as philosophy has done over and over again from Socrates to Bentham and since, by separating the self into a part which feels and a part which fears, controls, measures, and rules the feelings: which, in short, *has* the feelings? Why dig and then fall into those deep crevasses between reason and emotion, between action and passion? Without them choice ceases to be a mystery or an absurdity, and becomes a genuine mode of reflection. The central moral question is no longer, as the major modern traditions would have it, 'What should one do?', but 'How should one live?'; and 'life' becomes much more than conduct. As several of our philosophers insist, above all Nussbaum, Diamond, and Murdoch, literature is a mode of ethical reflection in which this central question is always at least as essential as it is in philosophy. It is encouraging to see how many more critics, as well as philosophers, there are thinking about literature in such ways in 1993 than there were in 1983.

The 'Kantian man' depicted by Iris Murdoch is lonely as well as divided. He is dissociated from others as well as within himself. Clearly the range of reflection on this kind of dissociation is both continuous with and as broad as the range on the other kind, but there is not space here to explore it at the same length. Raimond Gaita seems to me quite right to claim, in *Good and Evil*, that the 'serious contrast' is between 'non-reductive humanism', whose major progenitor is Aristotle, and various kinds of 'ethical other-worldliness', whose ancestor is Plato. It seems to me that the really interesting point on what one might call the spectrum of self-transcendence is the one where these two great schools meet. On one side of that imaginary central point (we can of course never find it) Aristotle will seem somewhat complacent; on the other Plato will seem rather authoritarian. On one side, only Plato's passionate mysticism quite answers to our need for spiritual transcendence; on the other, only Aristotle's diurnal tolerance quite captures our need for humanity. Lying more or less around this notional centre is a conception of the self, not as the old irreducible, impervious, and unchanging central core, but as a nevertheless 'substantial' and 'continually developing' permeable coalescence of affection and reflection, of 'attachments' and desires. Beside this there is an equivalent conception of a 'rich and

35

complicated reality' which transcends the self without necessarily transcending *everything*, and which infiltrates the self without dissolving it.[21] Then, just a little off centre, is what both Gaita and Murdoch call 'non-dogmatic mysticism', the sense that 'moral advance carries with it intuitions of unity which are increasingly less misleading'.[22] This is more or less the sense of an absolute good (or evil) which, far from being 'thin', is the thickest of all concepts. Much further off centre, at least on *my* spectrum, is the need of a MacIntyre or an Anscombe for a foundational and dogmatic metaphysics underpinning that sense. Off centre in the opposite direction is the need for an equally foundational and dogmatic humanism, defining itself by its refusal to recognise that same sense. I need hardly add that literature has been the mode of modern thought which has most consciously explored these various types of self-transcendence, when even philosophers have often simply assumed them, as the unacknowledged legislators of systems of thought.

There are two rarely associated thinkers whom I believe to be central to this conversation about literature and moral philosophy: a twentieth-century philosopher and a nineteenth-century critic. One could plausibly claim, as many of these philosophers explicitly do, that it is Ludwig Wittgenstein's thought about morality and art which lies behind most of these arguments. For Wittgenstein morality and art are both modes of *being*, not of fact or of fact-versus-value. This might be shown to be true, or at least nascent, even in early Wittgenstein: in the *Tractatus* and the 'Lecture on Ethics'. And of course the later Wittgenstein makes those famous pronouncements on meaning as use and on description rather than explanation as the proper solution to the problems of philosophy and of life. If Wittgenstein and Martin Heidegger are indeed, as many believe, the two philosophers who this century have done most to redirect their discipline away from its Cartesian and Kantian affiliations, then students of the two foremost disciples of Heidegger, Jürgen Habermas and Hans-Georg Gadamer, will hear many analogues of their thought in what I have been saying. But they are analogues, not echoes. These are two distinct conversations.

[21] The quoted terms are Iris Murdoch's, from 'On "God" and "Good"', 1969, in Murdoch, *The Sovereignty of Good*.
[22] Ibid.

What about the nineteenth-century critic? English literary criticism is a discursive practice which has existed in a more or less recognisable form for about 250 years: since Dr Johnson. It evolved as an unusual means (unparalleled, arguably, in other languages) of putting discursive, reflective, or philosophical prose into close contact with poetic and dramatic poetry; and although the scope of its material has since Johnson extended to include the novel, the more philosophical voice of criticism has retained its attentiveness and responsiveness to the voice of poetry. And that conversation of poetry and criticism has for most of its duration been predominantly ethical. It is David Bromwich's acute observation[23] that two separate subtraditions exist within this general critical tradition. The first includes Johnson, Hume, Burke, Hazlitt, Arnold, and, significantly, Wittgenstein. These writers believe, according to Bromwich, that criticism may be carried on without some founding version of reality or standard of objectivity, but just with the binding force of common habits of reading, and the long duration of certain opinions which acquire the force of custom. The other tradition is an essentialist one, seeking a single right interpretation and an epistemological method. This is the way of German idealism, of Coleridge, and of the latter-day Coleridgeans who have dominated modern academic criticism and literary theory. Bromwich believes that 'criticism is a language for discussing representations of the way people live and think and feel', not 'a map to a special province of truth'. For Coleridge poetry and morality must be grounded in some single great principle or Truth, visible to a trained clerisy but not to the ordinary reader, in which opposites are reconciled or held in synthetic tension and symbol plays a key revelatory role. For William Hazlitt, however, there is no founding principle and nothing for symbols to refer to, no reason why opposites *should* be reconciled, and an ordinary reader who always matters more than the clerisy. I believe Bromwich has a point, and that a critical practice which holds up Hazlitt and Wittgenstein as exemplary may well be of more use to us now than yet more of the one which has for so long held up Coleridge and, more recently, Heidegger. More use, for example, in trying to explain how it was that

[23] David Bromwich, 'Literature and Theory', 1986, reprinted in *A Choice of Inheritance: Self and Community from Burke to Frost* (Cambridge, Mass., 1989); and *Hazlitt: The Mind of a Critic* (Oxford and New York, 1983).

between the 1790s and the 1820s so many English-speaking poets failed to escape from that central Cartesian self, with its search for a theoretical account of the world and, often, its sceptical disillusionment with the eventual failure of the search. Yet at the same time some of the best novelists, so unlike each other in other ways – Austen, Scott, Edgeworth, Peacock – *did* escape these things. Why? And why, some years later, did Browning and Dickens escape, but not Tennyson or Mill? And does the question have any bearing, this century, on the poetry of Eliot and Yeats? Or the novels of Lawrence? Or more recent poetry and fiction: Pynchon and Bellow, for example? Or Martin Amis and A. S. Byatt? To take a particular case: Shelley's extraordinarily instructive ten-year passage from egocentric theorising to untheorised and self-forgetful evaluative description.[24] This is something a dissociated Coleridgean criticism cannot even see, as Diamond would have predicted: and yet such a criticism is what Shelley has mainly suffered. This criticism has looked either for excesses of lyrical feeling, or else for symbol and progressive social theory and Oedipalism and transcendentalism and scepticism and Platonism, etc. The seventeenth century taught us to pursue 'knowledge'; but as our moral philosophers are saying, as Wittgenstein and Hazlitt would agree, and as Shelley put it, we lack 'the creative faculty to imagine that which we know'.

[24] On this, see Simon Haines, *Shelley's Poetry: The Divided Self* (London and New York, 1997).

2

Martha Nussbaum and the need for novels

CORA DIAMOND

I

This chapter is about one of Martha Nussbaum's central claims in *Love's Knowledge*:[1] that there are some moral views which can be adequately expressed only through novels, and that therefore the study of such novels belongs within moral philosophy.

That claim is the second of the book's main claims. The first is that what view of life, of how to live, is conveyed by a text depends in part on formal features of that text. If we accept that point, it follows that formal features of various different sorts of literary texts may fit them for the expression of various views of life that cannot be expressed in other ways.

Suppose a philosopher seriously doubted both of Martha Nussbaum's main claims. Perhaps s/he doubts whether there are any moral views that only literary narratives of some kind can convey. How could we investigate that issue within moral philosophy except by giving careful attention to such texts, except by trying to see how their form *was*, or whether it *was not*, related to the moral thought conveyed by the text? It seems, then, that a doubt whether form and content are related in the way Professor Nussbaum thinks they are would commit us, just as much as would acceptance of her claims, to including an open-minded study of literary texts within moral philosophy.

[1] *Love's Knowledge: Essays on Philosophy and Literature* (New York and Oxford, 1990). Hereafter I use *LKn* as an abbreviation of the title.

So that is an argument that, even if Nussbaum's claims on behalf of the significance of literary texts were false, the sensitive study of those texts would still be important for moral philosophy: for there is, I should say, no adequate way of justifying the rejection of her claims except through study of such texts as those she herself discusses in her book.

Another way of putting this point: her book itself – through its commentary on certain novels – makes out an undismissible case. It succeeds in making the discussion of those texts important for moral philosophy whether or not her claims on their behalf are accepted, since she puts philosophers into the position of having to consider those novels and her commentary on them if they want to resist the kinds of claim she makes.

II

I turn now to the views of a philosopher who I think would disagree with my argument, R. M. Hare. Professor Nussbaum quotes a remark of Hare's: 'What are novels anyway but universal prescriptions?' (*LKn*, p. 166). When Hare came up with a similar remark thirty-odd years ago, he based it on the philosophical theory that one's moral view of anything in a novel (he spoke of one's moral opinion of its characters, but what he said was meant to apply as well to moral views of situations or actions) is a view concerning a *type* and not a particular. There are no concrete individuals in novels.[2] And so any moral judgment we are led to by a novel is necessarily universal. Moral philosophers do not have to do any careful reading of novels to know what they *can* offer us. They can present complex minor premises of practical arguments, they can try to lead us to major premises, universal practical principles, prescriptions, from which *what to do* can be inferred. If we already know the nature of moral thinking, there is nothing about what it might be which we need to turn to novels to see.

This is a very time-saving way of doing moral philosophy. The assumptions on which it rests were criticised years ago by Iris Murdoch: assumptions about what moral philosophy itself is (i.e., what its domain includes), about moral psychology, and about

[2] R. M. Hare, 'Universalisability', *Proceedings of the Aristotelian Society* 55 (1954/5), pp. 295–312, at p. 310: 'no work of fiction can be about a concrete individual'.

language and life. The assumptions themselves, she argued, were tied to a particular moral view, influenced by Kant, by Protestantism, by liberalism.[3] Martha Nussbaum's book may be seen as a sustained and detailed criticism of those assumptions, a demonstration that they are indeed not part of some neutral philosophical standpoint definitive of moral philosophy but belong to a moral view antithetic to that expressed through the novels she discusses.[4]

(The philosophical idea that novels cannot be about individuals is discussed separately by Iris Murdoch in her comments on Hare. That is, she does not treat it as part of the group of views distinguishing the moral philosophers she criticises. She says of Hare's view of novels that it is a strange view, since we *imagine* fictitious characters as concrete individuals. If our information about them is limited, that is also true of the real people we know; and what information we have is 'endlessly open to reinterpretation'. I do not think that Martha Nussbaum took in the full oddity of Hare's view.[5] In commenting on his remark, she says that Maggie Verver's judgments about Adam Verver (in *The Golden Bowl*) are responses to him as the particular person he is (*LKn*, p. 167), but Nussbaum does not (I think) see that Hare would take Maggie herself to be necessarily not a particular but a complexly specified *type*. Hare's view of novels is not merely 'strange'. Nussbaum's discussion of *Hard Times*[6] and of the Gradgrind view of imagination and stories suggests a connection between Hare's kind of utilitarianism and his seeing stories as presentations of 'types', that is, as not genuinely about individuals. Speaking about novels, she says that 'respect for a soul' is 'built into the genre itself' (p. 242); and it is precisely that conception of novels, of the kind of moral thinking they embody, that is

[3] Iris Murdoch, 'Vision and Choice in Morality', *Proceedings of the Aristotelian Society*, supplementary volume XXX (1956), pp. 32–58.
[4] See also *LKn*, p.290. As Nussbaum points out there, the assumptions underlying current philosophical approaches to ethics are given no justification within that body of work.
[5] I take the remark of Hare's, quoted by Martha Nussbaum, to be based on his 1954/5 view of fictional narratives; and it might be suggested that Nussbaum is perhaps more charitable to Hare in not taking his remark to be based on the theory of fiction he once held. I believe his theory of fiction is a part of the group of views he then expressed about particulars and universals, and which in essentials he still holds.
[6] See her chapter below, 'The literary imagination in public life', in part 3 of this volume.

rejected in Hare's theory of fiction. Respect for a soul is response to a concrete individual person: and it is just such a conception of the characters in a novel that Hare denies to be logically conceivable.[7])

Hare's remark, 'What are novels anyway but universal prescriptions?', interests me because it expresses in very condensed form an argument against my point about Martha Nussbaum's work: that she has made it a significant question within moral philosophy whether such novels as she discusses convey moral views that cannot be expressed in other forms, and hence has made the careful study of such novels (to see whether this is so) part of moral philosophy. I want now to develop an argument against Hare, but indirectly, via a consideration of Wordsworth's *Prelude*.

There is a tactical reason for considering *The Prelude* rather than novels. When it is suggested that novels might be significant within moral philosophy, many philosophers, including Hare, believe that the supposed moral relevance will be found in *what the characters do*. The characters – their dilemmas, their deliberation, their choices, their judgments, their conception of their situation – will supposedly be of interest to moral philosophers. But what is primarily important for Martha Nussbaum, in her treatment of particular novels in *Love's Knowledge*, is the activity of the novelist: his moral vision, his moral achievement. In discussing her claims, people tend to get distracted by the fact that she does direct attention to (among other things) the deliberations of characters in the novels. Her primary focus, though, is always on *how to live*, and how a novel can convey the novelist's view of *that*. I think that this has sometimes been missed because the subject of deliberation and its nature is indeed important to her: it figures significantly, she argues, in the view of life of the novelists she discusses. And it is also easy to take what the characters in a novel do as the centre of possible concern for the moral philosopher, because of the sheer dramatic interest of what they do and what happens to them. A claim comparable to that which Martha Nussbaum enters on behalf of novels can be made on behalf of *The Prelude*. But it is less easy, in the case of *The Prelude*, to misunderstand a claim about the relevance of the text to moral philosophy

---

[7] I return to this topic later, in section v.

as a claim about the relevance of deliberations and choices described within the text.

(That Nussbaum's focus is on the moral activity of the novelist has been plain, I should say, even in the earliest of the sequence of essays in *Love's Knowledge*. See the whole of part 2 of 'Flawed Crystals', but especially pp. 140–2. The 'example' relevant to moral philosophers is 'the entire text, revealed as the imaginative effort of a human character [the author]'. The views in the text 'derive their power' and their interest for moral philosophers 'from the way in which they emerge as the ruminations of such a high and fine mind concerning the tangled mysteries of these imaginary lives'. We could not 'see whether such views were or were not exemplary for us if this mind simply stated its conclusions flatly, if it did not unfold before us the richness of its reflection, allowing us to follow and to share its adventures'. That is a clear short statement of the fundamental argument of the book; its central 'examples' are not provided by what goes on within the novels, but by the novels themselves, regarded as expressions of the complex vision of moral thinkers, requiring the kind of statement given them by the novel. Nussbaum's aim has been missed even by such careful commentators as Richard Wollheim and Daniel Brudney. Wollheim says that 'Professor Nussbaum's principal reason for thinking that literature is a crucial element in moral philosophy is her view of moral deliberation': Maggie Verver's project, in the second half of *The Golden Bowl*, can thus help us see that moral philosophers have too simple a conception of deliberation.[8] The deliberative activities of a character are what constitutes the significant counter-example provided by the text. Deliberation, as presented in the text, is then relevant to the evaluation of philosophical theories (in something like the way a historical study, giving an interpretation of seventeenth-century physics, might help us evaluate philosophical theories about physics, and judge whether they were oversimple). Brudney discusses in detail whether Nussbaum is using an extended passage in *The Golden Bowl* as 'a counter-example to theories holding moral evaluation to be a matter of rule application', but concludes that her 'real theme' is the importance of the creative

---

[8] Richard Wollheim, 'Flawed Crystals: James's *The Golden Bowl* and the Plausibility of Literature as Moral Philosophy', *New Literary History*, 15 (1983), pp. 185–91, at p. 190.

shaping of action in the context of deliberation, shown in the passage from *The Golden Bowl*.[9] Here the idea is that a text like *The Golden Bowl* is useful to the philosopher considering theories put forward by philosophers, by showing something that those philosophers have failed adequately to consider.)

Like some of the novels that Martha Nussbaum has discussed, *The Prelude* is a work which is complex in the sense of including the expression of ideas about how it, or imaginative writing of the sort to which it belongs, bears on the moral thinking of its readers. It portrays the growth of Wordsworth's mind, but the role of imaginative development in his case – the case of Wordsworth as poet – is meant to show the importance of imagination in a full human life; and Wordsworth's aim is tied to his conception of the imaginative activity of the reader of his poem: what Nature has been to him, he may be to his reader.[10]

What relevance has this to moral thought? Wordsworth believed that 'truth in moral judgment' and 'delight that fails not, in the external universe' depend on a kind of liveness of being that combines creative activity with an openness of response to the natural and human world. His own story shows the development of those powers through the action on him, over a long period of time, of what he refers to as Nature. Wordsworth's poem is thus also meant to show how there can be a deadness or falseness in thought, including in particular moral thought, moral judgment, if our judgments do not issue from full imaginative life, do not have in them their connectedness to the soul's imaginative history and to the kind of love inspired by, tied to, imaginative life. What reason is, and what its relation is to moral thought and to human happiness, are explicable only through recognising reason as the 'moving soul' in the sort of development he traces. His own poetic power, he hopes, exercised in *The Prelude* itself, may contribute to the imaginative life of his readers in a way analogous to the workings of Nature on his own soul. (The ideas I have sketched

---

[9] Daniel Brudney, 'Knowledge and Silence: *The Golden Bowl* and Moral Philosophy', *Critical Inquiry*, 16.2 (Winter 1990), pp. 397–437. The entirety of section 2 is relevant; my quotations come from pp. 427 and 426.

[10] *Prelude* (1805 version), book XII, lines 278–312. See also M. W. Abrams: '*The Prelude* is a poem which incorporates the discovery of its own *ars poetica*' (*Natural Supernaturalism* (New York, 1971), p. 78); W. B. Gallie, 'Is *The Prelude* a Philosophical Poem?', *Philosophy*, 22 (1947), pp. 124–38; Joseph Gold, *Charles Dickens: Radical Moralist* (Minneapolis, 1972), pp. 176–7, for a comparison of *David Copperfield* with *The Prelude*.

bear also on the character of philosophical thought, and on the way in which the poem shows something that philosophical thinking can be.)

Moral judgments are not here seen as abstractly true or false, true or false out of connection with their life on their occasions of use, their rootedness then in the heart, the imaginative life, of the person who thinks the thought or makes the moral judgment. Wordsworth's own sense of the dignity of human life gets its imaginative sustenance from such particular 'tender scenes' as that in which he saw a labourer, cradling his sickly child in his brawny arms:

> He held the child, and, bending over it
> As if he were afraid both of the sun
> And of the air which he had come to seek,
> He eyed it with unutterable love.[11]

Sights like these, scenes of mountains looming over him at night, sensings of the souls of lonely places, experiences like that in which he waited for his father at the end of a school term, out on the fields on a stormy day, shortly before the death of his father – all these are now, many years later, part of his being capable of true moral thought, through their shaping influence on the affections and imaginative life.

I am presenting Wordsworth's ideas not because I take them to be right, but because I think it obvious that his conception of moral psychology – of what is active in our minds, in our moral thinking and responsiveness – is profoundly different from Hare's conception. Wordsworth's moral psychology can, in his poem, be seen to be inseparable from his vision of what fulness of human life consists in. The making of particular moral judgments is decisively *placed* within the more general picture, which includes an idea of the workings of the soul, a conception of fulness of life, and a contrast between the world as it appears to a dead habitual kind of perception and the 'active' universe.

---

[11] VIII (1805) 856–9. It is no accident that Wordsworth describes a man displaying 'female softness'. Compare his description of his wife: 'The reason firm, the temperate will, / Endurance, foresight, strength, and skill'. Wordsworth's picture of a good woman's character includes virtues that many of his contemporaries would have thought belonged especially or only to men. Here and elsewhere we can see his view that 'male' and 'female' traits need to be combined in us.

The poem shows us, then, an interesting kind of moral thinking; and I include as part of its moral thinking its taking its readers through, its working us into, its conception of the relation between imagination and moral thought. The kind of thinking presented includes the self-conscious treatment of the poetry as playing a role, or having a 'ministry', analogous to that of Nature in Wordsworth's own development.

Any serious argument that Wordsworth is doing what I have said he is would require careful discussion of the text, not just a few allusions to it. All that I want to draw from the account I have given is a single point. It would be extremely implausible to say of Wordsworth's poem what Hare says of novels: 'What are novels anyway but universal prescriptions?' Wordsworth's poem is not any universal prescription: 'Bring up children as I was brought up', or whatever. Why should not a poem embody a moral psychology that gives a place to imaginative life radically distinct from Hare's moral psychology? And why should that not be something that could be conveyed only by the poem? The *possibility* of views about morality and its nature, themselves actually a kind of moral view, needing to be worked through in a text like *The Prelude* – well, how can such a possibility be dismissed, without consideration of the poetry itself, except by plain dogmatic insistence that it cannot be so?

Hare's question, 'What are novels anyway but universal prescriptions?' was, I suggested, a condensed argument against considering novels as important within moral philosophy. But the argument relies for what plausibility it has on its idea of what novels can do: they provide full and complex descriptions of types of events, types of people, examples of what we may be invited to see as good or bad deliberation. Against this, I am suggesting that a novel may be an expression of moral thought in something like the way *The Prelude* is. And there is no plausibility in suggesting that the possible moral significance of *The Prelude* is limited to its containing descriptions of situations linked to universal prescriptions. The point of looking at *The Prelude* was to place it *with* novels like those Martha Nussbaum discusses, as presentations, through the use of narratives, of moral views in which there are links between some conception of moral psychology, a conception of language and the world, and a conception of how specific moral judgments may be related to views of life and human fulfilment. Her view of what novels may be is close to what I have suggested *The Prelude* may be. Now in fact the specific moral views with which she is concerned can be expressed only in novels which *do* present deliberation and choice. But that fact does not license the idea that the moral interest of the novels is that the cases they contain of deliberation support an Aristotelian theory or provide counter-examples to Kantian or utilitarian theories. It is not what the novel *contains* that is supposed to be an example supporting or tending to disconfirm this or the other theory put forward by philosophers. Philosophers have complex views about moral thought, expressed in philosophical prose. Poets or novelists may also have complex views of moral life, moral thought, expressible only through the kind of writing *they* do. That is the idea.

III

I have not yet mentioned one important part of Martha Nussbaum's argument that the novels she discusses should be included within moral philosophy. She believes that there is a kind of philosophical inquiry which, without the novels, would be seriously incomplete.[12] The philosophical inquiry she has in mind is the inquiry how one should live; it involves, besides the working out and full expression of particular answers to that question, a kind of reflective critical comparison of those answers. Since some important answers to the inquiry can, she argues, be presented only in novels, novels are necessary to the inquiry.

You might think that if you rejected Martha Nussbaum's conception of moral philosophy, as containing that sort of inquiry, you would be pulling the rug out from under her claims for the philosophical importance of studying those novels. I do not think that is so.

In section II, I argued for something I take to be central in *Love's Knowledge*, namely that the novels discussed in it *are* the moral thinking of the writers. They present an extremely interesting kind of moral thinking. *The Prelude* presents a somewhat different kind of moral thinking. Novels in which realistic narrative form is rejected may present further important kinds of moral thinking.[13]

---

[12] See especially *LKn*, pp. 24–5.   [13] See section IV, below.

If we are moral philosophers, whatever else we may think moral philosophy is or includes, we surely should take it to be concerned with moral thinking, its forms, their aims, possible objectivity, and so on. Martha Nussbaum gives us a strong case for the philosophical interest of the novels she discusses, a case which is actually independent of her conception of philosophy as itself including inquiry directed at answering the question how we should live. This is because she lets us see the novels as moral thinking, moral thinking interestingly different from what we usually consider in philosophy. Her achievement is indeed tied to letting us see the novels as themselves responses to the question how we should live. By taking novels in that way to be moral thinking, she puts herself at a substantial distance from most contemporary moral theorists, for whom moral thinking is the making of moral judgments, using either general moral terms like 'good' and 'bad', 'right' and 'wrong', or more specialised evaluative terms like 'just', 'courageous', 'generous', 'murder' and so on.

Think of Blake: Blake's moral thinking is in part a visionary attack on moral-judgment-making. If we as moral philosophers have a model of what moral thinking is, based on our preferred range of cases, we can indeed impose that model on all cases, ones that we look at and ones that we ignore.[14] But we cannot see what kind of loss that is for moral philosophy unless we do not just read Blake's poetry (say), but become aware of the complex relation between our desire to treat the poetry as falling within particular patterns of rational order (definitive of moral thinking, as we see it), and the poetry as subversion of that desire. Is the poetry itself tied to the subversion of desires and habits internal to moral-judgment-making of the sort philosophers usually have in mind? We need at least to be aware of that as a question.

Martha Nussbaum's success in showing the significance of literary texts for moral philosophy does not depend (as it might at first appear to do) on her wide understanding of what is included within moral philosophy.[15] Her readings of particular novels, and

---

[14] Reasons for not imposing such a model are discussed by Murdoch in 'Vision and Choice'; see note 3 above.

[15] The wide understanding of what moral philosophy includes *is* important for her overall project. In this chapter I am not directly concerned with her project, but rather with a question that may be asked from several different points of view, about the kinds of relevance literary texts may have to moral philosophy. There are, though, many ways of answering that question that I do not discuss at all.

her raising questions, through those readings, about the ties between text and moral vision, show us that there are no short cuts:
the *only* way to see what kinds of moral thinking may be found in
literary texts is by giving them sensitive attention, of a sort we are
not trained or encouraged, as philosophers, to give them. *We* look
for arguments, for theories, for supporting data or counter-
examples. The idea that we need to learn to read with a different
sort of eye, attentive to different sorts of things, may strike us as
very strange; but there are no short cuts for philosophers.

IV

I claimed in section 2 that *The Prelude* and the novels considered
by Martha Nussbaum can be relevant to moral philosophy in the
same sort of way. Here I look further at the interest of such works
for moral philosophy.

I used *The Prelude* to suggest what was wrong with Hare's
dismissive remark about novels. But I could have done that by
looking instead at novels of a radically different sort from those
discussed in *Love's Knowledge*. Those novels – classic realist novels
– contain scenes of deliberation and choice, and this is necessary
to the moral view they express. Think, though, of a novel like Kurt
Vonnegut's *Slaughterhouse Five* (or, to give it its full title, which
matters, *Slaughterhouse Five or The Children's Crusade: A Duty-
Dance with Death*[16]). What in that novel is morally expressive is –
centrally – the absence of coherent narrative development. The
'manner' of the novel is described on the title page, so that you
cannot miss it, as 'telegraphic schizophrenic'.[17] The author writes
about his problem: how to write a book about a massacre. But the
book certainly is not a universal prescription: e.g. (to take one
which might be 'read off' it), 'If you write a book about a massacre,
don't write it with parts for Frank-Sinatra-types or John-Wayne-
types.' The author has told his sons 'that they are not under any
circumstances to take part in massacres, and that the news of
massacres of enemies is not to fill them with satisfaction or glee'
(p. 19), but the book is not a corresponding universal prescription

---

[16] My quotations come from the Dell edition of 1988 (New York).
[17] More fully: 'THIS IS A NOVEL SOMEWHAT IN THE TELEGRAPHIC
SCHIZOPHRENIC MANNER OF TALES OF THE PLANET TRALFAMADORE,
WHERE THE FLYING SAUCERS COME FROM.'

addressed to its readers. The moral interest of the work cannot be taken to lie in how characters in it deal with morally demanding situations. The connection between features of the text (not only the 'schizophrenia' of the narrative but the organising use of irony) and the novel as moral thought is a main subject of this novel. The subject, that is, is how to think relatively decently (or whether there is even the possibility of thinking relatively decently) about our world, the world in which we massacre each other: the problems of *telling* about a massacre (thus also problems of *listening to someone telling about*, or of *reading about* a massacre). The moral activity of the novel lies in its treatment of that subject, of the relation between art, memory, and massacre.[18] A discussion of this type of novel could be used to make the same kind of point I made via *The Prelude*: we should not be derailed by the significance of deliberation and choice within the realist novel, and led by the structure of such novels to think that the moral interest of novels can lie only in how their characters deliberate and choose. But I did have reasons for choosing *The Prelude* rather than such novels as *Slaughterhouse Five*.

When Martha Nussbaum argues that novels like those of Henry James should be seriously studied within philosophy, her argument depends on her seeing those novels as giving 'a particular set of answers to the question "How should one live?"' (*LKn*, p. 36). She characterises their answers as, in a broad sense, Aristotelian. The view of life expressed in *The Prelude* does not, I think, belong in the family of Aristotelian views. It lacks some of the salient features of the family, but it does have *some* of those features. I want now to look at some of those resemblances, in order to give a further argument for the significance of literary texts to moral philosophy. In discussing the Aristotelian views, I

---

18 The tradition to which this novel belongs is described by Samuel Hynes in *A War Imagined* (New York, 1991). See, for example, his discussion of *All Quiet on the Western Front*, and the importance in that novel of pervasive irony, of the absence of coherent continuous narrative, and of the absence of narrative closure (pp. 425–7). Hynes connects those features of First World War novels to the questioning by the novels not just of particular values, but of 'the whole idea of values' (p. 426). See also Hynes's discussion of *Parade's End* (especially pp. 432–3), and the relation between Modernism in such novels and the unavailability of values. The role of art and the artist in a novel like *Slaughterhouse Five* has a complex relation to the role of art and artist in the classic nineteenth-century novel. What has happened to the figure of the artist is suggested by the description of the implied author of *Slaughterhouse Five* as an 'old fart', a 'pillar of salt', a 'trafficker' in literary techniques.

limit myself to two of the authors treated by Nussbaum, Dickens and James.[19]

The acknowledgment of mystery is an important theme for Nussbaum in characterising the literary texts she calls Aristotelian, and she draws special attention to the acknowledgment in those texts of the mystery in human lives.[20] There is an explicit expression of the sense of mystery in human life in book VII of *The Prelude*:[21]

> one feeling was there which belonged
> To this great city by exclusive right:
> How often in the overflowing streets
> Have I gone forward with the crowd, and said
> Unto myself, 'The face of every one
> That passes by me is a mystery.'

That sense of mystery is tied to Wordsworth's story-making imagination (his mind's going on to 'thoughts of what, and whither, when and how'[22]), but also to a spirit of response to life, expressed throughout the book: that there is far more to things, to life, than what we know or understand. Such a feeling is tied to a rejection of the spirit of *knowingness* often found in abstract moral and social theorising, a spirit which may recognise the existence of phenomena not yet satisfactorily explained or dealt with, but which is reductive in its idea of our relation to the world, and in what it takes understanding and knowledge to be,[23] a spirit that is

---

[19] Here, and elsewhere in the chapter, I ignore any questions that might be raised about the relation between the family of 'Aristotelian' views and the actual views of Aristotle. Since, in this section, I consider the philosophical interest of a somewhat different grouping of texts from the grouping important in *Love's Knowledge*, I should note at the outset Nussbaum's comments (*LKn*, p. 364) on the differences between Dickens and James. In several respects the sense of life expressed in *The Prelude* is closer to that in Dickens than it is to that in James.

[20] Compare also Nussbaum's remarks, in connection with Walt Whitman's 'Song of Myself', about the acknowledgment of mystery in nature, in 'The literary imagination in public life' in part 3 of this volume.

[21] (1805 version), lines 593–8.

[22] As if our stories went invisibly about with us. That is an image used by Dickens, at the end of *Dombey and Son*.

[23] See, for a good example, Daniel Dennett's 'The Moral First Aid Manual' (in *The Tanner Lectures on Human Values*, VIII (Salt Lake City, 1988), pp. 121–47): Dennett's comparison between the absence of computationally tractable methods of forecasting in meteorology and the absence of such methods in ethics (pp. 126, 129), his conception of the role of specialists in addressing the problems in arriving at an ethics 'manual' (p. 131), the example he chooses to give 'the ubiquitous features of real time decision making' (pp. 131–3), and his language throughout.

often 'restless' in its supposed wisdom, eager to re-order human lives in accordance with its rational plans. One picture of that spirit, discussed by Nussbaum, is Gradgrind; in the moral prodigy of book v of *The Prelude* we have another. (See also the passage in *Prelude*, book xii[24] about 'statists' and the hollowness of their conception of 'the wealth of nations'.)

In the 'Aristotelian' family of texts, we are shown how false moral, political, and social thought may be premised on abstractions, and how such thought lacks ties with, lacks nourishment from, the realities of concrete individual lives. For Wordsworth and for the 'Aristotelian' texts, dependence on abstract conceptions of humanity is linked to failure in imaginative life, which is contrasted with life nourished by imaginative response to individuals, and by stories. Here again Dickens and Wordsworth are particularly close. Wordsworth's great expression of what imaginative tales may mean to us when we are young ('oh, then we feel, we feel / We know, when we have friends') might equally have been Dickens's.[25] Wordsworth, like Dickens, blesses the tales, while contrasting that blessing with their condemnation by what is in effect Gradgrind rationalism.

That important resemblance between *The Prelude* and the 'Aristotelian' views is related to two others.

(1) When man is conceived in the spirit of an abstract rationalism, the connection between moral thought and its imaginative and emotional history disappears from view. The abstract moral deliberator has no capacities that can be shown only through their development, only through their still living connections with that development. The rejection of abstract rationalism is thus tied to a very different approach to moral psychology. A moral psychology may require presentation through a story of development, intended to lead the reader to make sense of the pattern of growth or change in a particular way. The Bildungsroman is then a form suited to the expression of certain conceptions of moral psychol-

---

[24] Lines 69–87 (1805); lines 64–84, book xiii (1850).

[25] *Prelude*, book v (1805), 546–7. See Martha Nussbaum's discussion of *David Copperfield* and the role of books as essential friends in David's life, *LKn*, pp. 230–1. The particular book to which Wordsworth gives most attention is *The Arabian Nights*, and it is specifically mentioned by Dickens in the passage Nussbaum quotes. Henry James uses it in characterising Gertrude in *The Europeans*: her reading of it while the others in her family go to church marks her difference from them, shows her to be imaginatively nourished in ways they are not.

ogy; and *The Prelude*, like *David Copperfield*, and like *The Ambassadors*, is a kind of Bildungsroman.[26]

(2) *The Prelude* and *David Copperfield* are not just stories of the development of their central character; they are stories of the growth of an artist: of a poet, of a storyteller. The figure of the artist is important for Wordsworth and Dickens (and indeed, as Martha Nussbaum shows, for James as well) in exploring and presenting more general ideas about human life, fulfilment, and failure, the role of imagination, responsiveness, and responsibility. Nussbaum argues that there is not just an analogy between moral imagination and the creative imagination of the artist, but something more: the Jamesian conception of moral value allows us to see how novels like his can be moral achievements, and how 'the well-lived life is a work of literary art' (*LKn*, p. 148). Dickens has a similar conception of how artistic creativity is related to moral life;[27] in section II above, I sketched Wordsworth's idea of that relation.[28] The idea of such a connection should be traced back to Blake.[29]

When Martha Nussbaum discusses the Aristotelian family of views, she contrasts them with Kantian, Platonic, Stoic, and Utilitarian views. I want to discuss a different contrast, also important in *Love's Knowledge*. It is tied to the things I have noted: the use of the figure of the artist to present a conception of human life, the connections between moral activity and creative imagination, the idea that a novel like James's might constitute a moral achievement. The texts I have described (which I shall refer to as 'artist'

---

[26] Compare Barbara Hardy's description of *The Ambassadors* as a 'middle-aged Bildungsroman' (*The Moral Art of Dickens* (New York, 1970), p. 28).

[27] See note 10, reference to Joseph Gold. His book can be regarded as a detailed argument for the claim made in the text about Dickens's conception of art in relation to moral life. See especially the introduction, the organising use of the quotation from Henry Fielding ('Life may as properly be called an art as any other' (p. 7), and the discussion of those Dickensian characters who are 'the artists of being human', who 'create whole worlds' (pp. 8–9).

[28] Compare also the connection Wordsworth makes between 'palsied imagination' and 'indurated hearts'. That is his description of the source of a kind of bad reading of his poetry (in 'Essay, Supplementary to the Preface' of *Lyrical Ballads*, 1815), but that particular connection is only a case of the more general connection between imaginative death and failure in responsiveness to what is of value.

[29] See F. R. Leavis, 'Justifying One's Valuation of Blake', in *Human World*, 7 (May 1972), pp. 42–64, especially p. 59, where Leavis writes of the continuity, important for Blake, 'from the inherent creativity of perception to the creativity, trained and conscious, of the artist', and ascribes to Blake 'a conception of human creativity that is at the same time a conception of human responsibility'.

texts) are opposed to some important philosophical ideas: the idea that there is some more or less isolatable group of uses of language characteristic of moral thinking (e.g., uses of 'moral words'), the idea that moral thinking, or moral language, may be given some general characterisation, which might then perhaps be illustrated by a few schematic examples. The 'artist' texts take a contrary view in part because of the importance in them of the idea that moral valuing may be alive or dead. (A good example of this, described by Nussbaum, is the 'refusal of life' in Maggie Verver's moral responses in the first half of *The Golden Bowl*; *LKn*, p. 142.) This possibility of livingness or deadness is absolutely central to moral thought: something that did not have deadness as a risk would not be moral thought (moral thought as understood in these texts). What is meant by livingness of moral thought (or any thought) cannot be given in advance, and is not tied to any particular linguistic forms. So too the understanding of something said or written (or painted, carved in stone or shown on a movie screen or whatever) *as* expressive of moral value (and also the understanding of *what* is expressed) depends on our own moral activity, our own 'energy of response'.[30] I am here suggesting that the 'artist' texts[31] imply an idea of what *reflection* about morality is, if such reflection is truly about *moral value*, an idea that contrasts with our usual philosophical reflection on morality. If we are engaged in reflecting about moral value, we need, as writers or as readers, to be exercising creative imagination: that is their view. The 'artist' texts imply that our standard philosophical approach to morality risks missing altogether what it aims at.

(When, at the beginning of *Love's Knowledge*, Nussbaum seeks to characterise 'ethical inquiry', she gives us this suggestion: it tries to answer the question how one should live. There is no easy way to tell which things, among those which people say or think, have a bearing on or express their conception of how to live. We might wonder whether or how a particular image (say), or a proverb

---

[30] I take the phrase 'energy of response' from Northrop Frye's description of what is demanded of the reader of Blake (*Fearful Symmetry* (Princeton, 1969), p. 7). But the idea of reading as requiring energy and activity in some way corresponding to that of the writer is explicit in Wordsworth and in James. Nussbaum emphasises the importance of the connection between 'energy of response' necessary in the reading of texts and that called for in the reading of life; see especially *LKn*, pp. 140–5.

[31] I mean the 'Aristotelian' texts and *The Prelude*. I have Blake in mind as well, and Martha Nussbaum might want to add Whitman.

('The cistern contains; the fountain overflows') expresses some-one's conception of how to live. And so one important thing about Nussbaum's characterisation of ethical inquiry is precisely that it points us away from the idea that moral thought or 'moral discourse' could be circumscribed in philosophy (even roughly) by some general specification of its essential features. Nussbaum's conception of ethical inquiry is not meant to be 'neutral' (see *LKn*, p. 24). What I want to bring out is its important tie to her philosophical method: we need to *explore* to find where and how there may be reflection on moral value; and we shall not be able to fix limits on where, in what sorts of texts, or using what sorts of words, it may be found.)

In philosophy we should be interested in how oppositions between modes of thought get expressed; and this is particularly important in the case of opposition to our own familiar modes of thought within our practice of philosophy. The texts I have been discussing – the 'artist' texts – have a view of what *valuing* is (and of what it is to have *valuing* as an object of reflection) which is opposed to our familiar philosophical way of thinking, and which is tied to their use of the figure of the artist and to their use of narratives. In philosophy we usually take for granted that we can delineate our field of study, say *morality*, and then get on with our work at the problems arising for philosophical consideration within that field (in whatever way exactly we conceive it). I want to suggest that, in the 'artist' texts, the use of the figure of the artist and the use of literary forms including narrative express a rejection of the very idea implicit in philosophical procedure of what *moral value* is.

So it looks as if my conclusion ought to be: in philosophy we need to look at 'artist' texts to understand their kind of opposition. But it is not quite so simple. For in our philosophical texts a central figure is the implied author. What s/he is *not* is an artist; s/he does not speak to us as someone who must respond with creative imagination and fulness of feeling. S/he is one or other kind of detached investigator, and is often modelled more or less on the scientist; his/her language, and the formal features of what s/he writes, may be more or less modelled on the modes of writing of scientists (including their informal exposition of the contents of logically systematised theories).[32]

---

[32] Compare also Martha Nussbaum's discussion (*LKn*, pp. 20–1) of professionalism in philosophical writing.

The 'artist' texts imply a view of the very subject *moral thinking*, namely, that it will not lie still to be investigated, but is made anew, and shaped in new ways, in our imaginative responses to life. The 'detached investigator' texts imply a subject matter that will lie still to be investigated. Yet I have said that philosophy needs to consider oppositions of thought, including oppositions to its own thought. It needs therefore to read and take seriously 'artist' texts, to explore how the literary features of such texts express opposition to *its* conception of moral inquiry. But to explore such texts seriously is to give up as its only central figure the impersonal investigator of a lying-still subject, and to take on as a new central figure the imaginative reader of texts. This, in a sense, it *cannot* do, so far as its conception of itself is tied to that of the figure of the 'detached investigator'.

If there is any way to draw a conclusion here, it is that the presence in (much) philosophy of that figure of the detached investigator works as a way to insulate philosophical thought from contact with what might challenge it most directly. Yes, we do need in philosophy to read novels; but reading them – *reading* them (in the sense *they* give that term) – is itself a revolutionary act.

V

In this last section I give what can be regarded either as a distinct argument for the claim that we need, as moral philosophers, to consider literary texts, or as an illustrative example for the argument of section IV. I start from a notion important in *Love's Knowledge*, that of particularity.

An appeal to particularity, as something of ethical value, may be meant in different senses. Professor Nussbaum makes that point, and explains it in the vocabulary that Hare developed. Hare drew attention to the fact that *universal* principles, principles which carry no essential reference to individuals, may be general, or may be as *specific* as we find appropriate: that is, they may incorporate reference to features which make a particular situation or particular person relevantly different from others covered by some general rule. But such features, if they make *this* particular situation or person relevantly different, might conceivably recur. A *principled* exception to a rule, through which it may be adapted to special circumstances, is itself a rule applicable to *all* cases relevantly like the exceptional case. If we are confronted with some case like that of the Kantian murderer at the door, asking for the whereabouts of his victim-to-be, we may, unlike Kant, think that the particularities of the case justify telling a lie. We may thus come to accept a principle about when lies are permissible, a principle less *general* than 'One ought never to lie', but no less *universal*.

An appeal to the importance in ethics of attending to the particularities of the cases confronting us may be entirely consistent with holding that in our moral reasoning we make use only of *universal* principles. To tell people to attend to the particularities of the situation may be to tell them to note the need for less *general*, more *specific* principles.

(Professor Nussbaum criticises moral theorists who insist that all moral reasoning is characterised by universality and who also desire moral principles to provide fixed, uniform guidance *in advance* of actual situations. She suggests that her criticism applies to Hare;[33] but Hare believes that highly specific principles (of the sort that might be arrived at by careful, unbiased reflection on a variety of complex cases) are not the sort of principles which ordinary people should use for practical guidance. Hare would grant Nussbaum's point, that the very highly specific rules which a 'universalist' might draw from a text like *The Golden Bowl* are not remotely likely to be suitable for a system intended to guide our actions. But he treats this point as an argument against encouraging people to consider the moral implications of novels. Reading novels, and thinking about fictional cases, is all too likely to lead to undesirable sorts of departure from general rules. He says that 'it would not be too much of an exaggeration to find, in the current prevalence of fiction as an art-form, the principal cause, or at least symptom, of the decline of moral standards which occasions so much concern'.[34])

The ethical importance of particularity in the sense just explained is an element of the 'Aristotelian' view as Martha Nussbaum describes it.[35] But she wants also to draw our attention

---

[33] *LKn*, p. 167; see the reference to Hare's project, suggesting that he thinks of principles as providing fixed, before-the-fact guidance.

[34] R. M. Hare, 'Principles', *Proceedings of the Aristotelian Society*, 73 (1972/3), pp. 1–18, at p. 9.

[35] See, for example, *LKn*, p. 38.

to something else, to particularity in quite a distinct sense, in which it cannot be explained in terms of repeatable features of situations or people (features perhaps repeatable 'only in principle'). How can this other sense of 'particularity' be explained? I shall explain using an example different from any of hers, addressed to children. In a poem, 'Ducks', Walter de la Mare presents for children first this kind of duck and then that: the Farmyard Duck, the Tufted, the Labrador, Pochard, Goldeneye, and so on. Then:

> All these are *kinds*. But every Duck
> Himself is, and himself alone:
> Fleet wing, arched neck, webbed foot, round eye,
> And marvellous cage of bone.
> Clad in this beauty a creature dwells
> Of sovran instinct, sense and skill;
> Yet secret as the hidden wells
> Whence Life itself doth rill.

Every Duck himself is, and himself alone. De la Mare is expressing and also teaching a kind of understanding of individual life, a kind of response to it. Every duck is *that* duck, is him*self*: a feeling for that can be in the child's attention to these creatures, and can thus also be in the child's ways of acting, in our ways of acting. The sense of life in the poem, the sense of the mystery of *this* feathered creature, with *his* one life, is akin to the sense of the mystery of individual human life felt by Wordsworth in the crowded streets of London: 'The face of every one that passes by me is a mystery': *each is himself*, this man, with this face, with his one life. There is *who he is*.

Response to particularity in this second sense enters moral life in a variety of ways. It might, for example, play a role in how we think of an attempt to rescue someone whom we do not know, perhaps someone in danger at sea. The urgency we see in the rescue may be tied to a sense of each person being who s/he is, with his/her one life. In order to be touched by that individuality of life we need not actually know the person him/herself. Indeed there are situations in which we keep from ourselves this awareness of the individual life of people whom we do not know, precisely because of the kind of difficulties such realisation can create for us, for example in official roles.[36]

---

[36] I am indebted to A. D. Woozley for discussion of this point.

But the sense of the particular person, of who he is, who she is, of *this* person, is central in our relations to friends, parents, lovers. The shaping importance of particularity in these relationships is a main theme of *Love's Knowledge*, and recurs in Martha Nussbaum's discussions of love, and of its connections with loss and with responsive, responsible action.

Hare treats with some contempt the idea that in ethics we need to consider particularity in this sense.[37] He believes that ethical appeals to such particularity rest on two confusions. One is the confusion between *generality* and *universality*. What he means is that someone who recognises that a very *general* principle gives bad results applied to some case or cases may not realise that the *specificity* of principle called for by such cases does not entail giving up *universality*. Whatever may be true of other moral thinkers, Martha Nussbaum is certainly not guilty of that confusion. What she says about particularity is carefully formulated to take into account the distinction between generality and universality.

The second confusion on which appeals to particularity supposedly rest is that of thinking that what can be *named* (the individual) cannot be described:

This confusion is peculiarly attractive to those who do not themselves like being described, especially by scientists and moralists. They have thus been led to say that *people*, and the situations in which people find themselves, are 'unutterably particular', and thus beyond the reach of any universal predicate or principle. ... But in fact individuals can be described as fully and precisely as we wish by the ingenious device (which is even older than the confusion of these philosophers) of putting the names of the individuals as subjects and appending predicates to them.[38]

The passage quoted is interesting, not only in its discussion of the alleged confusion, but also in its view of the emotional basis of that confusion. For Hare is certainly right in thinking that the appeal to particularity he finds confused *is* tied to emotions. And right that the emotions in question are attitudes towards certain kinds of description, descriptions in a certain spirit.[39] I

---

[37] Hare, 'Universalisability', p. 310.
[38] Ibid. For comments on this passage, and its will to exclude uncongenial forms of moral thought, see Murdoch, 'Vision and Choice', pp. 46–51.
[39] He is utterly wrong in thinking that the attitude towards such descriptions is a matter of dislike of *being* described in the relevant way.

want to focus not on that issue but on what Hare speaks of as the confusion of thinking that what can be named cannot be described.

Certainly a view that treats the recognition of particularity as important in ethics (particularity here not reducible to repeatable describable features of people or situations) *is* a view about the limits of the kind of description Hare has in mind. There is something important for ethics not captured by that sort of descriptive language, in which we put a name to an individual subject and append a predicate to the name. And Hare is also right that people who hold the view that he dislikes and finds confused may not merely believe that descriptive predicates do not as it were take us where we want to go; they may also attach a kind of significance to *names*.

Let me explain what I mean by that. Martha Nussbaum writes of the connection between what *loss* is to someone who has loved another person, and that person's sense of the particularity of the person lost, of who *s/he* is. That connection is often expressed through uses of the person's name, as if in uttering the name we were in touch with the person's particularity, in touch with *that* that we have lost.

In her writing about loss, Nussbaum quotes Dora Carrington's diaries, in which the repetition of the name 'Lytton' is tied to Carrington's sense of the particularity of the person lost.[40] A different sort of example is provided by the Vietnam Memorial in Washington. The power of the memorial is the power of the connection between the name of the dead person and the particularity of the loss: *he* or *she*.

What I have said so far about particularity is the background for my argument. I want to claim that ideas about particularity and its role in our lives, in our moral thinking and our moral responses, cannot be brought to awareness if we restrict ourselves to language conceived in certain sorts of ways. We need texts like literary texts (and like the Vietnam Memorial, like inscriptions on tombs, like the AIDS quilt); we need to be aware of them as the

---

[40] Compare the role of the name 'Nicoteles' in Callimachus' epigram (*Oxford Book of Greek Verse*, ed. Gilbert Murray, *et al.* (Oxford 1930), piece 516), in which the speaker mourns the loss of his twelve-year-old son; the shortness of the epigram, together with the placing of the name at the end, concentrate the expression of loss: the sense of what is lost, *who* is lost, is painfully present in the name.

kind of texts they are, aware of the language they use and what it does, if we are to hear the appeal to particularity.

Earlier I quoted de la Mare's poem 'Ducks'. Take a part of that quotation: 'Every Duck himself is'. Read that sentence, and at the same time understand the language in accordance with our philosophical way of thinking about language. Every duck himself is; that is, every duck is the duck that he is. That is a tautology. It does not say anything about particularity, does not say anything that we might need to learn, might need to listen to. What the line conveys has disappeared from view. It is important to the de la Mare line that what is said about ducks the poet would not say about chair legs; and yet if every duck is himself, so every chair leg is *it*self. So if de la Mare is not expressing of ducks something (self-identity) that is equally true of chair legs, what is it?

When we try to express our sense of the particularity of people, we often run into similar problems. We may speak of the importance of attending to the 'individual human reality' (say) of the person before us; we might say 'each person has his unique reality'. We mean there to say something about persons (possibly about some other things as well), not about any and every sort of object in the universe of discourse. But if we station ourselves resolutely in language used to pick out individual items and to describe them and generalise about them, using names and predicates and variables (and the ordinary language equivalents of variables), the attempt to express particularity fails entirely. For *every* particular item that can be picked out by a singular term is as much an 'individual reality' as any other: the *words* 'individual reality' cannot, within the language of straightforward description, do what we want them to do. An 'individual reality' is nothing, in that language, but something with the logical characteristics of an object. The head of every pin is an individual reality as much as is this man, this woman, this child, this dead man Lytton, this dead boy Nicoteles. Similarly with 'unique': all that we can do with the word 'unique' in ordinary descriptive language (of the sort philosophers use and take as their standard case of language) is get at the fact that some picked-out item uniquely instantiates certain properties. Or we may note that *every* phenomenon can be treated as unique in that it has its location in space and time.[41]

[41] See Richard S. Rudner, *Philosophy of Social Science* (Englewood Cliffs, N.J., 1966), p. 70, for a fuller statement of the argument.

Again, take the use of names. Names are important for us in expressing our sense of the individual reality of particular human beings. Our sense of such particularity, and our use of names to express it, have developed together. In Callimachus' epigram (see note 40, above), the name 'Nicoteles' seems almost to have in it all that the grieving father has lost: for him, his grief and that name cannot be separated any more than the grief and the boy can be. But what can we do with names, if we conceive of language as in standard moral philosophy? Hare tells us: we can make the name the subject of a descriptive sentence, and then go on to describe the individual thus named. (And Hare would not deny that there may be emotional associations with names.) Philosophers may then discuss and indeed disagree about the possible descriptive content of proper names. Do proper names have a sense through which the individual named is picked out? Whatever answers we give to questions in philosophy of language, there is one logical feature all such answers have in common. They will all be accounts of the kind of meaning names have, which are applicable to *all* kinds of individuals: people, chair legs, fragments of teeth, motes of dust, anything you like. They will all be accounts that abstract from the ways in which the expressive content of some kinds of proper names has developed with the development of our relations to each other, to the places we live and are attached to, the particular things and their stories through which we make sense of our lives. Philosophy of language is not intended to have direct ties with ethics, links with ideas about the good in human life including the good of attachment to particulars. And so the *language* it sees is not language that has in it shapings of expression and thought derived from, and contributing to, our ways of creating and maintaining such human relations.[42]

(I have spoken about our use of phrases like 'individual human reality' and of names in connection with particularity. Problems analogous to those I have discussed arise if we consider the use of demonstratives, personal pronouns and interrogative pronouns

[42] My argument is meant to supplement the discussion in Nussbaum's essay, 'Transcending Humanity', about the appropriateness, in philosophy, of 'thinking mortal thoughts'. Her argument focuses on ethics, mine, here, on philosophy of language, but the point is the same: 'that the emotions, and their accomplices, the stories ... are required in a fully human philosophy' (*LKn*, p. 389). My chapter, like her book, is about what a 'fully human philosophy' might be.

to express particularity. A good example of the use of interrogatives can be found in Samuel Beckett's essay on Proust. Writing about 'perhaps the greatest passage that Proust ever wrote', a scene that takes place a year after the death of the narrator's grandmother, Beckett says

For the first time since her death, since the Champs Elysées, he has recovered her living and complete, as she was so many times, at Combray and Paris and Balbec. For the first time since her death he knows that she is dead, he knows *who* is dead.[43]

Beckett uses the interrogative pronoun to express the weight of this knowledge, this coming by Marcel to connect what happened a year ago with his sense of the particularity of the dead woman. But note how different this use of the interrogative pronoun is from its use in ordinary descriptive language. To say (in ordinary descriptive language) that Marcel now knows who is dead is to say that he can answer the question 'Who is dead?', which of course he has been able to do all along. Beckett uses the stressed 'who' in a way which is connected with the use of proper names that I spoke of earlier, for example, their use in the poetry of loss.[44])

In a sense Hare is right, is justified, in ruling out the intelligibility within ethics of an appeal to particularity going beyond morally relevant specific differences in kind between cases. That is, such a limitation is inherent in the language within which we usually conduct moral philosophy, and within which we represent thought, including moral thought. The language of standard moral philosophy has the capacity to represent as of moral relevance only properties of situations or of people or of things. Moral attitudes are attitudes towards situations, people or things *as* having certain properties. The idea of the 'irreducibly particular' is a moral idea tied to language used differently, and studied, looked at, thought about, differently.

In her essay 'Love and the Individual', Martha Nussbaum writes that 'there is no neutral posture of reflection from which one can survey and catalogue the intuitions of one's heart on the subject of love, holding up the rival views to see how well they fit

---

[43] Samuel Beckett, *Proust* (New York, 1957), p. 28.
[44] See also Nussbaum's discussion of how knowledge and proper emotion are connected, *LKn*, p. 79.

the intuitions – no activity of philosophising that does not stand in some determinate relation to the love' (*LKn*, p. 329). She there implies (what she elsewhere explicitly affirms) that there is no language within which philosophising goes on that does not stand in some determinate relation to love. The truth of what she says is especially evident if we consider that relation to love expressible in the language of 'irreducible particularity'.

(In talking about this language, I have emphasised both our relations with particular people and also the imaginative sense of particularity that extends to those whom we do not know. The moral importance of this sort of language comes out for example in the difference it may make to our understanding of what is wrong with murder. There are radically different ways of thinking about the evil that murder is. No philosophical understanding of these differences can be reached unless we see how ideas about particularity and irreplaceability may enter such thinking, ideas which are missed if we restrict ourselves to ordinary philosophical language.[45])

Philosophy can refuse to consider the possible limitations inherent in its own language, can refuse to consider the kind of non-neutrality internal to its most familiar ways of writing and talking. But if we wish to look beyond, if we want to see possibilities for thought, we need to turn to such texts as novels, texts engaged in the shaping of the language of particularity.

[45] See, for example, Jonathan Glover, *Causing Death and Saving Lives* (Harmondsworth, 1977). Glover's discussion of what is wrong with killing babies makes it entirely a matter of the effects on other people and the possible lessening of the overall amount of worthwhile life; babies are, in a sense, replaceable. The language in which the issues are discussed imposes its own way of thinking about the issue of replaceability, about what can be meant by *the baby's* loss. See also G. E. M. Anscombe, 'Contraception and Chastity', in *Human World*, 7 (May 1972), pp. 9–30, at p. 25. James Conant drew to my attention the great importance ideas about human particularity have for Dostoyevsky, for example in the chapters 'Rebellion' and 'The Grand Inquisitor' in *The Brothers Karamazov*.

❖❖

3

The concept of dread
Sympathy and ethics in *Daniel Deronda*

❖❖

LISABETH DURING

This chapter is devoted to an English genealogist of morals who succeeded in being and doing even more than she knew she was doing, which was itself considerable. For Friedrich Nietzsche she was a 'little bluestocking', sullying her insight (into the vanishing of the divine) by replacing it with a shabby idealism. But I want to argue that George Eliot is the true, unknown candidate for Nietzsche's praise:

The English psychologists to whom we owe the only attempts that have thus far been made to write a genealogy of morals are no mean posers of riddles, but the riddles they pose are themselves, and being incarnate have one advantage over their books – they are interesting. What are these English psychologists really after? One finds them always, whether intentionally or not, engaged in the same task of pushing into the fore-ground the nasty part of the psyche, looking for the effective motive forces of human development in the very last place we would wish to have them found, e.g., in the inertia of habit, in forgetfulness, in the blind and fortuitous association of ideas.

(Nietzsche, *The Genealogy of Morals*, first essay)

The argument of this chapter is that George Eliot did know very well where the sources of 'human development' were to be found. In the nasty parts of the psyche, in passive, mimetic, regressive movements of dread and desire. But she did not always want to know that she knew that. In her last, most ambitious novel, she wants one character – the spokesman for the noble gospel of sympathy – to 'win'. That she identifies herself, as an aspiring 'great artist', with her character Daniel Deronda, is clear from a passage from the well-known essay, 'The Natural History of German Life':

The greatest benefit we owe to the artist, whether painter, poet or novelist, is the extension of our sympathies ... a picture of human life such as a great artist can give, surprises even the trivial and the selfish into that attention which is apart from themselves, which can be called the raw material of moral sentiment.[1]

Moral education, far from being irrelevant to art, is precisely what the artist, and in particular the novelist, can perform, no one better. For the pleasures of the novelist's 'picture of life' catch the vulgar unawares. The intense interest in eavesdropping on the affairs and the private tribulations of others, the same interest that enlivens gossip and is the more acceptable face of voyeurism, is just what the novelist counts on to achieve her effects.

What could be moral about such an interest? Perhaps that it surprises us out of selfishness without our noticing. Spectatorship, and by extension reading, was claimed by the eighteenth-century moralists who taught George Eliot as the 'raw material' of the moral consciousness.[2]

The novelist's imagination is, then, the training ground for an attention and an interest which, in its finest flowerings, is called sympathy. In this novel the privileged figure of sympathy and selflessness is a handsome young man in England who does not know that he comes from a race almost universally deprived of sympathy: a race chosen, if at all, only to be disliked. Deronda is the person the author loves. His is the ethical vision she would like us to approve. She does not want us, the captivated readers, to wish that the winner of the novel's power plays had been that virtuoso diva of dread, Gwendolen Harleth. Gwendolen is a primitive moralist, torn between her desire to enjoy the esteem and the admiration of her audience and her fear of self. While the first desire is a social, or socialisable passion, the second state is not. Fear of self is an uncanny emotion, mixed with the murkiest of psychic undergrowths. As social performer, Gwendolen would like to be

---

[1] In George Eliot, *Selected Critical Writings*, ed. Rosemary Ashton (Oxford, 1992), p. 263.
[2] On spectatorship as an eighteenth-century mode of the moral life, see David Marshall's brilliant study, *The Figure of Theatre: Shaftesbury, Defoe, Adam Smith, and George Eliot* (New York, 1986).

both the star and the director; intense absorption in the spectacle of others' lives and feelings is not in her line. George Eliot is reluctant to give her the power of sympathy. Yet Eliot does endow her heroine with a heightened sensitivity to the almost hallucinatory after-images of events and to their atmospheric prefigurations. In another age, she would have been blamed for her 'second-sight'. In this age, Gwendolen's susceptibility to aura does not allow her the moral intelligence she needs. She remains at the primitive stage of dread, a feminine daemon in a salon, afraid of the power she has and lacking that colder power that goes with moral indifference.

Gwendolen is the victim of her creator's ethical idealism, a sacrifice on the altar of Deronda's new social gospel. But many of the novel's first readers had to be dragged kicking and screaming to the scene of sanctification. *Daniel Deronda* was Eliot's most unpopular novel. It did not give its readers the ethical reassurance they had come to expect from her.

I Dread, or the world not so well lost

'Turn your fear into a safeguard', Daniel Deronda tells the distraught Gwendolen Harleth. 'It is like quickness of hearing. It may make consequences passionately present to you. Try to take hold of your sensibility, and use it as if it were a faculty, like vision' (p. 509).[3] Gwendolen is prey to a nameless dread that borders on hysteria. It is the concept of dread that connects the psychological-utopian experiments of this novel with philosophical critiques of the ethical universal. And it is dread, in its contagious, superstitious, demonic undoing of self-control, which calls into question the moral idealism of the English psychologists, 'those microscopic examiners of the soul', Nietzsche calls them, who require some way of explaining 'the provenance of the concept and judgment good'. How peculiar, then, that they dig in these murky places! What could motivate them? 'Could it be a prurient taste for whatever is embarrassing, painfully paradoxical, dubious and absurd in existence?'[4]

---

[3] All references to *Daniel Deronda* are from the Penguin edition, edited by Barbara Hardy (Harmondsworth, 1986); subsequently, page references appear in the main text.

[4] Friedrich Nietzsche, *The Genealogy of Morals*, trans. Francis Golfing (New York, 1956).

Some philosophers indeed would not want to deny their taste for the embarrassing and ambiguous, their fascination with those areas of the psyche where humiliation breeds. For Kierkegaard, dread exposes the self in its privacy, its deviation from the norm. Such a self is at the limits of individuation and ethical coherence. For Hegel, however (and his doubts may be shared by Eliot), the moment of deviation is a temptation to be resisted, a betrayal of relations to others. If dread confronts the self with its own negativity, it also severs the social subject from the concerns of the community.

If anything preoccupies *Daniel Deronda* – and here it does not renounce but problematises the concerns of *Middlemarch* – it is the question of a dialectic between self and totality. While on any acount of mental life acceptable to Eliot the self must be at the centre, that self can only be consummated through an expanding movement of sympathy, an opening towards something else, call that my identification with my culture. What could be more Hegelian in its demand for a transcendence of the internal dramas of the demonic soul? Read this way, *Daniel Deronda* is a novel of ideas wedded to its time and prophetic. For it studiously researches the conditions necessary to culture as a project of historical transcendence, an idea whose ramifications we are still learning to understand. On the account this novel offers, culture looks like a social identity in which the individual bears the responsibility of others whose lives he or she can hardly touch. Such a definition, I take it, is offered by the Jewish text of this internally split novel. Culture, or perhaps more precisely national identity, absorbs the individual into a larger scene of memory, feeling, recognition: it engages, to use Eliot's own terms, an expansion of sympathy. The Hebrew ethic which the author sanctions in this novel depends on such connections; the Jewish way of life, which Daniel Deronda's mother bitterly abjures, turns 'connectedness' into a good in itself.

Dread, however, attacks connections at their very core; it shatters the ground on which social relations flourish; it opens the abyss. Dread, which is inwardness at its most uncompromising, reminds us of a dimension of spiritual life which the comforting reconciliations of cultural identity do not admit. Emmanuel Levinas calls it the bad conscience, the state of pure passivity, the non-intentional state. In dread the reality of others is cut off; the world drops away.[5] Kierkegaard says of dread that it expresses the contradiction of selfhood, for the 'self' is what posited the general as the particular. Dread is the way this contradiction *feels* to the individual in a instant of passion and panic.

Gwendolen Harleth's fits of dread strike her down in the middle of motion. They are paralytic, sudden standstills which turn this plastic, mercurial woman into a statue. Her most striking crises occurs very early on in the novel, when in the middle of a party piece – a *tableau vivant* performed fetchingly by Gwendolen in her family's new house – the unfamiliar salon produces a horror of its own:

[a] movable panel, which was on a line with the piano, flew open on the right opposite the stage and disclosed the picture of the dead face and the fleeing figure, brought out in pale definiteness by the position of the waxlights ... Gwendolen ... stood without change of attitude, but with a change of expression that was terrifying in its terror. She looked like a statue into which a soul of Fear had entered: her pallid lips were parted; her eyes, usually narrowed under their long lashes, were dilated and fixed. (p. 91)

Gwendolen has little understanding of these attacks, which catch her at her most vulnerable, exposing a side she would prefer not to be seen, 'her susceptibility to terror'.

She wondered at herself in these occasional experiences, which seemed like a brief remembered madness ...

But the narrator cannot resist turning these involuntary exposures to moral account, hinting at the development of sensitivity, indeed of sympathy and a pious sense of the infinite, which one might expect to flow from such a remarkable nature. Will Gwendolen's dread be the means of her salvation? Or will she get lost in the sheer immensity of this uncanny interior world, lacking any trustworthy signposts to interpret it for her?

What she unwillingly recognised, and would have been glad for others to be unaware of, was that liability of hers to fits of spiritual dread, though this fountain of awe within her had not found its way into connection with the religion taught her or with any human relations ... Solitude in any wide scene impressed her with an undefined feeling of immeasur-

---

[5] See Levinas's paper, 'Bad Conscience and the Inexorable' (1981), translated by Richard A. Cohen, in R. A. Cohen, ed., *Face to Face with Levinas* (Albany, 1986), pp. 35–40.

able existence aloof from her, in the midst of which she was helplessly incapable of asserting herself. The little astronomy taught her at school used sometimes to set her imagination to work in a way that made her tremble: but always when some one joined her she recovered her indifference to the vastness in which she seemed an exile. With human ears and eyes around her, she had always hitherto recovered her confidence and felt the possibility of winning empire. (p. 94)

Dread is for her related to the dangers of solitude. Alone, she too easily loses any sense of her significance, a significance that so far seems wholly an extension and mirror of her will. In Gwendolen's last pathetic interview with Deronda, her spiritual adviser and lover *manqué*, the narrator shows the distance between them growing as they move towards a final parting:

The world seemed getting larger round poor Gwendolen, and she more solitary and helpless in its midst . . . She was for the first time feeling the pressure of a vast mysterious movement, for the first time being dislodged from her supremacy in her own world. (p. 875)

A properly educated moral subject, the narrator implies, would be able to recognise in these experiences of 'vastation' the analogous grandeur of Kant's 'moral law within'. Yet poor Gwendolen is no Kantian. She is closer to the pagan who Pascal discovers within his own civilised soul, for whom those vast spaces without limit are a nightmare. Kierkegaard also gave more sense of dread to the pagan, the primitive. Outside of a defined religious universe, where a sense of foreboding finds quick translation into an admissible fear of sin or at least transgression, the feeling of dread just floats. It does not help to bring the dread self to knowledge; it waits at the threshold of something it knows not what. It is, in a word, ambiguous.

Dread is fear in the face of nothing rather than something. Heidegger, who took over the notion, welcomes anxiety as the emotion which most throws me back on the self I was pretending not to be. For the 'what', the 'nothing', that dread is in fear of, is its own 'nothing', that absence or nullification of myself which I cannot figure in any representation but which lays chill hands on me, spinning me downwards into a vertigo that only an unmotivated act of resolution can arrest. Dread, then, has something very intimate to do with identity, and the way it feels to be a self. When that sense of self is most at risk I stumble on something which I cannot get rid of, which I cannot deny away. For this fear is an intentional emotion; it does not float in space. What I fear for in dread is myself.[6]

In Heidegger's analytic of existence, dread is the awakening which rips me away from a spurious social identity, a world where the opinions and interpretations of others wear the stamp of authority. None of those representations, he warns, can save me from the emptiness which awaits me in dread. This is something of what Kierkegaard also has in mind when he speaks of the 'freedom' of dread, which is at the same time 'the most egoistic thing'. But dread for Kierkegaard is more clearly a moral state, or at least a stage on the way to acquiring a moral consciousness. In dread what is opened up is the posssibility of freedom and therefore the possibility of being right or wrong, of sin and guilt. But dread is still rather unformed and ambiguous, indeed ambivalent about the very destiny which appears on its horizon. Contemplating my own freedom as a moral agent, Kierkegaard suggests, I feel attracted and repelled: the possibility of becoming guilty entices like the sweetest seduction, alarming and indefinite: 'In dread there is the egoistic infinity of possibility, which does not tempt like a definite choice but alarms and fascinates with its sweet anxiety' (p. 55).[7]

Dread, seductive and insecure, is (no surprise) feminine: 'it is a womanish debility in which freedom swoons'. But this is not because woman is the weaker sex, says Kierkegaard. Woman is more in dread than man because she is more sensuous. Her approach to the whole domain of goods and evils is qualified by her greater susceptibility to affect; intellectual reflection has less to do with it, enters on the scene later for her. 'If I picture to myself a young and innocent girl', he writes, 'and then let a man fasten upon her a look of desire, she experiences dread. If on the other hand I imagine that a woman fixes a desirous glance upon an innocent young man, his feeling will not be dread, but at the most a sense of abhorrence mingled with shame' (p. 60).

Thus the woman's feeling of dread picks out for her a special moral situation, yet one too ambiguous to strike most of us as

---

[6] Martin Heidegger, *Being and Time*, translated by John Macquarrie and Edward Robinson (Oxford, 1962), p. 181.
[7] Søren Kierkegaard, *The Concept of Dread*, trans. Walter Lowrie (Princeton, 1944). Subsequent page references appear in the main text.

comfortable; in dread the woman is both guilty and innocent. Dread has not yet 'done' anything; it hovers at the threshold of any act which could be marked as good or evil. But the more the self experiences dread, the closer comes the possibility of sin. The language here is theological, not secular. It is as a creature in a world haunted by overwhelming and uncomprehended powers that the dreading self feels lost, beyond control, deprived of free will and even of the power of responsibility. These are not the terms of a worldly, civilised morality: some would deny them moral relevance at all. If anything, the ethical moment which dread marks belongs to a morality of the uncanny. Gwendolen's theatrical, sensuous paralysis in her fits of dread gives us a glimpse into the psychopathology of the ethical life. What is such a thing doing in the hands of the great humanist, for whom only the hallowed image of Duty was allowed to replace the disappointing gods of her early religiosity?

I would argue that with the figure of Gwendolen Harleth, George Eliot has trespassed into areas of interior trauma and psychic unfreedom which her chosen secular morality cannot encompass. Between the supernatural and the social, the uncanny and the 'natural history' of moral life, the novel's emotional commitments are torn. The resolution it finally is unable to embrace is the rational reconciliation of passion and duty. Insofar as Gwendolen is one of the competing moral centres of this book, she prevents it from achieving closure on the expected harmony of virtue and happiness which Eliot hoped might be the outcome of moral 'bildung'. If the novel pulls in one direction towards Gwendolen's haunted, compromised world, where every moral act not committed preys on the fragile conscience like an unburied crime, it pulls in another direction towards the transcendence of the secular in utopian, millenarian visions.

II Daniel vs. Gwendolen – whose morality?

Daniel Deronda's official moral programme is the universal gospel of sympathy, which by the middle of her career was Eliot's intellectual compromise between the unsatisfactory alternatives of utilitarianism and faith. But the novel's deeper, less acknowledged allegiances are to a moral experience of ambiguity, complicity, and compulsion: a moral experience which is strongly feminine and, in practice, almost impossible to put into words. Gwendolen's significance in the elect company of Eliot's heroines – those 'frail vessels of human affection' – is, I believe, as a symbol of the woman isolated by her perceptions and unknown, even unknowable. Her stature is grander than Eliot wants to think.

The first indications we get of Gwendolen's uncanniness are, tellingly, in the scene of Gwendolen's aborted performance. It is her susceptibility to dread which at once makes her too volatile to be the poised, self-possessed *grande dame* she would like to act, and at the same time makes a mockery of her theatrical pretensions. Dread will characterise all her moral and psychic crises, as we see her drawn steadily deeper into a net of dissimulation and remorse: a net, it must be said, not of her own making. And the graphic portrayal of her dread appears at this relatively early stage in the narrative, when her conscience has no reason to be troubled and she enjoys a gratifying sway over the regard and interest of everyone around her. The invocation of dread drags ambiguity into Eliot's rational discourse on culture, moral sentiments, egoism, selflessness. And ambiguity is precisely what Gwendolen brings to the novel. Ambiguity is, one might say, her moral significance. In the story this novel tells, ambiguity – or being difficult to read – is also the heroine's final performance, when, exiled to a life of asceticism, she retreats from public performance and allows herself to become opaque. Shrieking and trembling, as we last see her when 'forsaken' by Deronda and left to nothing more consoling than her own spiritual guidance, she is at last framed, rather than annihilated, by solitude.

Let us look at a passage in the penultimate chapter of the novel. In a frenzy of revelations, Gwendolen has just found out that her confidant and possible lover, Daniel Deronda, is a Jew and that he not only intends to leave England for good – intending to set up a utopian community in Palestine – but that he is about to marry another woman, a Jewess. Hysterical after this trying scene, Gwendolen still manages to assure her mother, in words her mother will be the last to comprehend, that she means to live. The terms she accepts are those of independence and solitude, a solitude which before she could only experience negatively. She had been terrified of going on with her life without Deronda, although the other terms the narrators allows her for the expression of that terror are moral ones: he has, quite literally, had her soul in his keeping. Without him she doubts whether she would have had a conscience at all. Our brother, the narrator remarks, 'may be in the stead of God to us, and his opinion which has pierced even to the joints and marrow, may be our virtue in the making' (p. 833). And Gwendolen, who has no other God, is for a long while unable to differentiate between Deronda and her own self-enclosed world, between the sympathetic listener whom she depends on so totally and her own psychological states: 'She identified him with the struggling regenerative process in her which had begun with his action' (p. 841). Now, with this severance, she may begin to cultivate her own interiority; a subjective experience not constantly open to scrutiny, not endlessly 'monitored' by friend and foe.

As David Marshall writes of this scene, 'Deronda no longer stands as the privileged beholder and interpreter of Gwendolen's sentiments.'[8] Deronda's withdrawal can only appear brutal to her, dependent as she has been on him to dispel her horrible visions. But, by this moment of parting, Gwendolen has already lived through her 'horrible vision'. Her fears were real, and Deronda could not be there to dispel the hallucinatory threat. The pale and grotesque 'dead face' which had visited her when the alarming panel suddenly gaped open at Offendene recurred in the shape of her sadistic husband, whom she watched drown in the Mediterranean. The fleeing figure pursued by this apparition, which the painting had exposed, turned out to be her. Her uncanny premonitions can no longer prey upon her, making her feel guilty and shamed without any clear cause. For the reality which they foreshadowed had already come to pass. 'Murder' – Gwendolen's participation in the events that left her husband a corpse – has intervened. And Gwendolen's moral conscience is now her own affair.

Thus the last meeting between Deronda and Gwendolen is a foregone conclusion. Although she still reaches out for his sympathy, they are both coming to realise that her needs are elsewhere. Her story requires a different understanding. It is the relation between two moral discourses – the uncanny one which speaks of the integrity of an unknowable self and the moral enigmas of 'responsibility' in what I would call a Freudian sense – and the discourse of sympathy (rational, calculating, but humane)

---

[8] Marshall, *Figure of Theatre*, p. 211.

– which determines Gwendolen's fate. If Daniel and Gwendolen begin the novel in a striking and erotically charged connection (whose potential is quickly sublimated into that of confessor and penitent), the bond between them is broken, Eliot implies, by the incompatibility between the ethical codes they represent.

III What's wrong with sympathy?

Of course Deronda himself has other fish to fry. Although he seems to agree with his creator that his vocation is for the saving of maidens in distress, even before he meets Gwendolen his affections are pledged to a woman whose physical safety, rather than moral salvation, has become his responsibility. In a society which Eliot suspects of ethical as well as erotic deficiency, a man gifted with the power to nurture is going to be heavily in demand. Another imperilled woman, young Mirah, the Jewish waif whose wholesome if antiseptic image Eliot fondly believes will 're-make' the tarnished image of Deronda's own 'bad' Jewish mother, has become the object of his love: perhaps, the narrator suggests, because it allows him to relive a juvenile and narcissistic fantasy of his own (presumably suppressed) femininity:

Since the hour when he left the house at Chelsea in full-hearted silence under the effect of Mirah's farewell look and words – their exquisite appealingness stirring in him that deeply laid care for womanhood which had begun when his own lip was like a girl's – her hold on his feeling had helped him to be blameless in word and deed under the difficult circumstances we know of. (p. 813)

But while Mirah's need for him was able to evoke that 'care for womanhood' which he is willing to interpret as love, Gwendolen's call on his sympathies seems to move in a different direction:

It had lain in the course of poor Gwendolen's lot that her dependence on Deronda tended to rouse in him the enthusiasm of self–martyring pity rather than of personal love... (p. 813)

Mirah has the right to his sympathy because she shares his race: she is the past, the ancestry, the culture, which he has been denied by his mother's choice to have him raised as a Christian Englishman ignorant of his background. It is as if his disrupted and ambiguous upbringing could be corrected by his selection of a wife; choice might re-do destiny. Endogamy here becomes a powerful moral argument, as indeed it did in many nineteenth-century discussions of race, nationality, and culture, discussions which Eliot desired to bring out of the domain of the 'academic' and the 'exotic', and push into the faces of her good English readers. There are conditions under which the English virtue of sympathy becomes more than a civil tolerance to cover up deeper cultural incivilities. But these conditions are not likely to flatter the self-esteem of Gwendolen's counterparts and their friends.

In a famous passage, Eliot challenges the cosmopolitan and enlightened understandings of 'sympathy'. Just after Deronda has been heard musing about the newly eroticised image of Mirah, his reflections on her Jewishness lead him to a happy recognition of the new role, and usefulness, his commitment to their common culture was promising him:

> It was as if he had found an added soul in finding his ancestry – his judgment no longer wandering in the mazes of impartial sympathy, but choosing, with the noble partiality which is man's best strength, the closer fellowship that makes sympathy practical – exchanging the bird's-eye reasonableness which soars to avoid preference and loses all sense of quality, for the generous reasonableness of drawing shoulder to shoulder with men of like inheritance. (p. 814)

With such a claim, the moral vision Eliot had previously defended is put to the test, and found wanting. The social salvation of the race may not be brought about through the universal practice of interlocking sympathy. To use the idea of sympathy in the way she needs it to work here demands that the pressure exerted on it leaves the very doctrine distorted and unrecognisable. 'Pulling shoulder to shoulder with men of like inheritance' is seen as more rewarding, more exhilarating, and certainly more virile, than the dynamic of tenderness and dependence which had governed the operations of sympathy in Deronda's relations to Gwendolen. Yet the sacrifice of Gwendolen, who is made expendable by the higher duty of racial allegiance, is something more than a failure of sympathy.

At an early turn in the narrative we see Deronda, fluidly borne along by the fluid Thames, absorbed in a sympathetic identification which, in effect, dissolves his individuality:

He used his oars little, satisfied to go with the tide and be taken by it. It was his habit to indulge himself in that solemn passivity which easily comes with the lengthening shadows and mellowing light, when thinking and desiring melt together imperceptively, and what in other hours may have seemed argument takes the quality of passionate vision... He was forgetting everything else in a half-speculative, half-involuntary identification of himself with the objects he was looking at, thinking how far it might be possible habitually to shift his centre till his own personality would be no less outside him than the landscape... (p. 229)

His fondness for such Wordsworthian reverie is cut short by the sight of a maiden in distress. After rescuing Mirah and placing her into a safe refuge, Deronda's ability to remain in a pleasant, aesthetically flattering detachment diminishes dramatically. The narrator wonders sensibly whether it is his extraordinary talent for empathy which has, in fact, kept his life from taking shape:

His early awakened sensibility and reflectiveness had developed into a many-sided sympathy, which threatened to hinder any persistent course of action... (p. 412)

For there is a danger of sympathy taken too far, and Gwendolen can hardly be blamed for Deronda's excesses: the borders between self and other become blurred. Here Eliot seems to rehearse difficulties that may well be the price of any 'sublime', Spinozistic vision. As Hegel argued with great urgency in his 'Phenomenology of Spirit' (1807), monism is a threat to intersubjectivity, to our social and personal need to be recognised by others in our full distinctness, our 'difference', our otherness. When someone is the object of my too-interested imaginings, they lose any power they might have had to resist, to say no, to keep my understanding gaze out. The action of sympathy fills up all the empty spaces where a private subjectivity might come to exist. The object enjoying the sympathy is encouraged to think that the sympathiser truly 'lives' in them. And this has the effect of making it very difficult for the dynamic of sympathy to be reciprocal. The more you respond to and indeed uncover my needs, the less likely I am to imagine your life and needs apart from me. In this sense sympathy acts as an incentive to egoism, rather than as its corrective.

The measured operations of sympathy are tangential to the deep moral concerns of this novel, which are about the extreme and annihilating cases of sympathy. Such cases, as Hegel argued, are indistinguishable from the blindness of egoism. Poor Gwendolen wants to learn from Deronda's image of her how to see herself: she fervently believes it would be a better self-knowledge than any she could provide on her own. And this fallacy imprisons her in spiritual immaturity until she is forcibly torn from the mirror she had thought indispensable. Further, her absorption in the mirror of moral 'regeneration' which he holds up for her renders her incapable of noticing what is going on for him; his sympathy fails to sow the seeds of impartial sympathy that would develop her faculty of seeing and understanding a world outside herself. From start to finish she finds it impossible to imagine how other people radically different from herself and independent of her can even exist: her sympathy for Mrs Glasher arises partly out of a belief in the similarities between her disinherited state and that of Deronda's; her habitual response to the accidents of others was laughter; and the Jewish characters in the novel make as little impression on her mind as if they had the been the black-clad scene-changers in a play she was not watching very closely anyway.

So what good is sympathy to Gwendolen Harleth? My argument is that the failure of sympathy to perform the moral regeneration on Gwendolen that the novel keeps saying it will do is not a mere weakness of the novel's conception. It has to do with a cultural, as well as psychological, fragility which Eliot here recognises in the gospel of sympathy.

IV The divided path of *Daniel Deronda*: ethics and philosophy

The sensory and motor nerves that run in the same sheath, are scarcely bound together by a more necessary and delicate union than that which binds men's affections, imagination, wit and humour, with the subtle ramifications of historical language... And there is an analogous relation between the moral tendencies of men and the social conditions they have inherited.   (George Eliot, 'The Natural History of German Life')

At some points in this discussion readers may well be tempted to ask 'Is this a novel masquerading as a philosophical treatise?' It is not an easy question to answer. *Daniel Deronda* stages a

debate between competing conceptions of moral psychology, between competing ideas about how moral characters and emotions are formed, and why. For it is, I believe, a novel about
culture and its ethical possibilities. At a fundamental level, choices of what kind of society we want, what form of culture and
tradition we feel adequate to inherit, are moral choices. They
create, or fail to create, the conditions under which moral life
would be possible and moral subjects flourish. As we have seen,
Daniel Deronda is premised on the very real power and effects of
sympathy. But the gospel of sympathy of the eighteenth-century
British Enlightenment is at the same time what it puts into question. The theatre of sympathy and spectatorship is, for Deronda,
the intended hero, superseded by the larger act of sympathy
which is 'partial', by a conversion to the culture of his ancestors
and a commitment to political action which, Eliot argues, 'makes
sympathy practical'. What philosophically and culturally was
wrong with sympathy?

As I understand it, the philosophers' doctrine of sympathy
argues that the seat of moral judgment (or practical reason) is to
be found in the passions, not in reason. Yet moral perceptions, if
they are to be useful at all, must be general; they must apply to
you as well as to me, and that essentially, not accidentally. So
that the necessary passage between a sense of what is right and
wrong which refers only to individual experience and a sense
recognised as 'common' – public, available to general scrutiny,
acceptable to most – requires that the passions, which I feel
directly, socialise themselves. In short, moral communities need
shared passions, or more precisely, they need passions that can
be transferred from one individual to another. It seems a weird
requirement.

Yet something like this does indeed happen. In reading books,
in watching plays or events in the street, I am able to enter
imaginatively into the emotional world of another. My passions,
or something like passions which attach themselves to me, return
to me already mediated through a leap of identification and
exchange. I can indirectly but often quite vividly feel the plight or
pleasure of another. And that is all I need to make the move into
the space of social identity: the theatre of sympathy in which my
spectatorship interests me in others, and in which I learn (something even harder) to act as a spectator to myself. Socially engaged

in this public play of imagination and imputed feelings, my natural egoism is left behind.[9]

At its most extreme, the doctrine of sympathy should allow for a kind of transcendence which Eliot values very highly: the kind where I might find myself saying 'I can get lost in you.' Or, as the French philosopher Emmanuel Levinas would put it, 'one is for the other before being for oneself'. If it could do this, the commonsensical, worldly-wise doctrine of sympathy would certainly be a candidate for moral and cultural respect, even amazement. For it might be able to construct an image for love that would avoid the platonic ontology of collapsing two into one. Levinas writes: 'Man's relationship with the other is *better* as difference than as unity: sociality is better than fusion. The very value of love is the impossibility of reducing the other to myself, of coinciding into sameness.'[10] Even the notion of responsibility, which is hard to connect genealogically to the internal moral thermometer of pleasure and pain, as Nietzsche pointed out, could be supported by an extension of sympathy: events which I have nothing to do with, people whom I cannot imagine, identify with, or even like, would be suitable objects of concern to a universal faculty of imaginary enactment.

But can Hume and Smith be taken so far? Does the theory of sympathy have this kind of potential?

The truth is that sympathy has its limits. It relies on the power of imagination. But imagination, as the eighteenth century tended to understand it, is a reproductive, mimetic faculty: it converts past

---

[9] The theory of sympathy that I am describing owes most to Adam Smith, who gave the most polished version of an investigation into the 'moral sentiments' begun at least by Shaftesbury and Hutcheson, if not earlier. See his *The Theory of Moral Sentiments* (Indianapolis, 1976), section I. But see also David Hume, *A Treatise of Human Nature*, part III, 'Of the Other Virtues and Vices', for further analyses of the theatrical 'artifice' of man's moral nature, and the habit of emulation which moulds us into a social image and tempers our self-concern: 'Sympathy, we shall allow, is much fainter than our concern for ourselves, and sympathy with persons remote from us, much fainter than that with persons near and contiguous; but for that very reason, it is necessary for us, in our calm judgments and discourse concerning the characters of men, to neglect all these differences, and render our sentiments more public and social.' (*Enquiry Concerning the Principles of Morals*, part II, p. 580.) David Marshall has given the most interesting accounts of the eighteenth century intersection between theatricality and sympathy in both his books, *The Surprising Effects of Sympathy: Marivaux, Diderot, Rousseau and Mary Shelley* (Chicago, 1988) and *The Figure of Theatre.*

[10] See his work entitled *Time and the Other*, from which I am using the extract published in *The Levinas Reader*, ed. Sean Hand (Oxford, 1989), pp. 38–54.

impressions into new combinations, but those have to be impressions already inclined towards each other. Without the structure of resemblance – a slightly internalised form of contiguity – the imagination can do little to fuse the old with the new. In the social sphere the same restrictions apply. 'Likenesses' between me and the other have to be, at least, imaginable. Too great a difference or divergence threatens to evoke merely monstrosity. The force of imaginative projection is constrained by propriety, by what associations and affinities are 'suitable', appropriate. Hence an ethics controlled by imagination will have great difficulty accounting for the incommensurable. If I am to imagine an interchange between you and me, I have at least to picture you being a spectator like myself, imagining yourself into the actor's role, turning aside so that the role does not become too serious and my sympathy descend into partiality. But what if you are so different, so other, that the discourse of spectacle and beholder may have no purchase on you? On the far side of sympathy, what is needed is an ethics which will go beyond the proper and will not be afraid of imagining an identity with the repellent, the ostracised, the ugly, and the unloved. The ethic Eliot has in mind has grown too large, too unwieldly and speculative for the terms of 'Britishness'. It turns out to leave even Hellenism behind: it is an Hebraic ethic, an ethic of history, responsibility, prophecy, transcendence.

Conclusion: culture and an end to sympathy?

In writing *Daniel Deronda*, Eliot hoped to uncover a rationale for social idealism in a world disrupted by modernity. In *Middlemarch* she still favoured the idea of identity through interdependence: the community in which each independent part, pursuing its own conception of the good, returns unwittingly to a common language. *Middlemarch*'s ethical commitments are divided between two philosophies which Eliot and her contemporaries struggled to reconcile. One was a quasi-Hegelian idealism, the other a naturalised empiricism. Idealism sees relations everywhere; empiricism famously cannot ground them anywhere. While the incompatibility between these philosophies was difficult to resolve in the field of science or metaphysics (William James probably came closest), it proved more amenable to the world of socioethical existence, and thus (to make a long story short) to the novel. The surprising effects of sympathy uncovered the idealist within the empiricist, the elusive relation within the unconnected event and character. Far more powerful than a self-interest which divides is an all-penetrating sympathy which sees that self in others.

Now in her most ambitious creation, a world split into the awkward dialogue of English high society and Jewish Messianism, Eliot has not abandoned the figure of sympathy. But she finds it in a strange location. English society has lost the tradition and lacks the values which can nurture community between different individuals, disparate situations. Sympathy requires a leap of the imagination, and a willingness to transcend the egotistical self. While the natural world provides any number of examples where the singular organism or part freely abandons its own immediate ends for the sake of something else, Eliot no longer believes that the purely artificial structures of society – even in the most developed cultural forms – will reproduce this mechanism. Contra the received Hobbesian wisdom, nature may be altruistic but civilisation is not. So what is to become of the great Victorian elixir of life, the spiritual cure-all called renunciation? Eliot (here in agreement with Freud and Nietzsche) suspects that no one in modern society would choose it for its own sake. The motivation must be traced to deeper or more atavistic levels of causation, which for her in this novel turn out to be racial, familial, biological. Determined by blood, or (ideally) by the living inheritance of a prized culture, the individual finds herself capable of sacrifice and self-denial. Impulses to care for and protect others, otherwise inexplicable, make sense if I am acting on the promptings of a cultural destiny.

Thus in the conflicting resolutions of this novel, the possibility of being ethical, at one moment given the most deterministic if not sociobiological justification, is at the next moment consigned to the uncanny. The roots of cultural identity in Daniel Deronda himself are hidden, esoteric, melodramatic. He does not know who his parents are, what is his nationality or race, how he has come to be where he is and what expectations there may be for him. All he knows is that he suffers from an overdeveloped susceptibility to the needs and dreams of others, that he cannot screen out their designs on him. From this excess of sensitivity and responsiveness comes a character apparently unsuited for most active forms of English aristocratic life – the political, the commercial, even the scholarly and the artistic. Yet it equips him to feel the deficiencies and hopes of others, without knowing very well what to do with them, how to satisfy them.

Eliot's point seems to be that the psychological capacity for moral behaviour must first have an emotional source: one would not desire justice for others if one did not all too acutely feel their pain as if it were happening to oneself. So far this is a fairly commonplace version of the kind of physiological reductionism in ethics which was being argued by associates like Lewes and Spencer, and criticised by Continental thinkers with a sense of English culture like Nietzsche. Yet Eliot is not content to produce Deronda as a wonderful freak of nature: the triumph of nerves over instinct explaining, as Nietzsche might, the anomalous appearance of a moral consciousness. She wants to argue that his 'gift' is no aberration once he is recognised as the unconscious product of a different culture. His sympathy would not then be diffuse, a sign of Romantic hypertrophy which Nietzsche clearly wanted to call 'decadent'. For Eliot, 'becoming-Jewish' legitimates Deronda's otherwise puzzling selflessness. It converts passivity into power. But the price is cultural separation, even ethnic isolation.

Deronda is more sensitive than an Englishman, he feels the plight of others and therefore is obsessed with redressing wrongs because he is racially and culturally a Jew, member of an outcast people. Grandcourt, the English solipsist as psycho, presents a frightening image of what his culture's values can lead to if unchecked, uncontested by other, rival claims. But is the only alternative to this a voluntary embrace of cultural determinism? Is that moral nihilism which we are always being told about only to be resolved within the terms of particular traditions, within independent and culturally exclusive communities who no longer share a universal language? By invoking the 'magic' of culture Eliot naturalised her uncanny moralist. But her solution, 100 years on, has lost its innocence.

4

❖❖

Against tidiness
Literature and/versus moral philosophy

❖❖

JANE ADAMSON

It is doubly ironic that during the last twenty years the ethical functions of literature – for centuries of prime concern to imaginative writers and literary critics – have been repudiated by a majority of literary theorists (all driven in various ways, as Mark Edmundson has recently argued, by the centuries-old platonic will to disenfranchise art), while at the same time so many philosophers have sought to re-enfranchise literature by arguing for its special value as a mode of moral inquiry.[1] This chapter responds to three philosophers whose work in this latter area has opened fresh ground: Cora Diamond, Martha Nussbaum and Iris Murdoch.

I Philosophy's turn to literature

In 'Martha Nussbaum and the need for novels' (chapter 2 of this volume) Cora Diamond endorses Martha Nussbaum's claims and outlines a qualificatory critique of them. I broadly agree with her arguments, but think they need to be taken further and, in the process, modified. Coming at this from the literary side I shall focus upon what seems to me a problematic *link* between (a) philosophy's 'need' of literature, and (b) some difficulties in the crossover from philosophical to literary modes of thought. To

---

[1] Mark Edmundson, *Literature Against Philosophy, Plato to Derrida* (Cambridge, 1995). Edmundson's detailed theoretical discussion provides a broader context for my argument.

recognise this link may be the best way to avoid a sort of transdisciplinary catch-22. For brevity's sake, I shall use the term 'philosophy' to mean contemporary analytic philosophy, and the term 'literature' to mean literary art of some depth.

Philosophy's 'need' of literature arises from what many philosophers regard as limitations of analytic philosophy. These are both procedural and substantial: they concern philosophy's characteristic habits of argument, and its relatively narrow conception of what constitutes moral reflection and moral life. In 'Against Dryness', Iris Murdoch laid the foundations for subsequent discussion:

> what we require is a renewed sense of the difficulty and complexity of the moral life and the opacity of persons. We need more concepts in terms of which to picture the substance of our being... It is here that literature is so important, especially since it has taken over some of the tasks formerly performed by philosophy... Through literature we can re-discover a sense of the density of our lives. [2]

On this view, which seems to me right, philosophy's 'need' of literature hinges on the *differences* between the two modes. And this being so, it is vital to identify the differences and keep them in mind, if the 'need' is to be fulfilled. Yet in practice these requirements are a source of difficulty. For although philosophers often acknowledge differences between literature and philosophy, the differences just as often come to be treated as negligible, or dissoluble, or even entirely compatible. Frequently they get suppressed, or drop from view. One upshot is an overtidy picture of the relationship, in which philosophy assimilates literature into its system virtually without trace, and thus without evidently benefiting in the process. An alternative outcome, also unbeneficial, is an overcosy notion of their coming-together, as lean philosophy and rich literature join in a marriage of happy complementarity, somewhat along the lines of Jack and Mrs Sprat. As far as platter-licking goes, this sort of union works splendidly. But the difficulty here – in view of the ancient quarrel between these newly weds – is that this picture omits the big questions about how the partnership

[2] Iris Murdoch, 'Against Dryness: A Polemical Sketch', *Encounter*, 16.1 (1961), pp. 16–20, reprinted in *Revisions: Changing Perspectives in Moral Philosophy*, ed. Stanley Hauerwas and Alasdair MacIntyre (Notre Dame, 1983), pp. 43–9. Her phrase 'we need', repeated six times, is echoed by both Nussbaum and Diamond.

actually works when the honeymoon is over. For instance, who calls the tunes? And are there any spheres of interaction where the two do not rhyme nearly so tidily as 'lean' and 'clean'?

Instead of thinking of the relationship of literature and philosophy solely in terms of abstract differences, it is thus instructive to take a leaf out of literature's book and think of each one's distinctive *character*, and how they interact. This involves observing each one's operative values, concepts, desires, beliefs, and so on, as these emerge in its temper and style of mind. This raises questions about how individual 'character' is constituted transactively in what Charles Taylor calls 'webs of interlocution'.[3] It also raises others. For example – to think in a Shakespearean cartoon – it prompts the question of what might transpire if philosophy, like Julius Caesar, made uneasy by its lean and hungry adherents who 'think too much', were to say 'let me have men about me that are fat' ... only to find it had put Rome's fortunes in the hands of Falstaff. And, as with the relationship between lean-spirited Prince Hal and Falstaff in *Henry IV, Part One*, it prompts the questions of whether philosophy and literature influence each other for good or ill; whether their differences of character, which are also the ground for mutual attraction, are deeper than might initially appear; and whether the relationship alters as different agendas arise. Could it be that, after embracing plump Jack's vitality, Hal may find Plato-like reasons to banish him? Or could it even be that, as in that strange romance of ancient rivals, Caius Martius and Aufidius in *Coriolanus*, the outcome following the honeymoon may be not just extreme disenchantment but a resurgent will on the host's part to annihilate the old enemy?

Iris Murdoch tellingly contrasts the dryness (smallness, clearness, self-containedness) of post-war fiction with the bigger, sprawlier, and (in her word) 'messy' novels of the nineteenth century, which concern, not desiccated abstractions, but 'real various individuals struggling in society'.[4] This contrast between something self-contained and something messier which tends to sprawl and burst at the seams (like Henry James's image of novels

---

[3] Charles Taylor, *Sources of the Self: The Making of Modern Identity* (Cambridge, 1989), p. 36. On some of the literary issues, see Adamson, 'Who and What is Henchard?: Hardy, Character and Moral Inquiry', *Critical Review*, 32 (1992), pp. 47–74.
[4] Murdoch, 'Against Dryness', p. 47.

as loose, baggy monsters) suggests another spectrum along which to think of the distinct characters of philosophy and literature. They can be compared in terms of philosophy's penchant for tidiness as against literature's more disorderly, spontaneous 'messy' character.

In *The Fragility of Goodness*, Martha Nussbaum invokes a distinction somewhat along these lines. Echoing Murdoch's terms, she emphasizes the sense of 'complexity' and 'difficulty' of moral life, which literature articulates and revitalises in the reader:

a whole tragic drama, unlike a schematic philosophical example making use of a similar story ... lays open to view the complexity, the indeterminacy, the sheer difficulty of actual human deliberation. If a philosopher were to use Antigone's story as a philosophical example, he or she would, in setting it out schematically, signal to the reader's attention everything that the reader ought to notice. He would point out only what is strictly relevant. A tragedy does not display the dilemmas of its characters as pre-articulated; it shows them searching for the morally salient; and it forces us, as interpreters, to be similarly active. Interpreting a tragedy is a *messier, less determinate, more mysterious matter* than assessing a philosophical example.[5]

These differences are key ones to keep in mind, not least because of all they imply concerning possible tensions in a relationship between the two. Philosophy, we might say, loves what is shipshape, trim, strictly relevant, goal-directed. It values clear distinctions, clean categories, orderly lines of argument proceeding to conclusions. Literature, conversely, being less fastidious and more adventurous, loves the 'messier' texture of what John Donne calls the 'mixt of all stuffes' jumble and 'vicissitude', the mysterious un-nailable fluidity of experience.[6] And as we shall see, their converse loves and desires go with converse aversions. Yet philosophy and literature may be the more worth bringing into conversation precisely *because* they are so often at cross-purposes.

Since the fruitfulness of their contact depends upon their different values, it is important for philosophy not to overvalue its highest goods. If these are given sovereignty, other goods go by the board. Many philosophers have argued in effect that ethical

---

[5] Martha Nussbaum, *The Fragility of Goodness: Luck and Ethics in Greek Tragedy and Philosophy* (Cambridge, 1986), p. 14 (my emphasis).
[6] *John Donne: The Elegies and The Songs and Sonnets*, ed. Helen Gardner (Oxford, 1965), p. 76.

thinking has suffered from being conducted in overtidy categories and false either/ors which simplify by splitting off and denying the reality and force of whatever does not fit the prescribed pigeonholes. These self-criticisms have led to an awareness of how overtidiness results in loss and shrinkage of concepts.[7] Tidiness is not amongst literature's hypergoods.

In *A Midsummer Night's Dream* or *Troilus and Cressida* or *King Lear*, the hurly-burly of moral experience cannot be neatly categorised into public/private, fact/value, vice/virtue, impersonal/personal, and so on: these works explore the blurriness and leakiness of such supposedly watertight compartments. Often these ambivalences are central to the dramatic design, as in *Coriolanus*, and in *Measure for Measure*, with its interest in various draconian attempts (and all that resists such attempts) to coerce order – by the imposition of 'strict statutes' and 'biting laws', for instance – and to shut out whatever does not conform. Both plays investigate the psychic roots and effects of various rigidly 'strict' or puritanically black-or-white mentalities. (The plays' tough scepticism makes it the more ironic that they have so often been subjected to over-neat, casuistical interpretations which annul their drama of questioning and reduce them to some unilateral statement, 'message', position.[8])

Philosophy's turning to literary texts in search of what Iris Murdoch calls 'more concepts in terms of which to picture the substance of our being' thus implies a recognition of the value of literature's 'messier' kind of moral inquiry. It implies a recognition that *literature works against tidiness*. Yet the problem, and the potential catch-22, is that philosophy's drive to definiteness, clarity, and the like makes it so averse to ambiguity, opacity, inconclusiveness. Willy-nilly, *philosophy works against untidiness*.

II 'Learning to read with a different sort of eye'

Cora Diamond's account of some problems in philosophy's incorporation of literature is cast in quite other terms, but describes

---

[7] Compare Murdoch, 'Against Dryness', pp. 46–9; Cora Diamond, 'Losing Your Concepts', *Ethics* (January 1988), pp. 255–77; and Simon Haines, 'Deepening the self: the language of ethics and the language of literature', in this volume, above.

[8] Reductive (usually cynical) interpretations of *Troilus and Cressida* have similarly flattened and sentimentalised it, as argued in Jane Adamson, *Troilus and Cressida* (Brighton, 1987).

going round a related mulberry bush. The picture I have sketched fits with hers at many points and suggests how her arguments need to be pressed further. Her fourth section concludes: 'Yes, we do need in philosophy to read novels; but reading them – *reading* them (in the sense *they* give that term) – is itself a revolutionary act.' The context indicates her view that this 'revolution' has two levels. First, if I may put it this way, reading novels is an act of rebellion against the current *ancien régime* within moral philosophy, and against the view that philosophy has little to learn from literature since literature is at best a sort of orchard full of juicy examples which merely illustrate issues that philosophy pre-formulates perfectly well on its own. Second, the 'revolution' involves the whole discipline of moral philosophy, including the work of those who take a wide view of ethics and see the 'need' of literature to extend and deepen it. It is directed at philosophy's characteristic preoccupations and style of mind. To read imaginative literature *imaginatively* is a 'revolutionary act' against philosophy's characteristic un-imaginativeness, and even (one might add) its *anti-imaginativeness*. To read it with your heart as well as head, with your whole soul as well as rational faculties, is an act of dare-devilry, challenging the sovereign powers, the gods of neatness, logic and clarity.

Cora Diamond goes on to claim a need for change in the mental practices of all philosophers:

The *only* way to see what kinds of moral thinking may be found in literary texts is by giving them sensitive attention, of a sort we are not trained or encouraged, as philosophers, to give them. We look for arguments, for theories, for supporting data or counter-examples. The idea that we need to learn to read with a different sort of eye, attentive to different sorts of things, may strike us as very strange.[9]

All these points are worth taking further. From a literary stand-point we might say that they make a Blakean claim about the need to cleanse the doors of perception. They also imply agreement with Blake's idea (and Shakespeare's) that different eyes see different worlds: 'As the eye, such the object'; and as the I, such the object. Together, they imply a recognition that styles of mind are grounded in states of soul.

[9] Cora Diamond, 'Martha Nussbaum and the need for novels', in this volume, above p. 49.

Jane Adamson

To someone more familiar with literature than philosophy, the idea of a need 'to read with a different sort of eye' is not likely to seem 'strange'. Literary texts abound in studies of individual mentalities, and explorations of the need to look through different eyes. Some even explore the effects of eyedrops. 'I would my father look'd but with my eyes', says Hermia in *A Midsummer Night's Dream* (I, i, 56). Looking with different eyes is what Shakespeare investigates. More to the point, it is also what he continually *does*. His imagination darts forth into the interior of other minds, looking now with Hermia's eyes, now Hermia's-with-eyedrops, now Puck's, Oberon's, Lysander's, Bottom's – including minds that are reluctant or unable to imagine anyone else's sense of reality. And the play similarly engages *our* imaginations in looking through all these other eyes, in each case 'attentive to different sorts of things'.[10] As Diamond suggests, the ability to make imaginative leaps is not one that modern analytic philosophers are trained or encouraged to develop. On the contrary. But it is something philosophy needs.

As well as activating this, many literary texts highlight complexities involved in looking through different eyes, whether one's own eyes, altered, or someone else's. Our language often screens these from view. We speak of 'putting myself in your shoes', as if I remained the same old me, with different footwear; or of 'reversing perspectives', or 'seeing it from your point of view', as if it were basically a matter of standing on a different spot. Literature often suggests, rather, that it is a matter of imaginatively becoming a different I: a changed self, a different character, with a different *gestalt*, other values and beliefs, another sense of reality (or what Thomas Hardy calls a different 'structure of sensations'), and with consequent new conceptual and perceptual abilities as well. [11]

This is a question of imaginative abilities, and of the possibilities and conditions of change, refocussing, growth. In raising such issues, Shakespeare's plays – *Twelfth Night, Much Ado About Nothing*, for example – also explore how hard it can be to look with different eyes at different sorts of things. Often, it proves impossi-

[10] Martha Nussbaum discusses this particularly well in relation to Dickens (see below, pp. 222–46).
[11] Thomas Hardy, *Tess of the D'Urbervilles*, ed. Juliet Grindle and Simon Gattrell (Oxford, 1983).

90

ble. It involves moral luck as well as moral effort. For Beatrice and Benedick in *Much Ado*, and similarly for Elizabeth and Darcy in Jane Austen's *Pride and Prejudice* and Emma Woodhouse in *Emma*, learning to read oneself and others with a different sort of eye involves being jarred out of one's previous modes of understanding, surprised into new perceptions, values, and beliefs. In *The Winter's Tale*, Leontes' experience reveals how self-impeding and incomplete such a revolution of thinking can be. And, like some characters, some members of the audience – including oneself, perhaps – may turn out to lack much capability for creative change.

How does one learn to see 'with a different sort of eye'? And what can block such learning? Literary texts suggest that much depends upon one's habitual eyes, and upon the magnitude of the differences between the old and new outlooks. Shakespeare's plays, and Webster's, and Middleton's, for instance, often investigate the possibilities of particular minds undergoing a sea change. But in dramatising such selves as Bottom, Shylock, Iago, Malvolio, and De Flores they raise the possibility that some modes of vision are so deep-rooted in the whole personality that they cannot be significantly modified, or only temporarily, and too late. In Shakespearean drama, as in psychiatry, deep change in a powerful mindset takes more than a quick fix. As rain hurtles down well-worn gullies so does our attention. Resolving that one needs it to run down different gullies is not sufficient to bring this about.

Literary texts often invite readers to notice how learning involves *un*learning. They bring home how extremely hard it can be to stop looking with old eyes, especially when what these see is still pleasing. Australian painters in the nineteenth and early twentieth centuries, especially those trained in Europe, kept on painting the light and colours as if these were European, and could not or would not, or simply did not *un*learn the old habit in order to learn to look with new eyes and see a different play of light, a different kind of landscape. To take a plunge, to allow change into one's eyes and mind, is indeed a revolutionary act. To achieve new insight entails loss – *loss of security, loss of the world as one previously knew it.*

As literary texts also often bring home, every outlook has its blind spots. And it is hard for even the sharpest-eyed leopard to see its blind spots, let alone change them. Philip Sidney in his

Defence of Poetry, in a playful run of witty aspersions on the differences between poetry, philosophy and history as modes of moral inquiry, comments (after Plato) on how 'the astronomer, looking to the stars, might fall in a ditch'.[12] Comedies, tragedies, satires, lyric poems, are full of selves who, looking for one thing, miss another, and fall in ditches. Such texts also suggest that we are always liable to do this when our looking is purposive, focussed upon something important to us. Jonathan Swift makes brilliant hay from the fact that it is so much easier to criticise others' presumptions than to face and tackle one's own. Someone trained to be ever-alert to at least seven types of ambiguity may find it hard to read a philosophical text in terms of its fixed, unambiguous, non-paradoxical categories. Someone trained in philosophy, where looking for arguments may become part of 'the texture of [your] being', may have trouble seeing other things, especially ambiguities that confound your categories.[13]

III   Two models of moral attention

Earlier I said that some of the key differences to focus on are those summed up in Martha Nussbaum's comments that literature's moral thinking is *'messier, less determinate, more mysterious'* than philosophy's, and that the business of reading a literary text is thus correspondingly 'messier' than interpreting a philosophical example. This means that really to *'read'* literary texts, 'in the sense *they* give that term', one not only needs to engage with 'messier' thinking than philosophy's; one actually needs to have the courage to think more 'messily' oneself – to think *with* the literature, following where it leads. This involves being able to bear untidiness. Learning this is particularly hard for anyone who is professionally obliged to be tidy-minded, especially one who is also temperamentally inclined that way.[14] But, as Cora Diamond argues, if philosophers impose upon literature a schematic model of moral thinking, the result will be a loss for moral philosophy.[15] To

---

[12] Philip Sidney, *A Defence of Poetry*, ed. J. A. Van Dorsten (Oxford, 1966), p. 28.
[13] Compare Iris Murdoch, 'Vision and Choice in Morality', *Proceedings of the Aristotelian Society*, supplementary volume XXX (1956), p. 39.
[14] A wonderful account of this is in Doris Lessing's portrait of her relationship with Gottfried Lessing in *Under My Skin* (London, 1994), chapters 13–21, for example p. 358.
[15] Diamond, 'Martha Nussbaum and the need for novels', above, p. 48.

avoid this, it is important not only to heed those features of literature's character that resist and oppose philosophy's, but also to notice how certain of philosophy's habits of mind resist and oppose those of literature.

The opening of one of Martha Nussbaum's essays on Henry James illustrates in miniature the mutually resistent characters of literature and philosophy.[16] As its title declares, '"Finely Aware and Richly Responsible": Literature and the Moral Imagination' examines questions of moral attention and moral perception. Literary readers may tend to trip over the philosopher's very determinate 'the' in the title, which indicates there is one such item rather than a plenitude of them. The title of an earlier version contained an equally definite article: 'Moral Attention and the Moral Task of Literature'. This echoed Iris Murdoch's terms 'attention' and 'task' in the passage of 'Against Dryness' I quoted earlier:

Simone Weil said that morality was a matter of attention, not of will. We need a new vocabulary of attention.
It is here that literature is so important, especially since it has taken over some of the tasks formerly performed by philosophy.

Although philosophers often speak of philosophy (and moral thinking generally) as a matter of 'tasks', the idea of literature 'performing' 'tasks' seems very strange. But, whatever of that, this passage implies, as I understand it, that if philosophy is to meet its 'need' and find a 'new vocabulary of attention' it will need to pay attention to literature's 'vocabulary of attention'. This is right. And Nussbaum's essay sets out to do just that, by examining what she calls 'the nature of moral attention and insight' as defined through James's 'words and sentences'.

Yet the essay's opening inadvertently reveals the potential pitfalls in this enterprise, namely that it involves 'learning to read with a different sort of eye'. It involves what Diamond calls the 'revolutionary act' of reading James in the sense *he* gives that term. The hard part is to stop reading with the eyes of a philosopher, looking for arguments, theories, etc. and to read instead with the

---

[16] Martha Nussbaum, '"Finely Aware and Richly Responsible": Literature and the Moral Imagination' (1987), reprinted in Martha Nussbaum, *Love's Knowledge: Essays on Literature and Philosophy* (Oxford and New York, 1990); an earlier version was published in *Journal of Philosophy*, 82 (1985), pp. 516–29.

eyes and ears of this novelist. Martha Nussbaum's opening paragraph comprises a sentence from one of James's prefaces, followed by an explication of it. To my ear and eye there is a mismatch between the two: a discordancy in tone, which goes with a discrepancy in meaning.

'The effort really to see and really to represent is no idle business in face of the *constant* force that makes for muddlement.' So Henry James on the task of the moral imagination. We live amid bewildering complexities. Obtuseness and refusal of vision are our besetting vices. Responsible lucidity can be wrested from that darkness only by painful, vigilant effort, the intense scrutiny of particulars. Our highest and hardest task is to make ourselves people 'on whom nothing is lost'.

In its tone and idioms and its whole manner the quoted sentence is classic James, speaking of 'effort' in a way that effortlessly expresses his idiosyncratic style of mind. The tone is genial, urbane, witty, serious yet tinged with irony, understated, meticulously precise, mildly comical. All these qualities come together in his sublime figure of 'the constant force that makes for muddlement'. These tonal colourings of his language suffuse and shape his meaning – his evocation of a novelist's 'effort really to see', and everything that makes this 'no idle business'. His attention is on this 'effort' of attention (and by implication, the challenge, the fascination), 'in face of the *constant* force', in the nature of things, which activates and complicates and pushes against the 'effort'.

Martha Nussbaum's gloss on the sentence conveys a different story and a different set of considerations. In its tone and its phrasing it conjures up and inhabits a different world. Or, to put this another way, we might say that James and Nussbaum here employ two quite different 'vocabularies of attention'. They speak in different moral languages. Where the novelist writes genially of an 'effort really to see ... in face of ... what makes for muddlement', the philosopher reads him in terms of a 'painful' 'task' necessitated by one's own 'obtuseness'. This vocabulary looks quite strange when viewed in the light of James's.

Another way to put this would be to say that James's sentence and the interpretative gloss represent two different kinds of moral reflection, which are in effect mutually antipathetic. One is evocative, the other prescriptive and admonitory. They articulate two different ideas or models of what moral perception involves, and two different ideas of why it is difficult. To compare them helps to specify the vital features of James's 'literary' idea, as distinct from the 'philosophical' one. This in turn helps to reveal the importance of not thinking them the same, especially if we proceed to make more general claims on this basis, as Nussbaum does, about 'our ethical task', and about James's analogy between 'the work of moral imagination' and 'the work of creative imagination', as well as about his analogy between 'moral attention' and 'attention to works of art'. James's account – and his practice – of 'the effort really to see' is indeed (as Nussbaum claims) an exemplary model of all these analogous activities of moral attention. By contrast, the philosopher's idea of 'the task of moral imagination' describes an enterprise of analytical inquiry and argument, which is in several respects at odds with the creative effort involved in actual moral living and in the writing and reading of imaginative texts such as James's novels or Shakespeare's plays.

James's sentence deftly links the 'effort really to see and really to represent' with its operative conditions, and with what is there to be seen and represented. The 'effort' is a busy business ('no idle business') because it encounters and faces (is made 'in face of') the *'constant* force that makes for muddlement' (the emphasis is James's). He implies that it is difficult 'really to see' because part of what needs seeing is what 'makes for muddlement', and how it does so. There is a slight smile in that phrase, and this edge of good humour sets the reader pondering what constitutes 'the constant force that makes for muddlement'. The phrase suggests the ceaseless energies and contingencies of people and things in the world which foil and elude our attempts at clarity. It also suggests an aptitude for muddle and even an attraction to it, perhaps, in the writer's mind, and one's own mind in reading literature. James's phrase is figurative, suggesting the *confusing* force of human passions, for instance – of love and hate and grief and fear and desire; and the unpredictable vitality produced in social interchange. Or we might think of the constant force that makes for muddlement as being embodied in particular individuals – in one's two-year-old daughter, for example, or fictional characters such as James's Maisie; or Iago, or Cleopatra; or Heathcliff; or the wyf of Bath.

The philosophical gloss interprets James's sentence in terms of a severe equation: inattention = vice, attention = virtue. The idea that (as James would agree) 'we live amid bewildering complexities' leads to an (oddly un-Jamesian) castigation of 'our besetting vices', our 'obtuseness' and 'refusal of vision'. This problem of moral perception is attributed to wilfulness; our 'refusal' must thus be reversed by will, by 'painful, vigilant effort'. Murdoch's point, recalling Weil's, that 'morality is a matter of attention, not of will', seems here to have disappeared.[17] Our 'hardest and highest task' is to 'make ourselves' infallible, to escape being muddled, bewildered, and blind.[18]

As I read it, James's sentence describes a directly contrary conception of the business of moral understanding. It suggests that the 'force that makes for muddlement' is a constant, ordinary part of life's complexity and density: one which positively excites the writer's 'effort really to see', as well as complicating the whole 'business' by making it always fallible and liable to muddle; and also one which generates perceptual energy and inspires moral imagination. To see 'in face of' this, and 'really to represent' it, the artist must constantly engage with real and potential muddlement, examine (from the inside as well as the outside) what it is and how it works.

The context of James's sentence lends support to this reading. It comes in his preface to *What Maisie Knew*, where he refers rather drolly to 'elements with which even the most sedate philosopher must always reckon'. Describing how 'the painter of life has indeed work cut out for him', he makes his remark about 'the *constant* force that makes for muddlement'; and goes on to say:

> The great thing is indeed that the muddled state too is one of the very sharpest of the realities, that it also has colour and form and character, has often in fact a broad and rich comicality.[19]

James's sense of muddlement as expressed in all his writings bears this out. As a 'painter of life' he positively thrives in the face of it: he manages 'to see and really to represent' 'the muddled state' as 'one of the very sharpest of the realities' because (along

---

[17] This comment on Weil in 'Against Dryness' is elaborated by Murdoch in *Metaphysics as a Guide to Morals* (London, 1992), pp. 52–4.

[18] This view can be ascribed to James only by disregarding the lightly jovial tone and implications of his remarks in 'The Art of Fiction' (*The Art of Fiction and Other Essays*, introduced by Morris Roberts (New York, 1948), p. 11).

[19] Henry James, *The Art of the Novel*, introduced by R. P. Blackmur (New York, 1948), p. 149.

with Dickens, say, and Swift) he is intrigued by its 'colour and form and character', and intensely alive to its comicality, as well as to its often darker sides. His sense of it often intermixes farce, comedy, satire, elegy, meditation, tragedy.

Along with 'muddle' and 'muddlement', words such as 'bewilder', 'confuse', 'confound' are favourites in James's lexicon. In his preface to *The Princess Casamassima*, he writes of 'our own precious liability to fall into traps and be bewildered. It seems probable that if we were never bewildered there would never be a story to tell about us.' And this suggestion spontaneously buds and bursts into a semi-facetious little fantasised drama in which James fancies how 'the wary reader ... warns the novelist against making his characters too *interpretative* of the *muddle of fate*, or in other words too divinely, too priggishly clever. "Give us plenty of bewilderment," this monitor seems to say, "so long as there is plenty of slashing out in the bewilderment too."'[20]

In his portraits of Isabel Archer in *The Portrait of a Lady* and of Strether in *The Ambassadors*, for example, James's fascination with complexities that can bewilder people's 'efforts really to see', makes him exceptionally attentive to the vagaries of attention, and to the ins and outs and stops and starts of self-understanding, which he shows to be always linked with people's efforts and failures 'really to see' the reality of others. Like Chekhov, and Proust, and Hardy, he is sensitive to the ways things can distract attention, and escape attention, and to the processes of what Hardy calls 'self-unseeing', or 'looking away', or being 'in a dream'.[21] Rather than dismissing these as 'obtuseness', he presents them as ordinary liabilities of consciousness, and by no means always lamentable. Like Shakespeare, he often explores (as in his portrait of Isabel Archer) how moral insight can become disabled when it is driven by will. High determination can result in *not* paying sensitive attention to things, but rather in simply imposing upon them one's preconceived ideas. Like Louie's in Christina Stead's *The Man Who Loved Children*, and like Gwendolen's in *Daniel Deronda*, Isabel's achievement of increased self-insight is portrayed as a painful, blunder-prone process (often one step forwards, two steps back) of unlearning some habits of mind

---

[20] Ibid., p. 63.
[21] Thomas Hardy, 'The Self-Unseeing', in *The Complete Poetical Works of Thomas Hardy*, ed. Samuel Hynes (Oxford, 1982), vol. 1, p. 206.

and gradually learning to read with a different sort of eye. It involves relinquishing many of her previous 'lucidities' and theories about life, and slowly coming to realise what Martha Nussbaum aptly calls 'the complexity, the indeterminacy, the sheer difficulty' of actual moral experience. For the reader, similarly, reading *The Portrait of a Lady*, or *The Brothers Karamazov*, say, or *Macbeth*, involves an always fallible 'effort really to see' in the face of what are often bewildering complexities. Moral experience here can include being plunged into an abyss of ambiguities. The reader's or audience's activities of attending and struggling to orient themselves thus draw their colour and energy and character from the quality of the writer's.

This 'literary' kind of attending, exemplified in these texts and called for in reading them, differs from that implied in the gloss's 'philosophical' model in this key respect: it involves abilities of patience, receptiveness, wise passiveness, as well as constant activity of mind. It involves a *two-way*, reciprocal relationship between the individual noticer and what is being noticed: an 'effort' not just 'in view of', but (much more intimately) *'in face of'* all that attracts, impedes, and complicates clear-seeing, and even confounds it. It is responsive, and dynamic, finely calibrated, nuanced, and metamorphic (for example, now widely focussed, now divided, now like a spotlight) . It refrains from prejudicial categorising tidiness. It is variable in quality and degrees of intensity (playful, or absorbed, vigilant, obsessed, and so forth), depending upon its object (this joke; this moral miasma; this predicate; this baby; this abstract idea; this death; or whatever it be).

In contrast, moral attention as projected by the philosophical model is differently constitutited, oriented, and motivated. Here, attention is a task directed at an outcome. Mess is anathema. Our 'liabilitity to fall into traps' is anything but 'precious'. Whatever is muddled must be eliminated: 'Lucidity can be wrested from that darkness only by painful vigilant effort'. This language (metaphorically suggesting a nighthawk) describes a kind of attention that is narrowly focussed and targeted at its object. Such attention is static and uniform. It is active, but not interactive. Inquiry here involves a knower and an object of knowledge. On this model, the moral inquirer is fully in command.

This purposive attention, dismissive of whatever is not 'strictly relevant', fits the requirements of tight logical argument.[22] But it is not however an apt model of moral attention in general. Nor is it an appropriate model for the moral attention involved in writing and reading literary texts; and nor, we may notice, for that involved in creating and responding to other cultural forms – film, painting, dance, for example – whose imaginative qualities analytic philosophy similarly tends to lack, and to need.

One crucial reason for this is that the 'task' of 'wresting' lucidity from darkness allows no scope for reverie; or playfulness; or fantasy; or wondering; or seeing 'what's invisible', or pondering the unknown.[23] Nor does it allow for the inattention or absent-mindedness, or absorbed and preoccupied attention, which – far from necessarily being 'vicious' – may be a precious and necessary condition of intense vitality and creative thought. By contrast, a Jamesian or Shakespearean mode of attending allows ample scope for reverie, and for discovering if the darkness itself may be what one needs to attend to, in order to see what it is, and to discern what it may hide, or hold. Seamus Heaney evokes this active-and-passive character of creative attending in his volume title, *Door into the Dark*; and when he writes that 'I rhyme / To see myself, to set the darkness echoing'; and in his delicate explorations of it in *Seeing Things*.[24] Like painters, poets have always seen, and thus enabled readers to find, how 'lucidities' sometimes really shine only when you forebear to seize them, and when, instead, you allow their light to glow; and grow.

For Coleridge, reading involves being 'carried' by willing desire to go *wherever the writing takes you*: being 'carried forward, not merely or chiefly by the mechanical impulse of curiosity, or by a *restless desire to arrive at a . . . solution*; but by the . . . activity of mind excited by the . . . journey itself'.[25] Similarly for Keats, reading involves a surrender or suspension of self and a readiness to be carried, as well as outgoingness, and a capacity to have one's whole being aroused into activity. He fancifully proposes an ideal life of excursive contemplativeness in which one may 'read a certain Page of full Poesy or distilled Prose', and 'wander with it,

---

[22] Compare Nussbaum, *The Fragility of Goodness*, p. 14.
[23] Seamus Heaney, from the title poem in *Seeing Things* (London, 1991), p. 17.
[24] Seamus Heaney, 'Personal Helicon', in *Death of a Naturalist* (London, 1966); ibid.
[25] Samuel Taylor Coleridge, *Biographia Literaria*, ed. George Watson (London 1967), ch. 14, p. 173 (my emphasis).

and muse upon it, and reflect upon it, and bring home to it, and prophesy upon it, and dream upon it'. He conjures this imaginative journeying as a 'happy ... voyage of conception' – not a matter of 'painful vigilant effort', but of 'delicious diligent Indolence!'[26] Creative attending is receptiveness, not restless appropriative desire: it is as a matter of awaiting visitation, of *'budding patiently'*, not *'buzzing impatiently'*:

> Now it is more noble to sit like Jove than to fly like Mercury – let us not therefore go hurrying about and collecting honey, bee-like buzzing here and there impatiently from a knowledge of what is aimed at; but let us open our leaves like a flower and be passive and receptive – budding patiently under the eye of Apollo and taking hints from every noble insect that favours us with a visit – sap will be given us for meat and dew for drink.

IV Moral capabilities

This value which creative writers find in interactive receptivity bears directly on several issues raised by Cora Diamond concerning what she defines as some (perhaps irreducible) incompatibilities between literature and philosophy. Agreeing with Martha Nussbaum, and with Wordsworth in mind, she points out that 'a further argument for the significance of literary texts to moral philosophy' involves their acknowledgment of 'mystery', their sense 'that there is far more to things, to life, than what we know or understand'; and that this style of thinking is 'tied to a rejection of the spirit of *knowingness* often found in abstract moral and social theorising, a spirit which ... is reductive in its idea of our relation to the world, and in what it takes understanding and knowledge to be, a spirit that is often "restless" in its supposed wisdom, eager to re-order human lives in accordance with its rational plans'.[27]

These ideas can be magnified by looking through a literary lens. Keats, again, often draws a contrast between two such styles of mind. The first is capable of truth-discovering because it is alive to what is questionable, and imponderable, beyond our knowing – it is aware at once of mystery and of doors into the

---

[26] Letter of 19 February 1818, in *The Letters of John Keats*, ed. Maurice Buxton Forman (London, 1952), p. 102.
[27] Diamond, 'Martha Nussbaum and the need for novels', above, pp. 51–2.

dark. The other tends to the sterility of knowingness by reductively closing off inquiry in QEDs. The former is most memorably defined in his letter about how 'the Chamber of Maiden Thought becomes gradually darken'd, and at the same time on all sides of it many doors are set open – but all dark – all leading to dark passages – we see not the balance of good and evil. We are in a mist. *We* are now in that state – We feel the 'burden of the Mystery' ... 'and it seems to me that [Wordsworth]'s Genius is explorative of those dark passages'.[28] By contrast, Keats describes his friend Dilke as given over to the mystery-averse unexplorativeness of one 'who cannot feel he has a personal identity unless he has made up his mind about everything'.[29] In face of this, Keats declares that 'the only means of strengthening one's intellect is to make up one's mind about nothing – to let the mind be a thoroughfare for all thoughts'. Significantly, it took a 'disquisition' with Dilke to spark Keats's most famous distinction between minds that have a sense of mystery and minds that do not: it took Dilke's exasperating knowingness to make Keats realise the great value of the opposite quality, which 'forms a man of achievement, especially in literature, and which Shakespeare possessed so enormously – I mean Negative Capability, that is when a man is *capable of being in uncertainties, mysteries, doubts*, without any irritable reaching after fact and reason'. The obverse is the sort of mind that avoids dark passages, is allergic to doubts, and which, even though it may temporarily tolerate some degree of uncertainty, is (as Keats fine-tunes it) incapable of *remaining content* with half knowledge'.[30]

These distinctions illuminate Diamond's point that philosophers need to learn from literature to attend to things other than arguments. This implies a recognition that not all kinds of ethical inquiry are constituted in arguments, theories, etc., directed at logical conclusions – that reading literature involves being able to 'remain content with half-knowledge' and to *refrain from 'aiming' and desiring 'to arrive at a solution'*. Seamus Heaney's 'The Pitchfork' defines a related distinction (and a choice) between two models of ethical attention and deliberation. First is the long-desired intellectual ideal represented by the pitchfork, 'Of all

[28] Letter of 3 May 1818, *Letters of John Keats*, p. 143.
[29] Letter of 17-27 September 1819, *Letters of John Keats*, p. 425.
[30] Letter of 21 December, 1817, *Letters of John Keats*, p. 71 (my emphasis).

implements, . . . the one / That came near to an imagined perfection: / When he tightened his raised hand and aimed with it, / It felt like a javelin, accurate and light.' But the satisfactions of the imperturbable pitchfork mentality give way to something new, when he 'has learned at last to follow that simple lead / Past its own aim, out to an other side, / Where perfection – or nearness to it – is imagined / Not in the aiming but the opening hand.' Yet just how hard it is for philosophers to relinquish the pitchfork ideal can be gauged from their deep preference for the aiming, not the opening hand. Philosophy's buzzwords concern buzzing, not budding. Even in arguing that philosophy needs to learn from literature to be less bent on closure, philosophers persistently discuss literature in terms of 'views', 'arguments', 'premises', 'answers', 'propositions', 'conclusions'. Endorsing Nussbaum's claims Diamond writes that the novelist's 'views' and 'conclusions' are given a particular 'kind of statement' by the novel (above, p. 43); that novels such as James's give 'a particular set of answers to the quesion, "How should one live?"'.[31] This conception of literature is modelled on, indeed exactly replicates, Martha Nussbaum's conception of *philosophy* as 'including inquiry directed at answering the question how we should live' and as involving 'the working out and full expression of particular answers to that question' (above, p. 47; 50). This is the operative conception of both literature and philosophy throughout Nussbaum's *The Therapy of Desire: Theory and Practice in Hellenistic Ethics*, of 1994.[32]

The idea of literature as authorial (often expressly didactic) 'statements', views, arguments, etc., is of course widely current, and always has been. Countless readers have espoused it over the centuries, as have many writers – Spenser, Milton, Shelley, Tolstoy, to name a few, with the host of classical shades who loom behind them. Plenty of literature indeed has a 'palpable design' on us (as Keats complained of Wordsworth), enjoining, bossing or 'bully[ing us] into a certain philosophy'; and plenty of readers

---

[31] Diamond also follows Nussbaum in saying that literary texts 'convey moral views' (p. 000); that a 'view of life, of how to live, is conveyed by a text' (p. 000); that Nussbaum's primary focus 'is always on *how to live*, and how a novel can convey the novelist's view of *that*' (p. 42); that literary texts are 'presentations . . . of moral views' (p. 46).

[32] Martha Nussbaum, *The Therapy of Desire: Theory and Practice in Hellenistic Ethics* (Princeton, 1994).

do not 'hate' but love being so instructed.[33] But Keats's stress on the positive value of negative capability implies a contrary conception, one that must be taken seriously by anyone who wishes to engage with the 'thick' moral thinking in literary texts whose own such capability calls upon the same in the reader. For Keats implies that inquiry into the possibilites of living well or ill – inquiry both on the writer's part and on the reader's – can be a process of questioning, pondering, doubting, which does not issue in prescriptive assertions, 'answers', or even in 'final vocabularies', but remains (in Nussbaum's phrase) 'unexhausted, subject to reassessment', and bristling with questions.[34] Keats also implies that this vital business of searching for the morally salient is of value in itself, that its worth is not tied to outcomes, or 'the working out and full expression of particular answers', the resolution of 'mystery', or any ultimate tidying up of all the mess and muddle. As Philip Sidney writes in *A Defence of Poetry*, 'the poet ... nothing affirms'.[35]

Cora Diamond is therefore right to say that in reading literature one needs to stop looking for arguments, etc. – especially when the literature in question is dramatic, speculative, explorative of dark passages, and fissured, polysemous, not univocally polemical. Instead, one needs to notice how such texts throw open the *question*, 'how to live?' – how they frame it, focus it, bring it alive, and particularise it, rousing the reader to dream and muse and 'bring home to it', as Keats says, without closing it off in what Coleridge calls 'fixities and definites'. A literary text, on this account, is not a moral thesis. It is a foray, a many-sided experiential 'hypothesis', an adventure, a 'suppose'. It enjoins us only to 'imagine if ...' and calls our whole soul into the activity of doing so. Unlike forms of discourse that are cast in the indicative mood, 'thick' literature is cast in the subjunctive mood, so to speak. It deals in possibilities, ifs, conditionals. Its form is *interrogative*.

Hamlet for instance, is crammed with determinate views, conclusions, arguments, and the like, but these without exception come from Claudius, the ghost, Gertrude, the grave-digger, Hamlet, etc. None come from the horse's mouth. Shakespeare (as distinct from Polonius) provides no list of answers or ethical

---

[33] Letter of 3 February 1818, *Letters of John Keats*, p. 95.
[34] Nussbaum, *The Fragility of Goodness*, p. 15.
[35] Sidney, *A Defence of Poetry*, p. 52.

formulae. Chekhov's plays, Emily Dickinson's poems, novels such as Proust's, for example, all engage us in unargumentative exploratory moral thinking. Likewise, in *Rasselas*, Samuel Johnson evokes the flux and reflux of the young travellers' journey in search of answers to the question, how to live, on which they might base their 'choice of life'; he draws our imagination into their activity of seeking, which continually reveals fresh avenues of inquiry, in a search which is itself a form of moral living and which reaches only a provisional 'conclusion in which nothing is concluded', implying the continuation of moral reassessment, surprise, doubt, mental travelling, musing. A reader who is willing to 'be carried forward' on a 'voyage of conception' is thus engaged in in a quest which engenders precisely what Iris Murdoch calls 'a renewed sense of the difficulty and complexity' of moral experience, 'a sense of the density our lives'.

The word 'sense' is important here. A rich 'sense' of the density of our lives involves bodily senses as well as mind, one's 'whole soul' and imagination, emotions as well as thoughts. The phrase 'our lives' suggests that what we read has personal implications for ourselves, that 'our lives' are constituted in community with other lives. Such a 'sense of our lives' is quite different from an abstract 'conception' of life or Life, or a set of 'views about life', or an answer to 'how one should live'. Imaginative writers have always valued these distinctions and built them into their idea of moral inquiry. This is why they are often less than in love with the merits of linear logic. Reaching towards a 'sense of the density of our lives' is not predominantly a matter of arguments, formulae, reasons, or ideas. It is a matter of moral practices and personal capabilities of experience, including imaginative experience. Keats wrote: 'I have never yet been able to perceive how any thing can be known for truth by consequitive reasoning – and yet it must be. Can it be that the greatest Philosopher ever arrived at his goal without putting aside numerous objections. However it may be, O for a Life of Sensations rather than of Thoughts!'[36] D. H. Lawrence (who, like Keats, loves to shock the virtuous philosopher) similarly values 'sensations' over intellectual ideas, and often cajoles or laughs his readers into valuing other modes of understanding besides 'consequitive reasoning', 'Thoughts'. In

---

[36] Letter of 22 November 1817, *Letters of John Keats*, p. 67.

'Why the Novel Matters', he genially canvasses many points in common with and at odds with Cora Diamond's argument about 'the need for novels'.[37]

Lawrence's sense of literature's power to engage 'the whole man alive' and his stress on vibrant living as distinct from theorising about Life chime with Keats's conviction that reading involves imaginatively *feeling things 'to the full'*: 'we find what [Wordsworth] says true as far as we have experienced and we can judge no further but by larger experience – for axioms in philosophy are not axioms until they are proved upon our pulses: We read fine things but never feel them to the full until we have gone the same steps as the Author.'[38] This is how literature engages us in moral thinking, and how it 'can inform and lead into new places the flow of our sympathetic consciousness'.[39] And as T. S. Eliot remarks, 'A thought to Donne was an experience. It modified his sensibility.' 'Thoughts' which have such vivid immediacy as the odour of a rose impact upon and subtly *change the self who thinks them.*[40]

V Impersonal investigation vs. imaginative inquiry

To think of the business of reading in these terms helps to bring out the significance of Cora Diamond's argument where she elucidates the 'revolutionary' nature of philosophy's turn to literature. Observing that 'philosophy needs to consider oppositions of thought, including oppositions to its own thought', she defines this opposition in terms of how, in each case, the 'implied author' relates to and constructs the subject of moral inquiry. In contrast with 'the implied author' of '"artist" texts' such as *The Prelude* or *David Copperfield*, 'the implied author of a philosophical text … does not speak … as someone who must respond with creative imagination and fullness of feeling. He is one or other kind of

---

[37] D. H. Lawrence, 'Why the Novel Matters', reprinted in *D. H. Lawrence: A Selection from Phoenix*, ed. A. A. M. Inglis (Harmondsworth, 1971), pp. 182–8; see also, for example, 'Morality and the Novel' (1925), ibid., pp. 175–81, and 'Surgery for the Novel – or a Bomb' (1923), ibid., pp. 189–93.

[38] Letter of 3 May 1818, *Letters of John Keats.*, p. 141. Nussbaum endorses this strongly.

[39] D. H. Lawrence, *Lady Chatterley's Lover* (Harmondsworth, 1961), ch. 9, p. 104.

[40] T. S. Eliot, 'The Metaphysical Poets' (1921), in *Selected Essays*, 3rd enlarged edition (London, 1951, 1980), p. 287.

detached investigator, and is often modelled more or less on the scientist'. Detached investigator texts 'impy a subject that will lie still to be investigated', whereas 'artist' texts imply a contrary 'view of the very subject *moral thinking*, namely, that it will not lie still to be investigated, but is made anew, and shaped in new ways, in our imaginative responses to life'. In these respects, Diamond suggests, the two modes are indeed so contrary that a radical change is needed when philosophy turns to literature – a change so basic that it may be impossible: '[F]or philosophy to explore "artist" texts seriously is to give up as its only central figure the impersonal investigator of a lying-still subject, and take on as a new central figure the imaginative reader of texts. This, in a sense, it cannot do, so far as its conception of itself is tied to that of the figure of the "detached investigator".'

The literary conceptions of literature and reading that I have been considering imply that a change from an impersonal inquiry to one involving creative imagination is much more than a change from one 'central figure' to another, and much more than the adoption of a different investigative paradigm. Such a change is not a simple matter of 'giving up' one 'figure' and 'taking on' another. The idea of 'taking on' presupposes an autonomous agent in full control of the terms and parameters of the inquiry. But the change in question is not just a change of seeing: it is a change of being in relation to what one is 'in face of'. It is a change from a mode of analytic deliberation to a mode of proving things on our pulses, budding patiently, experiencing one's thoughts as sensations, in ways that modify one's sensibility.

Whereas the impersonal investigator stands apart and in command, analysing an object, the inquirer who responds with creative imagination is thus not wholly separate, aloof and in full control, but mixed up in the subject of inquiry, immersed, implicated, participating in it and imaginatively becoming one with it. This is how, as Coleridge says, Shakespeare *'darts himself forth, and passes into all the forms of human character and passion, the one Proteus of the fire and the flood'*, moved by 'that sublime faculty, by which a great mind becomes that which it meditates on'.[41] And this is how, as Keats says, the 'chameleon poet' merges with what is being contemplated, losing a separated ego-bounded

---

[41] Coleridge, *Biographia Literaria*, ch. 15, p. 80; and *Samuel Taylor Coleridge: Shakespeare Criticism*, ed. Thomas Middleton Raysor (London, 1967), vol. 1, p. 188.

identity. To an impersonal investigator's eye, a sparrow is a member of a certain class of creatures with itemisable specifications and behaviours; in the 'darting-forth' perception of Keats, its reality affects his own: 'if a Sparrow come before my Window I take part in its existince and pick about the Gravel'.[42]

This kind of non-detached, responsive way of being-in-relation entails the surrender of intellectual dominance and cognitive security. It entails risk-taking, and a capability to be in mystery, without defensively reconstructing the world to fit one's desired shape and pattern. It involves imaginative excursiveness, a going-out of oneself, and also a letting-into oneself of things that may delight, surprise, shock, challenge, intensely disturb. Thus, in the face of *King Lear*, Dr Johnson's capability for feeling things to the full makes him 'so shocked by Cordelia's death' that for many years he could not endure to read the play again.[43] In his sense of it, *King Lear* is anything but a 'lying-still subject' for impersonal inspection (like a patient etherised upon a table?): it 'agitates our passions', and 'fills the mind with a perpetual tumult of indignation, pity and hope. So powerful is the current of the poet's imagination, that the mind, which once ventures within it, is hurried irresistibly along.'

Johnson's inextricable mix of passive and active images of the mind – 'it fills the mind' ... 'the mind that ventures ... is hurried irresistibly' – acknowledges that the reader who 'ventures' is exposed to peril: of being swept out of oneself, thrown into a tumult, lost in darkness, spontaneously moved to peck the gravel, or bite the dust, of being 'carried forward' into unmapped country, hurried into *terra incognita*. He writes rather as if *King Lear* has this overwhelming effect on every mind. But of course many minds do not 'venture'; they remain unable or unwilling to be moved, agitated, swept along. Instead, the investigator's mind stays aloof, in charge, at a safe remove, assured of certain certainties. As Susan Sontag noticed, interpreters often stay free of tumult by pre-emptively defending themselves against what she calls real art's capacity to make us 'nervous'. By reducing the art to

---

[42] Letter of 27 October 1817, *Letters of John Keats*. pp. 226–7; letter of 22 November, 1817, *Letters of John Keats*, p. 68 (Keats's spelling).
[43] *Selections from Johnson on Shakespeare*, ed. Bernard H. Bronson and Jean M. O'Meara (New Haven and London, 1986), p. 240; the following quotation is from p. 238.

its content, for instance, and interpreting *that*, 'one tames the work of art'.⁴⁴ Many interpretative strategies serve as protective buffers, guarding the interpreter from the risk of being interpreted by the text. Comparable kinds of intellectualising have similarly defensive effects in philosophy (and science), as Cora Diamond observes: 'the presence in (much) philosophy of that figure of the detached investigator works as a way to insulate philosophical thought from contact with what might challenge it most directly'.⁴⁵ Similarly, in Iris Murdoch's view, 'the insistence that morality is essentially rules may be seen as *an attempt to secure us against the ambiguity of the world'*.⁴⁶ Whatever one's field (medical or social science, politics, humanities), a standard insurance policy against being overpowered by one's subject is to stipulate in advance of an inquiry what is 'strictly relevant' to it, and to exclude anomalies, inconsistencies, imponderables, and whatever else would complicate it, as irrelevant 'noise'. But – as all these writers make clear – to insulate and secure oneself against ambiguity is to shut out that very 'sense of the density of our lives' which literature abounds in, and which philosophy seeks to recapture in turning to literary texts.

Cora Diamond's conclusion would seem to be right, that so far as philosophy's conception of itself is 'tied to the figure of the detached investigator' it cannot incorporate imagination into itself. Nor can it more casually adopt or 'take on' imagination as an add-on, an extra string to its bow. It would seem that the two modes of inquiry, literature's and philosophy's, are not just inimical but mutually averse, even adverse – that each calls into question, subverts, and threatens to disrupt or oust the other. Philosophy would seem to be faced with a choice of incommensurable goods. To admit imagination into its way of thinking is to lose the intellectual contol and tidiness to which it has devoted itself. The conclusion may seem unavoidable that its analytic requirements and practices cannot co-exist in any very fruitful relation with those of literature.

Yet what if, in face of literature, philosophy takes the risk of loosening its grip on the impersonal, imperturbable 'pitchfork'

⁴⁴ Susan Sontag, 'Against Interpretation', in *Against Interpretation and Other Essays* (New York, 1961, 1966), p. 8.
⁴⁵ Diamond, 'Martha Nussbaum and the need for novels', above, p. 56.
⁴⁶ Murdoch, 'Vision and Choice in Morality', p. 50; my emphasis.

ideal, and the will to control which its 'aim' implies? What if a loss of super-tidiness is accepted as a necessary condition of a desirable gain in depth of moral understanding? The opposition between detached analytis and imaginative engagement can then start to become productive, a real tension in which the former is not presumed to be of paramount value, and is not presumed to function best in segregation from the latter. Chaucer's idea, and Blake's, are both to the point: 'By [its] contrarie is every thing declared'; and 'Without contraries, is no progression'.[47]

To examine properly the issues here would require detailed demonstrations of critical reading of literature as both an imaginative and philosophical activity. It would further require such reading to bring home how Chaucer's art, or Blake's – or that of Shakespeare, Keats, Pope, for instance – is itself exemplary in just this way, in coupling great imaginative abilities with great reflective and analytical abilities: much of their creative power is generated in the (sometimes tumultuous) strife and churning and give and take between these contrary sides of the writer's mind. And it would discover how a similarly creative oscillation or tug-of-war can occur in the reader who ventures it, between the imaginative-responsive side of the mind that darts forth into the messy experience of the drama, and the interpretative, pattern-making side of the mind in seeking to assess and make some rational sense of it all. As in ordinary attempts at self-understanding, where one's 'effort really to see' is made in face of all that makes for muddlement, and where 'seeing' thus requires the ability to step back and scrutinise and analyse and seek a shape and pattern in one's experience, as well as ability to be engrossed and to prove things on one's pulses, so does literary reading involve these same abilities, each pulling and pushing and sometimes grating against the other.

This productive resistance provides a working model of how philosophy and literature may similarly draw energy from their 'againstness', but a key point to notice is that this is not fixable in a formula, a theory, or a set of rules. It only emerges in practice, in the more or less untidy and surprising business of writing or

---

[47] Geoffrey Chaucer, *Troilus and Criseyde*, in *The Works of Geoffrey Chaucer*, ed. F. N. Robinson, 2nd edition (Oxford and London, 1957), p. 389; William Blake, *The Marriage of Heaven and Hell*, plate 3, *The Complete Poems*, ed. Alicia Ostriker (Harmondsworth, 1977), p. 181.

reading individual texts. It is necessarily fluid, provisional and ever-liable to change, being at times harmonious, at times discordant or embattled. One way to envisage the diverse possibilities of their liaison is to recall Coleridge's series of graphic metaphors in describing internal conflicts in *Venus and Adonis* and *The Rape of Lucrece*:

In Shakespeare's poems the creative power and the intellectual energy wrestle as in a war embrace. Each in its excess of strength seems to threaten the extinction of the other. At length in the drama they were reconciled, and fought each with its shield before the breast of the other. Or like two rapid streams that at their first meeting within narrow and rocky banks mutually strive to repel each other, and intermix reluctantly and in tumult, but soon finding a wider channel and more yielding shores, blend and dilate, and flow on in one current and with one voice. [48]

Even if one shares Coleridge's yen for reconciliation, it nonetheless makes sense to question whether the harmony achieved by such a quarrelsome couple can be more than provisional, and whether this does not paradoxically enhance its value.

[48] Coleridge, *Biographia Literaria*, ch. 15, p. 180.

PART II

Ethics and agency

❖❖❖❖❖❖❖❖❖❖❖❖❖❖❖❖❖❖❖❖❖❖❖❖❖❖❖❖❖❖❖❖❖❖❖❖❖❖❖

5

What differences can contemporary poetry make in our moral thinking?

❖❖❖❖❖❖❖❖❖❖❖❖❖❖❖❖❖❖❖❖❖❖❖❖❖❖❖❖❖❖❖❖❖❖❖❖❖❖❖

CHARLES ALTIERI

The invitation to write this chapter arrived at a most opportune time. I have been trying to think through a book that sets the contemporary against the postmodern by arguing that there are several features of contemporary literature and visual art, even work promoting itself as postmodern, that have strong claims upon us. But these claims have been blunted by the ambitious, overgeneralised abstractions dominating our rhetorics about the postmodern. Crude theory in effect colonises the art and limits its capacity to serve as 'equipment for living' as we enter the twenty-first century. Now I have the opportunity to work on one of the most important of these features – the possible ways in which these contemporary experiments have the power to modify our approaches to moral thinking.[1]

These modifications will not stem from direct ethical arguments; nor will they depend on the dramatic engagements with exemplary dilemmas that occupy most philosophers seeking to bring literary works into moral theory. Most contemporary art and literature with even the slightest experimental ambitions tend to be extremely wary of making any ethical claims for themselves.

---

[1] I accept Martha Nussbaum's distinction in *Love's Knowledge: Essays on Philosophy and Literature* (Oxford and New York, 1990), p. 169, between ethical theory, which investigates substantive moral positions, and a broader moral philosophy. For her this broader moral philosophy is 'a general and inclusive rubric covering many different types of ethical investigation'. Subsequently, page references appear in the main text.

I can partially finesse this problem by relying here on contemporary poetry, which is considerably less cynical and/or less insistent on transforming the moral into the political than is the visual art most celebrated by postmodern theorists. But even then we cannot avoid that wariness but instead treat it seriously as carrying a possible moral weight, or at least as asking us to qualify what we do in the name of the moral weight.

Rather than seeking idealised moral experience from these poems, I will concentrate on two features of what we might call contexts for representing moral agency: how the poets come to grips with those aspects of contingency that make universal prescriptions impossible, moral realism insensitive, and judgment problematic; and how they compensate for their suspicion about universals by developing what I will call a grammatical vision of social interdependency. These poets will not substantially change the anti-foundational, anti-Kantian approaches popularised by Richard Rorty and Bernard Williams. But they do put pressure on the specific ways we understand the concrete implications of these positions. Almost all Anglo-American philosophers assume that these contingent agents are still governed by a latent and workable reasonableness, without really exploring the internal pressures that might limit or even misdirect such reasonableness. And, more important, these philosophers assume an interest in social welfare and a concern for others that they do not scrutinise very carefully, largely because all the alternatives seem incompatible with ethical theory. Williams for example is content to base the social aspect of moral care on a basic common sense, and Rorty goes so far as to ground the social dimension of ethics in a version of direct sympathetic sensibility adapted from eighteenth-century philosophy. The poets we will attend to, on the other hand, experiment with aspects of agency very difficult to reconcile with reason, and consequently they have to explore alternative ways of imagining the social bonds fundamental to moral consciousness.[2]

[2] I hope I have said enough to indicate that I also hope to separate what we find in these poems from standard postmodernist slogans content with claims that the subject is irreducibly decentred, and hence bound to oscillate between anxious instability and provisional ingenuity. In a longer version of this chapter I argue that close attention to the arts is necessary to resist the tendency to sloganising inseparable from theory's appropriation of the sensibility the arts had first articulated. In particular I emphasise that the arts elaborated what began as simply a thematics of irreducible fictionality until those themes became relevant for our general claims about self-knowledge, judgment, and intersubjective bonds.

Taking up these two features also requires working through a related issue disciplinarily closer to literary criticism. For even if one cannot directly ground moral thinking on the work of these poets, the effort to discover how they address such concerns at all should make a difference in the ways we envision philosophers linking moral philosophy to literary texts. It is striking, or ought to be striking, that all the influential work in this vein is done on novels and plays, none more recent than Proust's writings. To most philosophers, and most literary critics interested in moral discourse, confining oneself to such work seems unproblematic: contemporary literature is uneasy with moral concerns, and the lyric as a mode lacks sufficient dramatic context for works to serve as rich concrete embodiments of moral sensibility or interpretations of moral judgment. But perhaps we pay a substantial price for such exclusions. Relying on traditional works of art also seems to entail using literature for nothing more than supplementing traditional moral vocabularies or shoring up contemporary therapeutic recastings of traditional wisdom. Contemporary writing might prove somewhat more challenging to our assumptions about the powers of moral judgment and the social interests we attribute to moral sensibility. And attending to lyrics intensifies the demand to focus on the elemental habits and orientations that shape agents, rather than on the working out of specific moral judgments. Lyrics usually do not provide much contextual framework, and hence do not emphasise measuring the adequacy of actions to situations. Rather they concentrate on the ways specific qualities of attention, patterns of self-projection, and direct concerns for an audience shape our interests in being certain kinds of persons. With lyrics the test of imaginative power is far more immediate than those elicited by the action in representational novels and plays. Lyrics invite such close attention to elemental relations among their parts that ways of speaking seem inseparable from the most intimate dispositions of the psyche, while formal intensity becomes a test of just how richly the attitudes projected open into satisfying existential states.

These are not merely theoretical issues. Challenges from contemporary thinking and, less directly, from the projective powers called up by the lyric, prove especially telling when we look concretely at the most influential recent philosophical treatments of literary materials, those of Stanley Cavell and Martha Nussbaum.[3]

Nussbaum's *Love's Knowledge* is the more telling for my project. The basic questions she poses to literature – 'How should a human being live?' (p. 15), or 'What is it for a human being to live well?' – lead us deeply into the ways classical texts engage the world. But to sensibilities shaped by contemporary art and critical discourse, such formulations carry dangerous presuppositions. For them it is by no means obvious that even her heroes Henry James and Marcel Proust thought in such terms. Neither writer seems very comfortable speaking about 'human being' or about 'our lives', as if there were only one window in the house of fiction. And the concept of 'should' seems an odd one for writers so attentive to the idiosyncratic aspects of lives or to the fantasy structures that seem to underly all public pronouncements. Clearly Proust's mother is not our mother; nor are his loves necessarily exemplary for us, although he clearly hopes that how we engage with the specificity he presents will affect our capacities for sympathy and even for indirect self-knowledge.

This is not to deny that we are implicated in Proust's relation to his mother and to his lovers. The basic issue for contemporaries is how to frame that sense of implication without either losing its fantasy dimensions to a language of rational judgment (instrumental or perfectionist) or forcing it into the status of heroic act and universal exemplar. But sensitive as Nussbaum is to nuance, to the limits of opera-driven heroic dreams, and, increasingly, to the ways that novels also resist confinement to moral languages, she still takes literary projections as having the generality of philosophical argument, even if they renounce abstract means to secure this sense of good for 'human beings'. And she assumes that there is no violence done to texts if one takes them as responding thematically to philosophical questions, even when the texts may have quite different concerns for a

---

[3] My most sustained criticism is in *Subjective Agency* (Oxford, 1994), but that case depends in part on my treatment of modernist values in *Painterly Abstraction in Modernist American Poetry* (New York and Cambridge, 1989). Let me also acknowledge three exceptions to my charges – Richard Eldridge's recent work on contingency (although based on Wordsworth), Bernard Williams's *Shame and Necessity* (which goes so far back for its examples that it directly addresses contemporaneity), and Richard Wollheim's writings on art (which are smart enough never to talk about morality).

moral dimension to experience. Thus we find Nussbaum asserting 'And so our interest in literature becomes (like Strether's in
Chad) cognitive' (p. 171). But 'cognitive' is an inordinately abstract and impersonal way of casting the network of desires,
fears, and partial identifications that bind Strether to Chad. It
imposes a mode of thinking that requires insisting on novelists as
sharing the form, if not the method, shaping philosophers' moral
concerns. Then the novelist's characters must be seen as motivated by the kind of cares that require justification in philosophical terms; authors must subsume individual fears and emotions
to some generalising judgment; and readers must be staged so
that their primary interest is in being edified by philosophical
wisdom, rather than, say, in simply coming alive by participating
in the mix of passions and projections that powerful imaginative
writing elicits.

Let me conclude my argument by citing one test case illustra-
ting the gulf between Nussbaum's approach and what contemporary writing asks of its audiences. Nussbaum takes James as a
great philosopher about love (which, on at least one occasion, p.
360, she makes sound like only morality on a higher plane). She
cannot even entertain the possibility that James's fiction is so acute
on that topic because he is continually trying to understand or
justify his own fear of the sacrifices love exacts and the muddy
binds it imposes on consciousness. James does not rely on a
simple binary between a cold formalist aesthetic and one open to
love (as p. 146 argues). Rather his later texts put in action a
complex set of tensions simultaneously binding his imagination
to particular sensibilities and seeking the distance art gives as his
way of winning a necessary distance from the price exacted by
specific commitments. James the writer manifests a presence severely complicating what one might want to claim as the moral
force of the actions performed by his characters, so we must
suspect that even writerly sympathy (as well as moral idealising)
can serve primarily to gain freedom from what others might
demand of us in the flesh.[4]

---

[4] Compare to Nussbaum the following general description of James's writing in
David Minter, *A Cultural History of the American Novel* (New York and Cambridge, 1994), p. 5: 'The discourse of imaginative contemplation, the discourse of
profit and loss, and the discourse of sexual conquest merge in James's work, each
converted, as it were, into the currency of the other.'

Charles Altieri

I

I am not claiming that the question of living well proves irrelevant for contemporary writers' attitudes towards literary experience. I argue only that we need more indirect and intricate ways first of understanding how idiosyncratic, and often unheroic, living well can be, then of seeing how the contingent projections of literary texts may still sustain generalised reflections that lead to possible communities, if not to perspicuous predicates about human being. There may be a satisfying way to talk about 'our lives' and even to develop some version of normative force, so long as we locate most of that force in the specific workings of the texts as they use their formal resources to give resonance to their own senses of contingency. Then we will find ourselves having to develop moral vocabularies that pay much greater attention than is now the norm to the complexity, self-division, and emergent or event-based aspects of moral life.

For example, if we can get clear about how thick, opaque, unstable, and mobile this contingency is, we may emerge with a different attitude towards Bernard Williams's belief 'in truth, in truthfulness, and in the meaning of an individual life'.[5] For it becomes harder to accept the British tradition's faith that we need not worry much about agency, since for them if we can get the principles clear, people's good sense and basic good interests will take care of the rest. Similarly we will find versions of individual agency that cannot be 'owned', in Stanley Cavell's sense, because there is a constant interplay between the effort to perform or represent the self and the manifestation of the dependencies and slippages that make spacing an important figure for postmodern psychology. And finally, if we see how difficult it is to formulate social bonds that can fully acknowledge the differences that such contingency entails, yet still help define grounds for caring about those others, we may come to appreciate those experiments in contemporary poetry attempting to foster what I have called a grammatical sense of intersubjective interdependency.

Let us begin with a contemporary poet who on the surface has no affinities with postmodern experiment. Robert Hass's *Human Wishes* sets itself the task of understanding how it might be possible to develop for oneself an 'habitable Space, lived in beyond

[5] Bernard Williams, *Ethics and the Limits of Philosophy* (London, 1985), p. 198.

wishing'.[6] Wishing is the antagonist here because it reduces 'the interval created by if' to a mode of passive self-evasion. Wishing preserves compassion with 'the innocence of all the suffering on earth' (p. 13), but its loss of active direction traps the poet in the fear that he is inseparable from the figure of a gazelle whom three jackals are eating while he can do nothing but watch. That figure ends the first section of the volume, charging what follows with the task of reimagining the self's relation to collective suffering and the terms by which it can imagine itself actively aligned with its fate without yielding to the role of noble self-pity.

Hass tries to meet these demands by developing a voice that can be intimate without letting any single encompassing image of the self take control. Then the habitable becomes something not reducible to narcissistic mirroring structures, and will becomes something we discover in the specific attitudes the poetry explores rather than in any overt interpretation of what values those attitudes might instantiate. More overtly experimental writers would resist those mirroring structures by some version of writerly dispersal insisting on a moment by moment contingency that prevents the entire text from any overt coherent scenic structure. Think for example of how Lyn Hejinian's *My Life* handles autobiography. But Hass is perhaps subtler and more useful because he builds this dispersal into the very processes of constructing and negotiating a scene, so they can be directly adapted to typical existential scenarios. Take for example the opening of his 'Apple Trees at Olema':

> They are walking in the woods along the coast
> And in a greasy meadow, wasting, they come upon
> two old neglected apple trees . . .
> Trout lily, he said; she said, adder's tongue.
> She is shaken by the raw, white, backlit flaring
> of the apple blossoms. He is exultant,
> as if some thing he felt were verified,
> And looks to her to mirror his response.
> It is afternoon, a thin moon of my own dismay
> fades like a scar to the east of them.
> He could be knocking wildly at a closed door
> in a dream. She thinks, meanwhile, that moss
> resembles seaweed drying lightly on a dock.

[6] Robert Hass, *Human Wishes* (New York, 1989), p. 4. Subsequently, page references appear in the main text.

> Torn flesh, it was the repetitive torn flesh
> of appetite in the cold white blossoms
> that had startled her. Now they seem tender
> and where she was repelled she takes the measure
> of the trees and lets them in. But he no longer
> has the apple trees.

On the level of imaginary demand this poem represents the speaker's continuing need in the present, the place of 'my dismay', to be the kind of self that can get another to mirror his own response. But the poem also embodies a demand for and an example of another mode of consciousness that finds its identity in a constant, mobile interplay of differences. He tries Adamic naming; she counters. That countering introduces a second perspective permeating the scene with possible differences, and the wariness that fear of such differences breeds. On her own, she handles being shaken well enough to reach an equilibrium with the trees, but by then he has shifted his attention to other objects. These differences in spatial focus then prove intense enough to trigger a difference in time as the speaker shifts for a brief moment to his pain in the present, which we must also take as generating and framing the entire remembered scene (much as the fading moon remains a scar).

But that shift to the present also has positive affects. By refusing self-pity, by forcing the self to maintain flexibility as observer of both agents, the poem comes to a version of what makes habitable space:

> The light catching in the spray that spumes up
> on the reef is the color of the lesser finch
> they notice now flashing dull gold in the light
> above the field. They admire the bird together,
> it draws them closer, and they start to walk again.
> A small boy wanders corridors of a hotel that way.
> Behind one door, a maid. Behind another one, a man
> in striped pajamas shaving. He holds the number
> of his room close to the center of his mind
> gravely sad and delicate, as if it were the key,
> and then he wanders among strangers all he wants.

Because the mind remains open, treating 'he' with the same distance it does 'she', there remains a possibility that in the present it can also remember how they could make adjustments building to a shareable sense of wonder. At first that sense is entirely particular, then it modulates into the elaborate concluding conceit defining the sense of empowerment available to both persons as they reflect on what they have discovered. Yet it remains crucial that even what they eventually share will not erase the boundaries separating them. Each will have the confidence to walk among strangers, but that also means each will have to remain at least partially a stranger. However the poem also somewhat modifies what we can mean by 'stranger'. For once we break identity down into this capacity for infinite adjustments – to scenic features and to the metaphors that tell us who we are as we respond to those features – parts of our lives are always potentially overlapping others.

The rest of *Human Wishes* applies this sense of what we might call 'modular agency' to the painful process of working through a divorce and beginning a new life marked by all the senses of separateness that breaking up a family generates. That accounting is too complicated to be traced here. But I want to note three of its features that bear directly on the issue of how poetry might elaborate models of agency that can affect our moral philosophising. First, the distance and the mobility we see in 'Apple Trees at Olema' take the form of refusing ever to directly thematise the large thematised conflicts that lead to the divorce, since such abstract, highly overdetermined materials cannot but foster both endless self-justification and endless self-pity. Instead Hass concentrates on small moments where we see various shared pleasures and senses of connection haunted by increasingly unreconcilable differences in perspective. Eventually the tension proves so great that the speaker himself becomes too bitter and quietly self-ironic to make the adjustments that would be required to save family peace.

Second, it is important to note the foundation Hass develops for hoping that he can establish a less tormented relation with another lover. In class I call the key moment the dynamic of the 'purple underpants', because of the role they play in resolving the entire volume. 'Squaw Peak', the volume's concluding poem, prepares for this resolution by a beginning so tinged with sadness that the speaker says he cannot even know which sadness it was that came over him as he began walking in the mountains with the woman he addresses. Then after exploring possible causes of sadness and the necessary silences between them, they start rushing back to the cabin they are sharing with several others. She starts to run, and his attention is suddenly entirely occupied:

> and you ran like a gazelle,
> in purple underpants, royal purple,
> and I laughed out loud. It was the abundance
> the world gives...
> Things bloom up there. They are
> for their season alive in those bright vanishings
> of air we ran through.

My avant-garde students hate the purple underpants because they so preciously mark the moment of connection and so neatly transform the gazelle being eaten as she watches to the gazelle who opens life to new movement. But I try to convince them that all these traits elicit important aspects of understanding what is at stake for Hass's understanding of human contingency. He is willing to risk embarrassment here because he wants the sense of excess itself to dramatise what chance can provide. So long as we remain adaptable it may be just such excess, just such a flirtation with embarrassment, that provides an occasion for linking the intense demands of intimate needs to the purely surface materials the world offers. Even the most casual features can suffice to put different beings on the same path, so that it then becomes possible to run together through what is already in the process of vanishing.

This is not a sentimental way to register how little love can do and how much that matters. The poem might be sentimental if it were contained within the parameters of a dramatic lyric, with the poet somewhere outside manipulating events. But Hass's perspective is very different; indeed this perspective constitutes the third and perhaps most important feature of his engagement with the thematics of contingency. In Hass there is no irony, in fact no distance at all, separating the voice that speaks the poem from the poet. Instead Hass works very hard to prevent the poem from collapsing into the status of composed artefact. What matters is the composing – not as the creation of a work but as the effort to establish a speaking voice inseparable from the poem's own process of working through the adjustments it needs in order to be responsive to the opportunity to get beyond self-protective silence. Poetic voice here is not transformed by art; the personal voice becomes itself an artistic instrument rendering shifts in emotional tone and exploring possibilities for connecting to other persons. Poetry becomes simply intensified direct speech whose task is to make continuous adjustments both to what can be located within remembered events and what can engage an audience to provide the kind of pressure keeping the speaker himself open to self-qualification. For Hass this is a plausible version of truthfulness – an effort to achieve transparency by breaking images of the self down to elemental details from which we can maintain some ironic distance and a corresponding resistance to using gestures towards openness in order to seduce whomever it gets to listen.

II

For John Ashbery, Hass's way of embedding voice in the details of a life dooms it to constant efforts at seduction. Even metonymies for the self seek mirrors. To avoid that need, or at least to live self-reflexively with such temptations, Ashbery experiments with more radical modes of contingency, so that it becomes more difficult either to contain that voice within the narratives by which it claims responsibility or to make the self dependent on a projected audience whose approval it craves. Yet he is not content with self-protective irony. His most recent work uses such wariness to reconfigure our senses of subjective agency – with results that can seem quite flat until we grasp the stakes involved in his enterprise. Take for example the climactic anticlimax offered by the last sentence of his long quasi-autobiographical poem *Flow Chart*: 'It's open, the bridge, that way.'[7] The flatness of course is part of the point, part of the resistance to treating autobiography as dialectical discovery of deep patterns within one's psyche. The most Ashbery can offer is this totally secular, non-transcendental version of Rilke's 'open', achieved by developing the freedom to keep constructing bridges that allow one to engage fully in passing from one path to another without having to rely on any abstract principles of judgment. Where Rilke dreamed of breaking through convention to a sense of a pure open in which the spirit

---

[7] John Ashbery, *Flow Chart* (New York, 1991), p. 216.

breathes native air, Ashbery dreams of an openness that is purely horizontal – not a break through into some pure state but a mobility that keeps all states in an uneasy enough interchange that the contingent, marginalised subject becomes visible as the power invested in particular kinds and directions of linkage. And hence where Hass's voice served primarily as an instrument allowing him to develop the kinds of identification celebrated in the closing lines of 'Apple Trees at Olema', Ashbery's similar instrumental immediacy consists largely in weaving relations capable of resisting that very temptation.

We have to go back more than twenty years before *Flow Chart* to find the abstract generalisation most useful for placing this version of the open clearly within the concerns of traditional moral philosophy. Early in 'The System', the third of his *Three Poems*, Ashbery sets his own thinking in a complex relation to the efforts to break through to a sense of vital presence that then governed experimental poetics. For him such a raw commodity must be filtered through the distancing intimacies of an ironic urban sensibility musing on 'the magic present that drew everything – the old and the new – along in the net of its infectious charm'. Then one has an angle from which to risk philosophy:

Surely it would be possible to profit from the options of this cooperative new climate as though they were a charter instead of a vague sense of well-being, like a mild day in early spring, ready to be dashed to pieces by the first seasonable drop in temperature... What actually was wanted from this constructive feeling? A 'house by the side of the road' in which one could stay indefinitely, arranging new opportunities and fixing up old ones so that they mingled in a harmless mass that could be called living with a sense of purpose? No, what was wanted and was precisely lacking in this gay and salubrious desert was an end to the 'end' theory whereby each man was both an idol and the humblest of idolators, in other words the antipodes of his own universe, his own redemption or his own damnation, with the rest of the world as a painted backdrop to his own monodrama of becoming of which he was the lone impassioned spectator.[8]

Twenty years later this monodrama re-emerges as Ashbery prepares the conclusion to *Flow Chart*. As it is, everyone now finds himself inferior: repeat, everyone. There is unrest; the

---

[8] John Ashbery, *Selected Poems* (New York, 1985), p. 130. Subsequent page references appear in the main text.

shadow of the ball carries over. I am left to repeat standards that have no particular relevance for me. It seems as if one is doomed either to accepting this sense of inferiority or collapsing into some form of harmonious mass, drugged into ignoring both the tension of the new and the pathos of the lost? But suppose instead we tried to appreciate what this sense of an open way (rather than an 'open road') affords moral thinking. The end of 'end' theory requires the possibility of a constant beginning lightly enough held to allow a version of contingency not based on the substance afforded by a harmonious mass. And, as Richard Rorty put it, it requires a version of values that can be modified without invoking external criteria. How both possibilities can in fact be realised then becomes a matter of qualities that the poetry itself displays – not as art but as simply a way of thinking attentive to its own processes.[9]

There is for example in much of Ashbery an elaborate play on the possibility of discursive transparency that simultaneously pursues and qualifies (without quite parodying) the ideal of 'truthfulness' fundamental to Williams's commonsense individualist version of contingency. In Ashbery transparency remains an ideal, but its pursuit cannot be separated from reminders of the irreducible dimensions of fictionality underlying the idea of truth. Not only is truth itself a construct likely to blind us to what falls outside the categories it demands, but transparency also involves projections of self and of audience that become problematic when we look at what goes into producing such phenomena. So the resistance to pure transparency that we find in Ashbery's flattened but not erased metaphors makes assertion inseparable from uneasy questioning. What determines how we decide on parameters for what is and is not a representation of 'self', and how do we avoid partially composing as audience a community preselected to secure a given version of transparency, which then

---

[9] Comparison with Wallace Stevens may help clarify what this Ashberyan 'open' involves. Stevens too rejects a poetry based on received ideals and transcendental ambitions, and he imagines poetry communicating not by statement but by implicating the lives of other people in its movements. But for him there is still a shadowy drama of ends that leads him to speculate on heroes and first ideas, while for Ashbery all imaginative work is simply a process of working out places to stand as certain culturally and personally embedded fantasies unfold. Readers do not approach some common ideal that remains just out of reach; rather they find affective attachments in the very ways that our various projections carve up the emotions brought into play by our sentences.

entails obscuring other, less flattering possibilities? There are no positive answers to these questions. For the questions themselves assume we can stand outside such phenomena sufficiently to make fixed cogent decisions. For Ashbery, rather than seeking answers we do better to pursue different ways of listening and questioning that are content to move around within the openness we win by our refusals. Understanding can be nothing more than a matter of surfaces that manage to touch or share for a moment a sense of common direction, always mediated through the irreducible residues of subjective fantasy and remembered social scenarios:

> Night after night this message returns, repeated
> In the flickering bulbs of the sky, raised past us,
> taken away from us,
> Yet ours over and over until the end that is past truth,
> The being of our sentences, in the climate that fostered them,
> Not ours to own, like a book, but to be with, and sometimes
> To be without, alone and desperate.
> But the fantasy makes it ours, a kind of fence-sitting
> Raised to the level of an aesthetic ideal.   (*SP*, p. 88)

Contingency then is less a matter of circumstance *per se* than of how one can possess specific sentences by investing in what they bind us to. So lyric itself comes very close to serving as our finest philosophical instrument for dealing with agency because its abiding question is what is involved in making those investments. Happiness may consist simply in feeling one's sentences eventuate from oneself, rather than from elsewhere; and love in feeling that the sentences have their ultimate source in the direction of address calling them forth. But there are also darker, more complex movements among sentences that define the limits of our social relations, as I think is the case in the intricate thinking that constitutes 'Cups With Broken Handles':

> So much variation
> In what is basically a one-horse town:
> Part of me frivolous, part intentionally crude,
> And part unintentionally thoughtless.
> Modesty and false modesty stroll hand in hand
> Like twin girls. But there are more abstract things too
> That play a larger role. The intense staccato repetitions
> Of whatever. You don't know and we don't know either.

From there it's a big, though necessary, leap to
The more subtly conceptual conditionings: your opinion
Of you shaped in the vacuum-form of suppositions,
Correct or false, of others, and how we can never be ourselves
While so much of us is going on in the minds of other people,
People you meet on the street who greet you strangely
As though remembering a recent trip to the Bahamas
And say things like: It is broken. But we'd heard
You heard too. Isn't it too bad about old things, old schools,
Old dishes, with nothing to do but sit and wait
Their turn. Meanwhile you're
Looking stretched again, concentrated, as you do not pass
From point A to point B but merely speculate
On how it would be, and in that instant
Do appear to be travelling, though we all
Stay home, don't we. Our strength lies
In the potential for motion, not in accomplishments, and it gets
Used up too, which is in a way more effective.[10]

This poem begins as if it were a chastened, interiorised Whitman catalogue defining the various aspects of the ego that provide variation within its fundamentally one-horse town. Then the very process of taking inventory forces the speaking voice out to the increasingly complex dependencies that it realises make possible its sense of effective agency. As Lyn Hejinian puts it, 'My portrait is a bowl and I tap it with a spoon.'[11] First there is a simple amusement at the co-presence of the various, somewhat contradictory orientations shaping his actions. But pure self-consciousness soon generates a less controllable sociality because each of these various selves can be addressed, and hence can position the speaker in the roles afforded by various personal pronoun positions. And then all boundaries between self and other begin to weaken, since the 'you' and the 'we' apply both to the individual agent and to the poem's developing anxieties about its readers, and hence its, and its speaker's legibility.

By the second stanza the 'you' takes on increasing distance, as if the effort at self-inventory only demonstrated that self-representation is impossible: our images for ourselves are the vacuum-form of suppositions demonstrating how much of ourselves is going on in the minds of other people – both literally in terms of

[10] Ashbery, *A Wave* (New York, 1984), p. 51.
[11] Lyn Hejinian, *The Cold of Poetry* (Los Angeles, 1994), p. 113.

what we take from those others and figuratively in terms of the conceptual conditionings we share. And the subject whom we seek through those images now becomes so abstract and so defined as object of a quest that it no longer quite correlates with the speaking voice. That is why the speaker is so easily displaced by the other voices of people met in the street.

And yet being reduced to the margins is not necessarily being silenced. This second stanza grows vague and difficult because it must do very complicated work in handling the possible presence of what is absent on the surface (or, at least, it takes a hypothesis about that supressed subject to make sense of the stanza's vagueness). Initially the speaker remains present simply by the strange precision that he gives to his rendering of the pressure from the minds of other people. Then, perhaps because the 'people''s speech is so utterly banal, it also proves lusciously duplicitous, with its range of personal pronouns open to the possibility of another reading that is made possible by our sense of how the initial speaker must be hearing it. The voice of the other ultimately offers a surprising theatre in which to appreciate how the displaced person might also possess these sentences.

At first the people are content with conservative clichés. But their hostility soon emerges in their twitting their interlocutor by mixing concern for his welfare with digs about his merely speculative poet's existence. Having projected a fantasy of power, this voice finds itself capable of wielding a pompous and imperious 'we'. But that very process is at once so general and so vague that the original speaker's possible reading of their language also becomes part of the poem. This double reading is most evident when the people begin to assert an imperious 'we all stay home', just when the original speaker must be dying for some kind of travel, some escape. Yet actually staying at home would be the best way of staying away from them. So it seems plausible to imagine his agreeing with the form of the sentences while giving them a very different import. And once this possibility appears, it seems clear that his version of 'our strength' lying in a 'potential for motion' promises a possible flight from the territory that the speaker's 'we' seems to control. In fact this promise that a strength that is used up may be more effective becomes for him a wish that the public voice may itself be used up, and there may emerge some other way of relating to other people not so limited by the broken handles everywhere evident here.

Underlying this slippage, and the resulting possibilities, is Ashbery's mining the marvellous duplicity of the 'we', a duplicity fundamental to ethical theory because of the dramas of inclusion, exclusion, and differentiation it allows (and conceals). Here as the 'we' is undermined it is also oddly reinforced, because its semantic range turns out to include with the proposed likeness a possibility for differences that frustrates the effort to form a community. In this case the people's version of musing ironically defines desires that give the original speaker a form for his own possible escape from that very naming. He cannot escape the 'we', but he can, perhaps must, resist its authority if he is to find any expressivity for his contingent being. That escape, moreover, is not a matter of locating some inner authenticity; it is simply enacting a capacity to tilt language so that his own relation to available sentences remains in the foreground.

III

It is now time to build on these poems in order to spell out three aspects of Ashbery's work that help redirect moral thinking away from 'end' theory and towards a full appreciation of how mobile, contingent agency both invokes and resists the 'we' fundamental to abstract ethical theory. First, we are confronted with how complex contingent subjective agency is.[12] On the simplest level we have to acknowledge how our senses of power and of obligation as subjects are inseparable from a constant dialogue among pronoun positions, which must be taken into account when we talk about judgment and responsibility and moral assessment. Moreover each of those morally loaded concepts brings with it its own fictive 'you's' and 'we's' that carry a range of fantasies. Responsibility is also performance for internalised others, and judgment is a stylised imitation of roles we identify with, without quite finding identity in. Even our most intimate feelings about ourselves stem in part from forces consciousness cannot control and are shaped by

---

[12] The best critical work on the basic affective qualities shaping this contingency is Herman Rapaport's essay on Ashbery in his *Between the Sign and the Gaze* (Ithaca, 1994). Rapaport's book offers a powerful development of one aspect of the postmodern heritage – which he calls 'extimacy' – to capture the various ways that the intimate and the external permeate one another.

how we envision others as models and respondents. Finally, even this talk of self and others must be severely qualified because 'so much of us is going on in the minds of other people'. On many occasions subjective agency can only be understood by treating self and other as irreducible dyads: judgment is determined by how agents embedded in interpersonal situations work through the intricate dependencies that give meanings to their actions. Consider how difficult it is to attribute responsibility to the ways married couples interact with each other or with their children.

The second theme leads us back to the ways we can positively characterise individual moral agency. For the very multiplicity of roles that we play and stances we take within the sentences we inherit allow considerable room for self-definition, if we know where to look. For Ashbery, we cannot find a locus for personal responsiveness and responsiblity either in concepts or in images. The person is not something we see or reason to but a mobile force we come to recognise by the patterns of adjustments we make to the sentences that someone speaks:

> underneath the talk lies
> The moving and not wanting to be moved, the loose
> Meaning, untidy and simple like a threshing floor.   (*SP*, p. 88)

So the person's talk must provide exemplary access to what lies beneath it, or perhaps alongside it, as post-structural theory prefers to say. That is why Ashbery plays transparency against enigma and self-definition against self-undoing. The language of his lyrics often seems painfully discursive in its efforts to be clear. Yet in order to provide a context or motive for that clarity, or to register the implications of the casual metaphors arising within the efforts at precision, the poems also generate internal slippages and strange juxtapositions reminding us of how little we understand, and how generous we have to be not to foreclose on what is there to be understood if we can find the best angle of address. Sentences can be descriptions or can be more complex speech acts, but what matters most is how their overt shape is an effect of something that cannot be stated but must be carried by the framing of the discourse. No 'end' theory is sufficiently subtle to address such framings. Rather we do much better to imagine ourselves and others always in the middle of processes that only partially reach the surface, or, perhaps better, that are so much of the surface and its folds that our ingrained assumptions about depth only allow us partial recognitions.[13]

Finally, it is crucial to realise how thoroughly Ashbery recognises the limits to any dialogical model that idealises the instability of subjects, is content with calls to let the other be, and assumes that emphasising the process aspects of desire deepens our capacity to form intersubjective bonds. As we see from a passage early in *Flow Chart*, the play of discursivity against self-conscious irony demonstrates just how provisional and frustrating the open must remain. Moral philosophy, or even moral adequacy, cannot be made the vehicle of deep self-satisfaction without putting at risk the very possibility that there may be a version of morality still capable of making feasible demands upon us:

> What we are to each other is both less urgent and more
>
> perturbing, having no discernible root, no raison d'être,
>   or else flowing
> backward into an origin like the primordial soup it is so easy
>   to pin
> anything on, like a carnation to one's lapel. So it seems we must
> stay in an uneasy relationship, not quite fitting
> together, not precisely friends or lovers though certainly not
>   enemies, if
> the buoyancy of the spongy terrain on which we exist is to be
>   experienced
> as an ichor, not a commentary on all that is missing from the
>   reflection
> in the mirror. Did I say that? Can this be me? Otherwise
>   the treaty will
> seem premature, the peace unearned, and one might as well
>   slink back
> into the solitude of the kennel, for the blunder to be read as
>   anything
> but willful, self-indulgent.   (*Flow Chart*, pp. 10–11)

[13] I think it is very important here, and in most discourse about the arts, to distinguish this sense of middles from celebrations of indeterminacy. Most of these celebrations fail to motivate the indeterminacy by attaching it to significant values. And even those that do provide motives ignore the fact that an emphasis on indeterminacy is still bound to models of discourse where determinacy is the ideal and indeterminacy its scandalous enemy twin. Ashbery's work seems to me to attempt working free of that entire binary pattern in order to emphasise the rewards of attempting to align ourselves to what circulates through sense. His is a radical version of Cavell's attunement, one willing to pay the price exacted by the music we actually make as we speak.

The uneasiness with its own quite precise generalisation is probably the most striking feature of this speaking voice. That uneasiness, Ashbery tries to explain, may be the only provisional guarantee we have that we are trying to respond to the relevant contingencies in the present without imposing on them an idealising commentary against which they will seem inadequate and the speaker bound to return to self-protective solitude. And yet the uneasiness entails difficult social relations. If understanding is undone even as it is taking form, then at best we have tangential relations with others as they enter and leave our spheres of influence or affect our enterings and leavings. And if understanding another person cannot be primarily a matter of concepts or even images, then the only stable relations we can have depend on our learning to participate in the play of pronoun positions and to hear that loose meaning underneath the talk.

Yet rather than apologise for such uneasy relationships, we may do better to accept the values they make possible. On the most general level, such acceptance entails our renouncing any hope in abstract universals or general consequentialist calculi as providing moral foundations. We can use such principles, but only on grounds provided by personal relations – for example if my desire for the respect of another or my care for preserving mutual trust leads me to act in accord with universals. So my commitments derive from specific ways of negotiating the ways in which we do not quite fit together, but need each other even more because of that very fact. We can still try to live in accord with the bonds that stem from our desire to possess the sentences we utter as investments in some ongoing social theatre. But that theatre will remain fractious, and there will be many persons and many kinds of suffering it excludes because they do not have the immediacy to compel us to engage in the difficulty of working through the particular differences or demands they involve.

This view need not be entirely bleak. It shares a good deal of Cavell's concern for attunement, thankfully without his Emersonian individualism or his optimistic sense of how far that attunement can extend. And it shares even more with Wittgenstein's resigned personalism: we can measure our personal relationships only by the qualities that develop from our ways of going on within them. Even what seems perverse or destructive from an objective point of view may establish significant bonds of care and commitment. The only measure of wellbeing we can develop will concern our capacity to balance the pain we are willing to suffer with the intensity and sense of harmony our actions manage to produce, so long as in the process we do not become unbearable to others, or to other aspects of ourselves. And even that sense of limits is constantly negotiable, depending on how much we care for those others and what ideas of ourselves we can live with. Ultimately our sense of ourselves and our relations to other people will vacillate between feelings that we slide along hard, opaque surfaces and the sense that for a moment we completely share investments in the specific sentences that certain actions and attitudes allow us speak: 'what is is what happens in the end / As though you cared' (*SP*, p. 226). Ashbery's lyrics, then, establish the complex powers and constraints by which we come to live within this 'as though', as though it had to suffice for all our talk about ends.

Such talking will not necessarily produce actions that we can agree are moral; nor will it provide stable public measures of morality. And it may even be the case that the more we become aware of what is involved in acknowledging the contingent aspects of morality the more we will be convinced we need to make the sacrifices necessary to restore impersonal universals. But we will only fully appreciate what these options involve, or how we might find alternatives to them, if we allow poetic experiments in agency like these to become basic features of the grammar within which we judge what moral judgment must entail.

6

Moral luck in Paris: *A Moveable Feast* and the ethics of autobiography

❖❖

RICHARD FREADMAN

Where there is most insight and reason, there is least luck; and where there is the most luck there is the least insight.

(Aristotle, the *Eudemian Ethics*)

Hemingway's autobiographical volume *A Moveable Feast* begins (after preliminary scene-setting) with an image of adulterous desire and draws to a close with a lament to his betrayed wife and son. The first description is of a young woman whom Hemingway sees in a café:

I've seen you, beauty, and you belong to me now, whoever you are waiting for and if I never see you again, I thought. You belong to me and all Paris belongs to me and I belong to this notebook and this pencil.

(p. 6)[1]

At the end Hemingway is temporarily reunited with wife and child in the mountains:

When I saw my wife again standing by the tracks as the train came in by the piled logs at the station, I wished I had died before I ever loved anyone but her. She was smiling, the sun on her lovely face tanned by the snow and sun, beautifully built, her hair redgold in the sun, grown out all winter awkwardly and beautifully, and Mr Bumby standing with her, blond and chunky and with winter cheeks looking like a good Vorarlberg boy.   (p. 210)

[1] Ernest Hemingway, *A Moveable Feast* (New York, 1964). Subsequent page references appear in the main text.

This chapter considers the ethical terms and implications of the narrative's passage from the inaugurating moment to its concluding statement of regret.

I Autobiography, ethics, and luck

In the introduction to his classic autobiography *World Within World*, Stephen Spender foreshadows discussion of 'certain moral problems'[2] and says that he has tried to 'write of experiences from which I feel I have learned how to live'.[3] However modest, the latter remark points to deep and perhaps inevitable links between autobiography and ethics, for most autobiographers are ethicists in the sense that they pose, however directly or indirectly, consciously or unintentionally, answers to the Aristotelian question, 'How ought a human life to be lived?' Answers, of course, vary enormously; but the autobiographer, at least in most strains of the Western tradition, can scarcely engage with the question without negotiating a set of familiar and interrelated ethical questions: 'To what extent is the subject of the narrative the product of circumstantial determination and/or self-scripting choice?' 'To what extent, and in what ways, are the subject's vision of life, and the life itself, susceptible of moral evaluation and justification?' 'What modes of interaction with other selves does the narrative evince and recommend?' And so on. Here, too, the narrativisation of such issues may be explicit or implicit, deliberate or inadvertent; and the same applies to the presence of another issue which is closely related to the ones I have just noted: the issue of luck.

For the autobiographer, as for anyone, luck is a strange and disturbing phenomenon. Because it confronts us with our vulnerability to the unpredictable and uncontrollable realm of the contingent, it can seem terrifying and inimical to the rational conduct of a life; yet, as Martha Nussbaum has noted in her superb study of luck and ethics in Greek tragedy and philosophy, *The Fragility of Goodness*,[4] its very connection with the world of chance, risk,

---

[2] Stephen Spender, *World Within World* (London, 1951), p. vii.
[3] Ibid., p. viii.
[4] Martha C. Nussbaum, *The Fragility of Goodness: Luck and Ethics in Greek Tragedy and Philosophy* (Cambridge, 1986).

and protean variability can render luck exhilarating and make it seem constitutive of any life we can imagine living or wishing to live. My interest here is not principally in luck as a general phenomenon, but in the particular conjuncture between luck and ethics about which Nussbaum, Bernard Williams, Thomas Nagel, and others have recently written: in what has been termed moral luck.[5]

The concept of moral luck is complex and much-debated, but in essence it contests the Kantian claim that dutiful rational moral agents and their intentions are not subject to the vicissitudes of external contingency, to luck. As Bernard Williams puts it, the Kantian position is that 'Both the disposition to correct moral judgment, and the objects of such judgment, are ... free from external contingency, for both are, in related ways, the product of the unconditioned will'.[6] Kant, we recall, writes that

Even if, by some special disfavour of destiny or by the niggardly endowment of stepmotherly nature, this [good] will is entirely lacking in power to carry out its intentions; if by its uttmost effort it still accomplishes nothing, and only good will is left (not, admittedly, as a mere wish, but as the straining of every means so far as they are in our control); even then it would still shine like a jewel for its own sake as something which has its full value in itself. Its usefulness or fruitlessness can neither add to, nor subtract from, this value.[7]

The contrasting position, which we might loosely designate as Aristotelian, holds that moral agents, intentions, and outcomes are to some degree subject to contingency, to luck, and that the Kantian image of moral self-sufficiency is untenable, both conceptually and with respect to practical moral conduct. In this chapter I want to consider a philosophically unself-conscious 'autobiographical' work which is marked by recurrent, indeed almost obsessive, references and appeals to the contingent in moral conduct, to what is in effect moral luck: Hemingway's *A Moveable Feast*. I do so on the assumption that extended narratives – novels,

[5] Bernard Williams, 'Moral Luck' in *Moral Luck: Philosophical Papers, 1973–1980* (Cambridge, 1981), pp. 20–39; Thomas Nagel, 'Moral Luck' in *Mortal Questions* (Cambridge, 1991), pp. 24–38. I would like to thank Dr Alex Segal for drawing my attention to some of the philosophical connections noted here and for his helpful early comments on some of the ideas I develop in this chapter.

[6] Williams, *Moral Luck*, p. 20.

[7] Immanuel Kant, *Groundwork of the Metaphysics of Morals*, trans. H. S. Paton (New York, 1964), p. 62.

plays, poems, autobiographies, memoirs and other forms – can offer context-rich and specific descriptions of ethical situations and concerns; descriptions which complement more specialised philosophical accounts, and which can provide kinds of detail and emotional involvement which are hard to attain in 'conventional' philosophical discourse. Such indeed is one of the contentions of the 'turn' to the ethical in literary studies and philosophy. Yet I believe that this 'turn' should not focus merely on the sort of exemplary narrative text which expertly complements and deepens philosophical understandings. The 'turn' should also retain something of the evaluative emphasis of earlier forms of ethical criticism; it must have something to say about texts which are not exemplary in the sense just described – about what their ethical (and related aesthetic) limitations are, and about what these limitations tell us about the structure of our ethical concepts and the narrative articulation of our ethical visions and commitments. In saying this I am not advocating a return to the sort of avenging critical judgmentalism that wants by attitudinal fiat to cast out all but the greatest texts, or to condemn a novel for its alleged failure to be appropriately condemnatory of, say, adultery or hypocrisy. I am arguing for an evaluative dimension which works through the importation into criticism of specific ethical concepts, and which takes evaluation down two axes: one which concerns the text and its status as an ethical–aesthetic document; the second which factors literary articulations of particular ethical concepts into øur more general assessments of those concepts. This chapter, then, offers an account of Hemingway's autobiographical rendering of the concept of moral luck together with some reflections on that concept. In the process it has something to say about the ethical milieu that has conferred upon Hemingway the status of a cultural legend.

In *The Old Man and the Sea* the old man muses, 'Luck is a thing that comes in many forms and who can recognise her?'[8] In order to help make sense of the various forms of luck that occur in *A Moveable Feast* it will useful to make some initial distinctions. For expository purposes I draw upon Thomas Nagel's influential article, 'Moral Luck'. Nagel identifies kinds as follows. First, there is constitutive luck: 'the kind of person you are, where this

---

[8] Ernest Hemingway, *The Old Man and the Sea* (1952; London, 1974), p. 117.

is not just a question of what you deliberately do, but of your inclinations, capacities and temperament'. Second, circumstantial luck: 'the kind of problems and situations one faces'. I propose to subdivide this kind into two subsidiary forms: metaphysical luck, by which I mean the underlying metaphysical condition which functions as a kind of background to all of one's experiences; and cultural luck, the kind of cultural environment in which one finds oneself. Third, 'luck in how one is determined by antecedent circumstances' (I shall term this agent-determinative luck). Fourth, 'luck in the way one's actions and projects turn out' (I shall call this outcome luck).[9] A further and important qualification is that the notion of luck used here does not carry any implication that the event or influence in question is uncaused. Luck refers merely to the impingement on his/her life of that which is outside of the agent's control.

II Luck in art, racing, and love

Initial impressions of *A Moveable Feast* tend to focus on its charm, its apparent slightness and the various cultural myths that converge between its covers: the artistic life in Paris in the thirties; the life of the Lost Generation; the complex fate of American expatriates in Europe; and of course the legend of Hemingway himself, as writer, *bon vivant*, and man of action. The mix is memorable, the writing is generally relaxed and light, as if to suggest that not too much is going on beyond the effort of memorialisation itself.

But closer inspection of the kind for which Hemingway had great disdain reveals deceptive complexity. One measure of this is the book's hybrid generic character. It is part memoir and part 'autobiography proper'; it veers between fictional invention and quasi-journalistic report; at some levels it is a sad twenties-style story of failed passion while at others it is a moral fable about the destruction of love from without. It is also an autobiographical Künstlerroman in which the artist as young man learns his craft in a complex cultural and social milieu.[10] Then there is a confessional element, complicated by the text's posthumous editorial and pub-

---

[9] Nagel's definitions are given in *Mortal Questions*, p. 28.
[10] Though strictly a term for the novel of the 'education' of the writer, Künstlerroman will suffice for a case like *A Moveable Feast*.

lication history,[11] that pertains to the older man looking back on the failings of his younger self – a dimension that might incline us to think of this as a work of quasi-confessional autobiography. And threading its way through much of the above there is an ethical strand: an exploration of modes and motivations of moral conduct.

The ethical strand yields a kind of code, many aspects of which are familiar in Hemingway's fiction. Despite the suggestion of plenitude in the book's title,[12] the code unfolds within the characteristic Hemingway metaphysic of scarcity, of a world which cannot, ultimately, meet the needs of ordinary human beings, let alone the needs and aspirations of extraordinary ones. The code comprises various values and virtues. I will consider the interrelation between some of these later; for the moment it will be sufficient to note them (in no particular order). First, there is a powerful emphasis upon fidelity, an emphasis which incorporates both truthfulness and sincerity in personal relationships and a fierce emphasis upon authenticity in art, 'the true sentence' (p. 12), the fidelity to fact, which is the building block of literary realism. Second, there is a strong emphasis upon friendship – here epitomised by Ezra Pound – and the related virtues of generosity, honour, loyalty (Pound's admiration of his friends' work is 'beautiful as loyalty', p. 107). Third, a receptiveness to other people, and to experience in general – qualities Hemingway finds in the regulars at one of his favourite cafés, the Closerie des Lilas, people who are 'all interested in each other and in their drinks or coffees, or infusions, and in the papers and periodicals which were fastened

---

[11] The text was edited by Mary Hemingway and Harry Brague. Scholarship on the various manuscript drafts seems conclusively to show that the published text departs significantly from the one intended in Hemingway's final drafts. In particular, the published version omits some formulations in which he sought to take more responsibility for the break-up of his marriage with Hadley, and includes a key passage, which he had apparently decided to excise, in which he blames the 'rich' for the advent of Pauline Pfeiffer in his life. I discuss these matters later (pp. 147–8). For scholarship on the manuscript and publishing history of *A Moveable Feast* see Gerry Brenner, 'Are We Going to Hemingway's Feast?', *American Literature*, 54.4 (December 1982), pp. 528–44; Ronald Weber, *Hemingway's Art of Non-Fiction* (London, 1990), ch. 6; and, by far the most detailed treatment, including tabulation of the various manuscript emendations and drafts, Jacqueline Tavernier-Courbin, *Ernest Hemingway's 'A Moveable Feast': The Making of a Myth* (Boston, 1991).

[12] The title was selected by Mary Hemingway and Harry Brague from a list that Hemingway had left. See Weber, *Hemingway's Art of Non-Fiction* , ch. 6.

to rods, and no one was on exhibition' (p. 82). Fourth, the absence of 'exhibition' is one of many values which are associated with restraint and discipline: stoicism in the face of the hard facts of existence (this and related virtues are shown to be comically lacking in the profligate and hypochondriacal Scott Fitzgerald), discipline, particularly in respect of art, thrift, durability, courage – especially physical courage – and, importantly, self-sufficiency. Fifth, and in a contrasting vein, there are values that pertain to fullness, satiation, even in some cases to excess: the exercise of one's capacities, immersion in the full, unmediated, sensuous experience of life; the emphasis on action as the mode in which capacities are exercised, in which courage is demonstrated and, crucially, in which inner conflicts are deferred or dissolved through commitment to particular choices and sensations. Here the emphasis is on risk, submission, daring, and the sating of appetites – what he calls 'the fiesta concept of life' (p. 209).

So stated the code is unremarkable, though it is potentially interesting for its apparent inconsistencies. What brings it to life, of course, is the strangely equivocal power of this book's version of the Hemingway persona: a version which offers the self as at once exemplary in its heroic quest for artistic perfection, and as destructively flawed, a fit subject for a kind of gruff and intermittent moral self-scrutiny. Part of the appeal of the legend is apparent in this typical description of Hemingway preparing to work, from the sardonic chapter, 'Birth of a New School':

The blue-backed notebooks, the two pencils and the pencil sharpener (a pocketknife was too wasteful), the marble-topped tables, the smell of early morning, sweeping out and mopping, and luck were all you needed. For luck you carried a horse chestnut and a rabbit's foot in your right pocket. The fur had been worn off the rabbit's foot long ago and the bones and the sinews were polished by wear. The claws scratched in the lining of your pocket and you knew your luck was still there.   (p. 91)

What is typical here is the image of Hemingway as the heroically self-sufficient man, the post-Romantic chronicler of the ordinary who needs little more than a café table, a pencil and paper, a coffee, and his own fierce discipline to capture the hard facts of a common condition. Self-sufficiency, of course, is appealing in part because it seems to promise immunity from the unnerving flux of contingency, and the appeal of the Hemingway persona, here, in his fiction and in modern culture generally, derives in large part from this image of a man who is at once sufficiently susceptible to the facts to memorialise them in art, and self-sufficient to a degree that insulates him from the uncontrollable forces that make the shared condition the unnerving thing it is. (It is a significant aspect of the Hemingway legend that he suicided, thereby to some extent dictating the terms of death's otherwise arbitrary impingement.) Yet the passage is not all about control; it is also about flirting and indeed *engaging* with risk, trying your luck, the thrill of pitting the modes of control against the contingent, the sport involved in narrowing the gap between chance and consummate artistry by the exercise of discipline and expertise. The rabbit's foot suggests a link here between Hemingway the writer and Hemingway the hunter: each magnetised by risks they feel compelled to master. As the chapter continues with a report of Hemingway's ferocity towards a pestering aspirant writer in the café we are reminded that in this case the hunter and the writer share another tendency: the propensity to destroy.

The tension between the ethos of discipline and control on the one hand, and of risk, submission, and contingency on the other, runs deep in the narrative. Indeed the contrastive pair contingency/control amounts to a kind of organising binary in the book which links what might (after Wittgenstein) be termed *families of activity*: activities which are disparate in some ways but which are conceptually and experientially similar in others. One such activity is art, a form *technē*, of skill which can restrain the powers of *tuchē*, of unordered contingency. Here Hemingway describes writing in a hotel room in Paris:

Up in that room I decided that I would write one story about each thing that I knew about. I was trying to do this all the time I was writing, and it was good and severe discipline.

It was in that room too that I learned not to think about anything that I was writing from the time I stopped writing until I started again the next day. That way my subconscious would be working on it and at the same time I would be listening to other people and noticing everything, I hoped; learning, I hoped; and I would read so that I would not think about my work and make myself impotent to do it. Going down the stairs when I had worked well, and that needed luck as well as discipline, was a wonderful feeling and I was free then to walk anywhere in Paris.

(pp. 12–13)

The passage combines several elements of the code: the emphasis upon truth-telling through writing about the familiar; the receptiveness to other people; the thrilling sensuous immediacy of Paris; but also the effort to negotiate the tension between control – or 'discipline' – and submission, in this case submission to the capricious riches of the 'subconscious' and its wellsprings of creative inspiration. The need for 'luck as well as discipline' encapsulates the tension to which I have referred: it is the play of contingency that renders the discipline of art necessary, just as the disciplines of art are required to organise and memorialise the contingent energies of life.

Another instance of this kind of activity to which the narrative often refers is betting on the races. Here is an example:

You had to watch a jumping race from the top of the stands at Auteuil and it was a fast climb up to see what each horse did and see the horse that might have won and did not, and see why or maybe how he did not do what he could have done. You watched the prices and all the shifts of odds each time a horse you were following would start, and you had to know how he was working and finally get to know when the stable would try with him. He always might be beaten when he tried; but you should know by then what his chances were. It was hard work but at Auteuil it was beautiful to watch each day they raced when you could be there and see the honest races with the great horses, and you got to know the course as well as any place you had ever known. You knew many people finally, jockeys and trainers and owners and too many horses and too many things. (p. 62)

Much of the deceptive charm and interest of *A Moveable Feast* is apparent here. The passage combines two characteristic movements of feeling: a capacity for apparently unreflective and unselfconscious sensuous experience, for submission to that which is 'beautiful' but also potentially risky and destructive – a kind of flirtation with a dangerous plenitude ('too many horses and too many things'); and in contrast, a reassuring sense of familiarity, a particular kind of 'work' that yields mastery, expertise, an inwardness about the activity that narrows the odds and reduces the risks.

Marital love is the third of a triad of related activities in the text. A passage from the chapter 'Shakespeare and Company' shows that for Hemingway luck is deeply implicated in love. Hadley says to Hemingway that '"we'll never love anyone else but each other"'. He replies, '"No. Never."' They then discuss which books they will borrow from Sylvia Beach's bookshop. Hadley says,

'And we're going to have all the books in the world to read and when we go on trips we can take them.'
'Would that be honest?'
'Sure.'
'Does she [Sylvia] have Henry James too?'
'Sure.'
'My,' she said. 'We're lucky that you found the place.'
'We're always lucky,' I said and like a fool I did not knock on wood. There was wood everywhere in that apartment to knock on too.   (p. 38)

The reference to James is significant not only because the couple's fate as innocents abroad in Paris echoes James's international theme, but also because James, who had a powerful influence on Hemingway in the twenties, was responsible for some of the most subtle and elaborate fictional treatments of intimate relationship that were known to him. Knocking on wood in the hope that your marriage holds up – this is the quintessential submission to circumstantial and outcome luck as the arbiter of marital fate. And the motif crops up again in the chapter which prefaces the one about the Fitzgeralds' destructive marriage, 'Scott Fitzgerald'. Hadley says,

'We're awfully lucky.'
'We'll have to be good and hold it.'
  We both touched wood on the café table and the waiter came to see what it was we wanted. But what we wanted neither he, nor anyone else, nor knocking on wood or on marble, as this café table-top was, could ever bring us. But we did not know it that night and we were very happy.
                                              (p. 176)

If the verb 'to hold' implies some sort of effort that might sustain a relationship the proposition here is actually quite the contrary: nothing, but nothing, can resist the contingencies that will destroy their love. One might refer to this kind of thing as the marble table-top view of human fate and agency. But consider now a more complex and powerful example from the fine chapter 'A False Spring'. Here again luck in love is associated, albeit ironically, with luck at the races. After success on the track he says:

'You said we were lucky today. Of course we were. But we had very good advice and information.'

She laughed.
'I didn't mean about the racing. You're such a literal boy. I meant lucky other ways.'
'I don't think Chink [the friend who had accompanied them] cares for racing,' I said, compounding my stupidity. (p. 57)

It is a nice irony that the 'stupidity' that in this instance and elsewhere marks the young Hemingway as a man oblivious to certain important truths about love here betrays him into misunderstanding Hadley's meaning and into a resultant defence of the kind of informed gambling that can to some extent counter the play of contingency. It is the hallmark of this 'stupidity' that he has no conception of what is needed, or even of the need, to contain the contingencies of love. A similar note of retrospective self-reproach occurs in a striking passage which metaphorically fuses racing and the later state of the Hemingway marriage:

Racing never came between us, only people could do that; but for a long time it stayed close to us like a demanding friend. That was a generous way to think of it. I, the one who was so righteous about people and their destructiveness, tolerated this friend that was the falsest, most beautiful, most exciting, vicious, and demanding because she could be profitable.
(p. 61)

This prefigures the advent of Pauline Pfeiffer and the resultant (or associated?) collapse of the marriage to Hadley. In the published version that results from Mary Hemingway and Harry Brague's editing this event is later attributed to circumstantial forces beyond Hemingway's control; here he accepts some responsibility, albeit responsibility that is mitigated by his having sought profit to assuage the couple's alleged poverty.[13]

Such inconsistencies in moral appraisal, equivocation between occasional concessions to responsibility on the one hand, and recourse to the dominant assumption that contingency governs all on the other, help to explain the oddity of tone and disposition that on closer acquaintance so characterises *A Moveable Feast*: its peculiar blend of moral timidity and fearless virility, of nascent self-awareness and crude self-justification. There is a feeling of inevitability about the recurrent lapses from mature recognition to the casuistry of self-mythification: having finally given up on the races

---

[13] Tavernier-Courbin conclusively demonstrates that this poverty was an invention of Hemingway's (*Ernest Hemingway's 'A Moveable Feast'*, pp. 90–4).

he tells us that 'it was enough just to be back in our part of Paris and away from the track and to bet on our own life and work' (p. 64). Like many other of the passages which assimilate love to betting, this one locates marital love in the realm of the contingent. Such unawareness of the ways of intimacy might seem like an unlikely self-reproach from a writer renowned, in some quarters at least, for his fictional treatments of relationships of love. But perhaps not. Hemingway's fictive relationships are after all embedded in a kind of quasi-determinism, a realm of metaphysical luck, famously encapsulated in the description of ants on a burning log late in *A Farewell to Arms*.[14] Frederic Henry's vision of human life as ant-like is soon to be confirmed by his lover Catherine's death after the stillbirth of their child. The Saint Anthony good-luck charm which she gives him early in the novel symbolically saves him while she perishes without its powers of protection against the remorseless contingencies that surround their wartime love. Love of this kind has a particular fascination for Hemingway; indeed, despite his schooling in James and other great novelists of character, Hemingway has great difficulty with the subtleties of intimacy that arise in situations not shaped and constrained by immediate external crisis or threat. In *For Whom the Bell Tolls*, Jordan muses, 'So if you love this girl as much as you say you do, you had better love her very hard and make up in intensity what the relation will lack in duration and in continuity. Do you hear that? In the old days people devoted a lifetime to it.'[15] Here, as elsewhere, we see a strikingly narrow conception of love: a conception lacking in emotional range and complexity, and one in which love is not only surrounded by hostile contingency but permeated by it. But what does such a lifetime as Jordan refers to permit? What is needed to maintain a viable relationship that has 'duration and continuity'? What part does contingency, luck, in fact play in such relationships?

Martha Nussbaum points out that love of any kind exposes the individuals concerned to the contingency of the Other's being, and to the fragility and chanciness of intimacy, its susceptibility to external influence and mutability.[16] But as extreme Hemingway-style assimilations of love and luck show, this view is (as

[14] Ernest Hemingway, *A Farewell to Arms* (London, 1929), pp. 282–3.
[15] Ernest Hemingway, *For Whom the Bell Tolls* (London, 1941), p. 163.
[16] Nussbaum, *The Fragility of Goodness*, p. 222.

Nussbaum acknowledges) partial at best, and it can be quite misleading. Betting comes in various shades, but there is always a moment of choice (or compulsion masquerading as choice) in which one submits to the flux of contingency. Submission to the spin of the roulette wheel is total: a complete forfeiture of control. (In an early letter, Hemingway boasts that he can even cut the odds by observing the behaviour of the wheel.[17]) Betting on the horses is different, certainly in a case like Hemingway's where he studied the form, talked to trainers and so achieved a more favourable configuration of contingency, risk, and mastery. Betting of this kind cannot influence outcomes, but it seeks to predict them through an inwardness with the activity concerned, and through a certain kind of preparatory work. Intimate, committed relationships are different again. Though such relationships do indeed expose lovers to the contingent, there is also a sense in which engagement with another person works in the opposite way. We could also say of relationships of love that though the unaffiliated Other is a locus of contingency in respect of Self, the consensual bonds of relationship are designed (at least in part) to bring that which is opaque, unpredictable, independent of Self, under degrees of control that come with knowability and commitment to shared projects. Indeed it is one of the painful paradoxes of relationships of love that while they ideally delight in the contingent otherness of the Other, control of this kind is an ineluctable feature of them – though the gender ideology and the gendering of control that often come with it are not. As much of the classic fiction Hemingway read will show, the nub here is the configuration of freedom, commitment, and control that arises, or more commonly, is achieved by the lovers. I say 'achieved' because if love is more than just passion, more than just submission to contingent and mutable bodily needs and drives, its most viable and substantial form seems to involve a certain kind of work, a moral work which includes negotiating and continually re-formulating the balance between commitment, control, and the freedoms of the Other.

Hemingway, of course, is renowned for the belief in the moral and therapeutic powers of work. As he says in *A Moveable Feast*, 'Work could cure almost anything, I believed then, and I believe

---

[17] Ernest Hemingway, *Selected Letters, 1917–1961*, ed. Carlos Baker (New York, 1981), p. 33.

now' (p. 21). He dedicated himself to work in Paris (and else-where) on writing, to work at Auteuil on the races; but he seems to have lacked any developed sense of work as a feature of, a prerequisite for, substantial relationships of love. The thinness of his conception becomes painfully apparent late in *A Moveable Feast* when he owns up to, and tries to explain, his involvement with Pauline. In this moment of what I shall call pseudo-confession he depicts himself as 'plunged into the fiesta concept of life' (p. 209), as in a state of risky deviation from the exacting demands of his code of discipline. He claims to be led on by 'the rich', in particular by a certain 'pilot fish' (p. 208: though he is not named the reference is to John Dos Passos). And then this:

> Before these rich had come we had already been infiltrated by another rich using the oldest trick there is. It is that an unmarried young woman becomes the temporary best friend of another young woman who is married, goes to live with the husband and wife and then unknowingly, innocently and unrelentingly sets out to marry the husband. When the husband is a writer and doing difficult work so that he is occupied much of the time and is not a good companion or partner to his wife for a big part of the day, the arrangement has advantages until you know how it works out. The husband has two attractive girls around when he has finished work. One is new and strange and if he has bad luck he gets to love them both.
>
> Then, instead of two of them and their child, there are three of them. First it is stimulating and fun and it goes on that way for a while. All things truly wicked start from an innocence. So you live day by day and enjoy what you have and do not worry. You lie and hate it and it destroys you and every day is more dangerous, but you live day to day as in a war.
>
> (pp. 209–10)

It seems that Hemingway's final intention was to omit this and to include a more balanced and self-accusative passage about the rich.[18] Nevertheless, this passage constitutes one of several versions he was contemplating and, like much of the material that was reinstated by the editors, it accurately reflects his underlying presuppositions. 'Infiltrated' captures nicely Hemingway's assumption that love is not just surrounded but permeated by hostile contingency. One of the problems with the explanation offered here is that even the snatches of marital description that are given of life with Hadley (some snippets were omitted by the

---

[18] See Tavernier-Courbin, *Ernest Hemingway's 'A Moveable Feast'*, pp. 177–80, 201–3.

editors[19]) lack the depth that is implied in this admission of marital degradation. Though we know Hadley to have been bright and quite sophisticated at the time of their marriage, she is generally given the sort of numpty-brained dialogue that characterises the intimate relationships in Hemingway's war novels, and the kind of exchanges between husband and wife that I have quoted have an evasive banality, a confected 'innocence' that is intended as a tragic contrast to the 'truly wicked things' that befall the relationship. But what they show is that for Hemingway living 'day by day as in a war' is less a betrayal than a condition of relationship, and that here, as in war, one is a plaything of 'luck'. Here again, 'work' figures, but it is writing work, and the claim is that, in effect, this work leaves the marriage even more open to contingent threats from without than it might otherwise have been.

This pseudo-confession lends credence to Jeffrey Meyers's acerbic claim about Hemingway that 'Self-justification was always more important to him than friends, wives and children.' [20] But it is interesting that here self-justification goes beyond the explanatory invocations of luck as cosmic contingency to luck as a mix of circumstantial and agent-determinative forms. Agent-determination takes the form here of an alleged 'innocence', a residuum of his straight-laced Oak Park upbringing; the circumstantial factors have to do with cultural luck – the encounter with a debased code of the kind dramatised in *The Sun Also Rises*: a hedonism that reposes in the very play of contingent appetite and excess that the code of disciplined work at art seeks to resist. Ernest and Hadley are presented as American innocents abroad and the culture they encounter as destructive of their tender – their fragile – love. The effort at self-exoneration is maudlin and basically absurd: as Michael Reynolds points out, 'Ernest was in fact ripe for an affair at this time and would have been a party to one if Duff Twysden had been willing'.[21]

Yet earlier, a similar attribution of blame is made with a poetic delicacy, and an existential suggestiveness, that are typical of Hemingway at his best. In the chapter 'A False Spring', the couple stand on a bridge watching the Seine. They have a feeling of

[19] Ibid., p. 180.
[20] Jeffrey Meyers, *Hemingway: A Biography* (London, 1985), p. 482.
[21] Michael Reynolds, *Hemingway: The Paris Years* (Oxford, 1989), p. 319.

'hunger' which is later for her assuaged by a lovely meal and the love-making that follows. But for him it is different:

> It was a wonderful meal at Michaud's after we got in; but when we had finished and there was no question of hunger any more the feeling that had been like hunger when we were on the bridge was still there when we caught the bus home. It was there when we came in the room and after we had gone to bed and made love in the dark, it was there. (p. 57)

Hemingway goes on again to reproach himself for 'stupidity', this time for trying to understand his feelings as he lies beside the now sleeping Hadley in the moonlight, and the chapter concludes with a rumination that is at once haunting and morally problematic:

> But Paris was a very old city and we were young and nothing was simple there, not even poverty, nor sudden money, nor the moonlight, nor right and wrong, nor the breathing of someone who lay beside you in the moonlight. (p. 58)

Together these passages intimate the presence of three forms of luck: implicitly, the cosmic kind that lies behind everything; the circumstantial–cultural kind that is the debased culture of Paris and Schruns; and, again implicitly, another kind – a form of constitutive luck, something that has to do with the needs and appetites, the whole psycho-physiological disposition of this autobiographical subject.

III Many sorts of hunger

Hours before the meal at Michaud's and Hemingway's moonlit rumination about his marriage, the couple are standing on a bridge watching the Seine and become aware that they are hungry. Minutes later they stop outside of Michaud's and he ponders:

> Standing there I wondered how much of what we had felt on the bridge was just hunger. I asked my wife and she said, 'I don't know, Tatie. There are so many sorts of hunger. In the spring there are more. But that's gone now. Memory is hunger.' (pp. 56–7)

This is one of the few intelligent things that Hadley is given to say in the book and it proves to be important. Hunger, of course, is a central feature of the Hemingway world and of the Hemingway legend. His books are preoccupied with gustatory and sexual appetites and their satisfaction. The legend, which has accorded extraordinary cultural status to a writer who, as both man and artist, was imaginatively and spiritually quite limited, is very much about the scale of Hemingway's needs and appetites: the need for adventure in love and war, in hunting big game, bull-fighting, and so on. Charismatic though this may in some respects be, it raises questions about the model of self, and by extension of the interaction between selves, which underlies Hemingway's work and reputation. *A Moveable Feast* brings these questions home with particular point.

The emphasis on hunger, here and elsewhere, needs to be seen in context of the overall emotional economy of Hemingway's world. I read the generative emotion of this world as a haunting intimation of nullity, a sense, in Sartre's words, that 'a nothingness haunt[s] being'.[22] 'What did he fear?', the older waiter in 'The Clean, Well-lighted Place' asks himself. 'It was not fear or dread. It was a nothing that he knew too well. It was all a nothing and man was nothing too.'[23] Characters live on the brink of – and sometimes succumb to – a feeling that is often described as an emptiness. One of the frustrations of Hemingway's writing, however, not least in *A Moveable Feast*, is that the rendering of these feelings seldom gets beyond the sort of primitive emotional notation that Hemingway found in the Mark Twain he so admired: one is lonesome, hollow, empty or, if things go well, one feels grand or swell. In much of Hemingway's work these emotional states and possibilities are expressed through existential binaries: emptiness/fullness, hollowness/fullness, loneliness/intimacy, pleasurable action/desolate passivity, hunger/satiation, and so on.

A title like *A Moveable Feast* tends to suggest that all may be well with the self so conceived: so long as your feast goes with you your needs will be met and your hungers assuaged. But of course neither life nor Hemingway's vision of it offer such reassurances. Martha Nussbaum notes that 'the activities associated with bodily desires not only exemplify mutability and instability in their own internal structure; they also lead us and bind us to the world of perishable objects and, in this way, to the risk of loss and the danger of conflict'.[24] In other words, they lay us open to contin-

[22] Jean-Paul Sartre, *Being and Nothingness*, ed. Hazel E. Barnes (London, 1969), p. 11.
[23] *The Complete Short Stories of Ernest Hemingway: The Finca Vigia Edition* (New York, 1987), p. 291.
[24] Nussbaum, *The Fragility of Goodness*, p. 7.

gency, to luck. We have seen that Hemingway's fiction locates human hunger in a metaphysic of scarcity where, more often than not, need meets capriciousness and privation. His response to this is not philosophically complex, but it is artistically fraught and powerful, and it has interesting implications.

In fact, I would argue that he has three responses, each finding expression in a particular model of self and of its interactions with other selves. The first is an essentially atomistic model which envisages for the self an incessant quest for satisfaction, a never-ending rhythm of fullness–emptiness–fullness, and so on. Aristotle's emphasis on the notion of 'replenishment'[25] is helpful here, and we might term this model a *need–replenishment* picture of the self. So conceived, the self is characterised by acquisitive and 'taking' relationships with the world in general and with other selves. Its quest for replenishment is compulsive, partly because it is pitted against a reality that at some level it knows to be unpitying, 'niggardly'; importantly, it is also fundamentally egotistical in that it accords Self absolute supremacy. George Eliot's references to the 'illusion of a concentric arrangement'[26] and to a sense of the world as 'an udder to feed our supreme selves'[27] are apt here, not least for their suggestion that many forms of egotistical hunger – including of course gustatory ones – are regressed, repetitions of infantile need. Another passage about writing in Paris captures something of the rhythm of emptiness and replenishment in which the atomistic Hemingway self is caught:

It was necessary to get exercise, to be tired in the body, and it was very good to make love with whom you loved. That was better than anything. But afterwards, when you were empty, it was necessary to read in order not to think or worry about your work until you could do it again. I had learned already never to empty the well of my writing, but always to stop where there was still something there in the deep part of the well, and let it refill at night from the springs that fed it. (pp. 25–6)

This deals with two of Hemingway's principal hungers: creative and sexual. Largely unwittingly, it establishes not only an economy of needs, but also a hierarchy among them.

---

[25] Aristotle, *The Nichomacean Ethics*, trans. J. A. K Thomson (Harmondsworth, 1976), Book III, xi, p. 138.
[26] George Eliot, *Middlemarch* (1871–2), ed. G. S. Haight (Cambridge, Mass., 1946), p. 195.
[27] Ibid., p. 156.

A second model of self and interaction is exemplified in this exchange from *A Farewell to Arms*:

'You see', says Catherine to Henry, 'I do anything you want.'
'You're so lovely.'
'I'm afraid I'm not very good at it yet.'
'You're lovely.'
'I want what you want. There isn't any me any more. Just what you want.'
'You sweet.'[28]

The impulse to fuse with another's being is familiar in Hemingway's fiction, and in some of his letters. (The desire to merge or exchange genders with one's partner, explored in the novel *The Garden of Eden*, is a related phenomenon.) It constitutes a reaction to the feelings of emptiness and isolation, of the nullity at the heart of things, and there are times in Hemingway's writing when its powers of consolation and protection seem almost magical. In *A Moveable Feast* this enchanted sense of unison is symbolically associated with the life that Hadley and Ernest have early on in the mountains, away from the debased code of Paris: 'In the night we were happy with our own knowledge we already had and other new knowledge we had acquired in the mountains' (p. 21). It also manifests linguistically, as in some of the conversational exchanges I have quoted where the couple speak an almost childlike idiolect of two, as if from a shared existential core of innocence. We might term this a *fusion* model of self and interaction. Here the self seeks to assuage its emptiness through the absolute solace of an intimacy that abrogates the boundaries upon which isolation depends. Such fusion also abolishes the distance, the difference, which allow contingency, be it circumstantial or the kind associated with linkage to the opaque and contingent qualities of the Other, to 'infiltrate' relationships of love.

Finally, there is a model of self as oriented towards and engaged in *reciprocity* with others. There are not many developed representations of this view in *A Moveable Feast*, and, not surprisingly given the deeply masculine quality of the Hemingway world, the best examples in fact occur not between Ernest and Hadley but between Ernest and other men, in particular Pound and Fitzgerald. Where it pertains to Ernest and Hadley it emerges

[28] Hemingway, *A Farewell to Arms*, p. 96.

most commonly through expressions of regret: regret that he was not more attentive to her needs, that he put work first, that, in the word that usually expresses his sense of regret, he was 'stupid' about their love. About his strictures on spending he says: 'I knew how severe I had been and how bad things had been. The one is doing his work and getting satisfaction from it is not the one the poverty bothers ... I had been stupid when she [Hadley] needed a grey lamb jacket and had loved it once she had bought it. I had been stupid about other things too' (pp. 50–1).

A Moveable Feast is torn between these three models of self and interaction, but ultimately it is egotism, the need–replenishment view, that prevails. The style of egotism involved is familiar enough. Like the depressive hunger that fuels its various needs, this egotism is in some sense characteristically male. The self is not seen, in the terms used by some feminist theorists of autobiography, as 'relational', as being constituted and realised through interaction with others, but as an already-given site of identity and goal-directed energy.[29] This self is also in some sense characteristically American, a latter-day version of the post-Romantic Imperial Self, isolate, purportedly self-sufficient and self-scripting. For the self so conceived, mutuality is likely to seem not just fragile, but also ancillary, secondary to the project of self-validation through action, creation, and first-person mythification. Thus if in Hemingway's world love has little power to resist the encroachments of the contingent, the same is not true of art. The above passage about writing in Paris shows, as does so much else in the book, that Hemingway's deepest need is for, and his deepest commitment to, art: love and sex have important parts to play in the replenishment of creative energies, but in this emotional hierarchy they are ultimately secondary to such energies and will be sacrificed to them, if need be. To some extent creativity needs help to renew itself, but, given the right circumstances, it will replenish its almost 'empty' 'well' in the night. Love, too, needs help; it also needs work. But, as we have seen, the real work here is devoted to art. If at times Hemingway seems aware of these shortcomings and even, almost, to apologise for his 'stupidity' in respect of them, the logic of the Hemingway legend, and of the Künstlerroman form

---

[29] For a feminist reading of Hemingway see Nancy R. Cromley and Robert Scholes, *Hemingway's Genders: Rereading the Hemingway Text* (New Haven, 1994).

through which the legend is here given expression, carry the promise of exoneration.

The need for exoneration, justification, is itself a kind of hunger; a kind that is familiar in much autobiographical writing. Hadley is right to say that '"memory is hunger"', and the comment is particularly apt for *A Moveable Feast*, a work whose desire to memorialise, to contain the play of contingency through writing, is complicated by its imperious need to justify, to shore up the Hemingway legend through appeals to the power of the contingent, of luck, in life.

IV Regret, justification and some one to be

In his essay 'Moral luck', Bernard Williams discusses an example, loosely based on the life of Gauguin, in which a morally sentient individual leaves his family in order to pursue a career as a painter. Williams argues that luck plays a big part in moral conduct, and that in this case the moral status of 'Gauguin's' decision to leave his family will be subject to various forms of moral luck, including, and perhaps principally, outcome luck – the success or otherwise of the artistic career that follows. If that career is successful, 'Gauguin' will, from a standpoint that is heavily conditioned by that success, deem his decision morally justifiable; if not, he will be subject to 'agent-regret': a form of regret that agents can feel towards their past actions, or actions in which they have participated. The degree to which 'Gauguin' does in fact succeed will depend on various forms of luck, some 'intrinsic' to his project, others 'extrinsic'. Only the former class will be a possible cause for agent-regret; but there is a sense in which the whole issue is clouded because the self which ostensibly chooses to leave family for art is itself to a significant degree a product of external, circumstantial determination. This recognition throws the whole Kantian projection into question.

This picture has some relevance to *A Moveable Feast*. Though Hemingway did not leave his wife and son for a career as a writer, we have seen that there is a sense in which his priorities rendered them secondary to that career and in which their secondary status left them highly vulnerable to the contingencies of the appetitive Hemingway soul. Interestingly, his posthumously published novel, *Islands in the Stream*, another work which replays his regret about leaving Hadley, features as its central character Thomas Hudson, an artist who likens himself and his life choices to the predicament of Gauguin.[30] The lament with which *A Moveable Feast* draws to a conclusion is a statement of something like agent-regret, and the book's moral fumbling and confusions in general are crude attempts at self-justification. The moral standpoint from which these utterances and attempts are made is complex. It is central to our understanding of the moral sequence described, and to Hemingway's understanding of it, that he writes from the standpoint of a literary legend. To the extent that literary success might on an account like Williams's justify the writer's neglect of wife and son, the justification is, as it were, already in place. Art constitutes its own moral justification. The use of the first-person Künstlerroman form reinforces the legend's potential power to expiate because this is a genre often predicated upon the assumption that the artist concerned has achieved a degree of success which renders the reconstruction of the history in which his/her talent developed interesting and worthwhile.

The moral standpoint here is further complicated by the particular nature of Hemingway's regret. To say that this is a form of moral regret is true, but it is not the whole story. Certainly the narrative evinces a sense of guilt and moral failure, and in so doing it summons, or is at least parasitic upon, some of the resources of traditional confessional autobiography in which regret charts a narrative path for a complex autobiographical self in relation to some larger system of value or discourse of self-awareness. Moreover, the element of what Hemingway termed 'remorse' in draft passages would have been more pronounced had such passages not been excised by Mary Hemingway and Brague.[31] Yet Hemingway's regret also has its non-moral side; a side which reflects the egotism of the Hemingway self. Here regret simply refers to the loss of something that in retrospect he wishes he had not forgone. *A Moveable Feast* was written in depressive advancing years in an effort (among other things) to recapture the 'innocence' of life with Hadley. Its closing sentence is: 'But this is how Paris was in the early days when we were very poor and very happy'. (p. 211). In fact, the moral and non-moral

---

[30] Ernest Hemingway, *Islands in the Stream* (New York, 1970), p. 7.
[31] Tavernier-Courbin, *Ernest Hemingway's 'A Moveable Feast'*, pp. 178–9.

concerns tend to merge: grief drives an egotistical review of life priorities which guilt takes up in its own more empathetic terms.

The attempt to review life priorities in this way amounts to an effort to ask how his life should have been lived and, by extension, how any life ought to be lived. Ethics enters the picture. However inadequately and implicitly, *A Moveable Feast* tries to distinguish between the 'good life' platitudinously conceived as bohemian indulgence, the fiesta concept – cafés, companionship, wine and writing – and The Good Life that is comprised of optimal human dispositions, activities and interrelations between these. That it cannot make this distinction with any real success is partly a matter of temperamental and intellectual limitation, partly of contradictions in the code which reflects these limitations, and partly the upshot of contradictions that are inherent in the constellation of values and activities in question – a legacy of conceptual and pragmatic incommensurability. In particular, the confusions of this text suggest that the sense of developed interiority that we expect in any representationally powerful autobiography, and a strong commitment to moral luck, are deeply incommensurable.

In fact, the Hemingway code is here riven with contradictions, but four are perhaps particularly noteworthy. The first is the tension between control and submission where the ethic of discipline, containment of contingency, pulls against the belief in submission to the unmediated play of experience and sensation. Second, there is a pull between fidelity as an absolute and overriding commitment to artistic truth and fidelity to those others who, in principle and in practice, cannot but take second place to art. Their betrayal is almost assured. If art has intrinsic value, and if a part of that value resides in its – in this case the fiction writer's – ability to render others as ends in themselves, the pursuit of that art may nevertheless treat others as a means in the quest for artistic perfection. Third, there is a discrepancy between the ethos of self-sufficiency and the belief, both aesthetic and interpersonal, in receptiveness, openness to others. Finally, there is a contradiction between the strong sense of agency which underlies Hemingway's belief in action and self-sufficiency and the attenuated sense of self-as-agent which is associated with his appeals to luck, particularly moral luck.

The last of these points picks up on Williams's concern about the actual provenance of the moral self in a world where virtually all aspects of such a self can seem, at least from an external standpoint, the product of luck. This concern is shared by Thomas Nagel, who notes that if we begin the process of attribution of self and acts to 'antecedent circumstances' there seems to be no end to the process of regress, and no beginning to the individual agent: 'The area of genuine agency, and therefore of legitimate moral judgment, seems to shrink under such scrutiny to an extensionless point.'[32] For Nagel and (I think) Williams, there is no conceptual solution to this bind. Both appeal instead to the sense we have by introspection that agency, though more circumscribed than the so-called 'good-condition' theorists might like to think, is real: 'We extend to others the refusal to limit ourselves to external evaluation, and we accord to them selves like our own.'[33] Nagel's great and memorable concern is that if we hold only to external evaluation – to selves and actions as they appear as parts of networks of cause and consequence – 'it leaves us with no one to be'.[34]

One of the great virtues of autobiographical writing is that it takes us beyond external evaluation, the spectator's view of other selves, and gives the sentiment, the logic, the experience of the inner world of first-person agents. Perhaps better than most other forms of discourse, it can express and help to reconcile the puzzling duality of the self; the two senses in which it seems implicated in thread-like worlds. From one angle it seems part and constitutive of a web, where all that surrounds it also shapes and partakes of it, and any movement of which it is capable within the exacting constraints of its medium reverberates out, affecting all with which it shares interconnections.[35] From another perspective it looks less like a conjuncture than a node, the product of narrative threads which converge to form an active entity which is able to gather and, to some extent, articulate and redirect the threads of its own and other people's narrative histories. It can do this in a variety of ways: with respect to others, through action, including moral action which requires moral sensitivity, reflection and work; with respect to self, through introspection and the sort of narrative articulation and self-constitution that are characteristic of autobiographical writing. Such writing cannot perhaps persuade us that there is a clear point at which antecedent circumstances end and the self begins, but it can help show how antecedence

---

[32] Nagel, *Mortal Questions*, p. 35.   [33] Ibid., p. 37.   [34] Ibid., p. 38.
[35] See Bernard Williams's invocation of this metaphor in *Moral Luck*, p. 29.

shades into the capacity for action, and what such action, and the developed forms of agency with which it is associated, look like. It can reassure us that it is possible to 'be' someone, and it can offer models of being for our intellectual and emotional contemplation.

Having said this, it must be conceded that *A Moveable Feast* lacks a productive sense of tension between a developed central self and a complex social – ideological, moral, situational – totality. Though its Künstlerroman and confessional elements are at times suggestive of such complexity, it continually retreats into a memoir-like modesty about self-revelation. These tendencies are apparent in its implicit and explicit engagements with luck. The thinness of self-description is reflected in the paucity of detail about constitutive or agent-determinative luck. The narrative begins *mediis rebus*: it does not accord the narrated self a past or a moral history; nor does its vignette structure allow for much sense of moral development. There is much about life-patterns, drives, needs, and compulsions, but virtually no introspection about possible sources of these patterns. The self is in many ways monolithic, a given: the good constitutive luck involved in having talent is taken for granted, and it is assumed that discipline can deliver a destiny of artistic greatness in the face of the contingencies that threaten other aspects of life. Outcome luck seems not to afflict the vocation of art. But for love, and the moral provenance of the self, things are very different. The recurrent references to 'stupidity' are suggestive of an element of constitutive luck which contributes to the break-up of the marriage; but the nature and history of such tendencies remain unscrutinised. The major appeals to luck are to its circumstantial forms: the metaphysical kind which surrounds and threatens all human activity, and the cultural form which Ernest and Hadley encounter in Paris and Schruns. It is here that Hemingway ultimately lays the blame for the collapse of his marriage.

Blame and the agent-regret that go with it are not assuaged by artistic success. Hemingway sees the self that arises from its earlier choices largely as a casualty. At some level the book laments that life is not a feast, that one cannot have the good outcomes without the choices and errors that helped to produce them, cannot have the current – legendary – writing self together with all that seems retrospectively desirable about earlier states and experiences of the narrated self. Here Hemingway the tough guy, the man of action, the stoical survivor in a world of scarcity and caprice, gives way to an altogether softer and more sentimental figure, yearning for a plenitude the books that made him famous expressly deny. His earlier caution that 'it is only when you can no longer believe in your own exploits that you write your memoirs'[36] is of little avail.

The emphasis on action constitutes an effort of simplification where the complexities that bedevil the self and its code can be deferred or dissolved. The line between action and evasion is fine indeed. So too is the line between courage and cowardice. The Hemingway who was decorated for bravery in battle and who habitually courted physical risk emerges from the published version of *A Moveable Feast* as something of a moral coward, unable and unwilling to take responsibility for choices that he sheets home to luck. On the last page of *A Moveable Feast* he looks back nostalgically to the time with Hadley when they thought they were 'invulnerable' (p. 211). He now wants us to know that this was an illusion. But the text over-corrects and responds to loss with an odd mix of heroic invulnerability, a monolithic memorialisation of self, and despairing moral fatalism that suggests that, ultimately, there is virtually no self left to be. The marble table-top view of fate and agency supplants the ethos of heroic responsibility. The icon of this world is not Kant's jewel but the rabbit's foot, the Saint Anthony charm.

It is ironic and highly unfortunate that the published version plays up the element of moral cowardice by omitting several expressions of remorse and personal culpability that Hemingway had finally intended for inclusion. However, the editorial history of the text does not in my view substantially affect the reading I offer here. The rationalisations offered in the published version were seriously contemplated by Hemingway among the many drafts he tried, and they are consistent with a conception of luck and agency which dominates not only earlier parts of the text, but his writing in general. Moreover, the draft expressions of remorse do not appear to take a high degree of responsibility. Appeals to luck remain prominent, though the appeal features a greater emphasis on constitutive luck ('fault of character'[37]) than does the

---

[36] Ernest Hemingway, 'Pamplona Letter', *Transatlantic Review*, 2 (September 1924), p. 301. Quoted in Weber, *Hemingway's Art of Non-Fiction*, p. 136.
[37] Tavernier-Courbin, *Ernest Hemingway's 'A Moveable Feast'*, p. 180.

published version. Whatever minor changes the increased emphasis on contrition might have for our sense of Hemingway the man, the published version has made a decisive contribution to the Hemingway legend. The ethical flaws in the published text reflect ethical flaws in the legend.

One such flaw is the failure to see that egotism constitutes a greater threat to relationships of love than even the unnerving impingements of luck. We know that it was Mary Hemingway and Brague who chose to put the chapter containing the lament to Hadley in *A Moveable Feast* last. Hemingway had apparently decided to drop the last four pages for fear of hurting Hadley and to end the volume with the chapters in which he emerges as a good and empathetic friend to the chaotic Scott Fitzgerald.[38] The impulse to protect Hadley while also securing his own status as a moral being is typical of the moral confusions that pervade the book. Such confusions let in a little moral light, but not a lot and not often. In 'A False Spring' he notes that when in their impoverished days Chèvre d'Or, a horse on which they had wagered, fell, Hadley 'cried for the horse, I remembered, but not for the money' (p. 51). He commends her for her uncomplaining attitude to the poverty to which his quest for artistic greatness had committed them and he seems aware, but only dimly, of the significance of this episode: his inclination is to curse their bad luck in losing their wager; she cries for the horse. His response is to lament a loss to the self; hers is outward-looking, emotionally cognisant of other beings and their tragic vulnerability to modes of ill luck about which there really is nothing to be done.

[38] Ibid., ch. 8.

❖❖

7

The unseemly profession
Privacy, inviolate personality, and the ethics of life writing

❖❖

PAUL JOHN EAKIN

Everyone thinks he is more or less the owner of his name, of his person, of his own story (and even of his image).

(Philippe Lejeune)[1]

The right of property in its widest sense, including all possession, including all rights and privileges, and hence embracing the right to an inviolate personality, affords alone that broad basis upon which the protection which the individual demands can be rested.

(Samuel D. Warren and Louis D. Brandeis)[2]

Children are always episodes in someone else's narrative.

(Carolyn Kay Steedman)[3]

Is there harm in life writing? Aside from writing something libellous, what would the harm be? I found such questions disturbing, for I had conditioned myself for many years to think rather of the good of life writing, of its natural place in a lifelong process of identity formation. Moral issues, of course, the rightness of a subject's acts or motives, frequently constitute a primary content of biographical and autobiographical narrative. But I was drawn

---

[1] Philippe Lejeune, *Moi aussi* (Paris, 1986), my translation: 'Chacun se sent plus ou moins propriétaire de son nom, de sa personne, de son histoire (et même de son image).' Subsequent references will be given in the main text.
[2] Samuel D. Warren and Louis D. Brandeis, 'The Right to Privacy' in Ferdinand Schoeman, ed., *Philosophical Dimensions of Privacy* (Cambridge, 1984), p. 85.
[3] Carolyn Kay Steedman, *Landscape for a Good Woman: A Story of Two Lives* (New Jersey, 1987), p. 122. Subsequent references will be given in the main text.

instead to focus this inquiry on the moral consequences of the act of writing itself. What is right and fair for me to write about someone else? What is right and fair for someone else to write about me? I discovered the beginnings of an answer to these questions in the legal and philosophical discussion of the individual's right to privacy.

I want to note at the outset that a distinctly individualist bias colours this discussion. Philosophers and jurists characteristically posit the capacity for action in an autonomous, free-standing model of selfhood – a distinct and clearly defined person who acts and is acted upon. Defining agency in this way helps both to identify the individual in whom privacy is vested and to assign responsibility for violations of that privacy.[4] Ethical determinations become more complex, however, if we conceptualise identity as relational rather than autonomous, for such a model makes it more difficult to demarcate the boundaries of the self upon which a privacy-based ethics of the person can be founded. Against the autonomous moral agent posited by ethical theory I want to set the relational self that is frequently portrayed in contemporary autobiography and memoir. Speaking of her relation with her mother, for example, Carolyn Kay Steedman writes, 'She made me believe that I was her' (p. 141); similarly, recalling his relation with his father, Philip Roth evokes a period when their lives were 'intermeshed and spookily interchangeable'.[5] As these examples suggest, in contrast to the supposedly self-determining model of identity that autonomy predicates, a relational concept of selfhood stresses the extent to which the self is defined by – and lives in terms of – its relations with others. If, as I contend, we are relational selves living relational lives, an ethics of privacy needs to address that fact.

Jeffrey H. Reiman argues that privacy is 'a precondition of personhood', '*a social ritual by means of which an individual's moral title to his existence is conferred*' (in Schoeman, ed., *Philosophical Dimensions*, p. 310, emphasis in original). Moreover, theorists of privacy seem to agree that space or social distance is a precondi-

---

[4] Robert Young observes, 'Autonomy is commonly held to be a presupposition of moral agency and hence of responsibility, dignity, and self-esteem' ('Autonomy and the "Inner Self"' in John Christman, ed., *The Inner Citadel: Essays on Individual Anatomy* (New York, 1989)). See also the essays collected in the Christman and Schoeman volumes.

[5] Philip Roth, *Patrimony: A True Story* (New York, 1992), p. 225.

tion of privacy. If we accept these hypotheses, ethical problems will arise in life writing when space is transgressed, when privacy is abridged, with the result that the integrity of the person is breached or violated. This is the proposition I will examine in this chapter. I will begin by exploring the link between privacy and personhood in the philosophical and juridical literature. Then I will test this thinking by applying it to violations of privacy and personhood to be found in relational lives, narratives of relational selfhood that require, by definition, sustained portraiture of other selves, usually family members.

I Privacy and inviolate personality

The American press seized upon the death of the late Jacqueline Kennedy Onassis in 1994 to mourn the passing of an ideal of privacy that this beloved public figure had, paradoxically, come to represent. No one needs reminding that we live in an age of intrusiveness, where each innovation in communications technology seems to create some new threat to the possibility of being left alone: we read daily about eavesdropping in the eaveless virtual space of cellular phones, about call screening, caller identification, and scrambling devices. It is surely a sign of the times that *access* is newly empowered as a transitive verb. The hunger of the public for the private lives of the rich and famous has spawned a breed of professional privacy busters – gossip columnists and paparazzi – and Onassis became the chosen prey of self-styled paparazzo Ronald E. Galella. Photographer Galella's single-minded pursuit of Onassis resulted in more than a decade of litigation, culminating in a Federal Superior Court judgment in 1982 that upheld Onassis's 'constitutional right of privacy' (Galella 1106). A particularly interesting feature of the case, and one which gives it special symbolic value for my purposes here, was that the series of judgments against Galella prohibited the photographer from approaching 'within 100 yards of the home of Mrs Onassis and her children; 100 yards from the children's school; and at all other places 50 yards from Mrs Onassis and 75 yards from the children' (1081). Space is the prerequisite of privacy, that '"right to be left alone"' which Galella, in the judge's finding, had 'relentlessly and shockingly invaded' (1106).

The legal history of the right to privacy invoked in this case dates from the publication in 1890 of a celebrated article by Samuel D. Warren and Louis D. Brandeis entitled, precisely, 'The Right to Privacy'. The article was occasioned by Warren's exasperation with intrusive coverage of his family's social life by the popular press of the period; revolutions in printing technology and photography exposed anyone deemed to be a celebrity – the Warrens were wealthy, socially prominent Bostonians – to the gaze of a mass-circulation audience.[6] Brandeis and Warren argued for 'a general right to privacy for thoughts, emotions, and sensations ... whether expressed in writing, or in conduct, in conversation, in attitudes, or in facial expression' (p. 82), a right so comprehensive and fundamental, in fact, that we might call it the right to personhood. Their own formulation, however, as we shall see, has proved peculiarly memorable, 'the right to an inviolate personality' (p. 85).

The subsequent legal history of privacy is rich and complex, turning especially on challenges to Brandeis and Warren's positing of a single, all-embracing right.[7] William Prosser, for example, reviewing seventy years of cases in 1960, found that 'the law of privacy comprises four distinct kinds of invasion of four different interests of the plaintiff'. I quote his description of these four torts to suggest something of the complex of issues with which the right to privacy has been associated in the law:

1. Intrusion upon the plaintiff's seclusion or solitude, or into his private affairs.
2. Public disclosure of embarrassing private facts about the plaintiff.
3. Publicity which places the plaintiff in a false light in the public eye.
4. Appropriation, for the defendant's advantage, of the plaintiff's name or likeness. (p. 107)

Countering the apparent reductiveness of Prosser's four-part analysis, however, is Edward J. Bloustein's 'Privacy as an Aspect of Human Dignity: An Answer to Dean Prosser' (1964), a defence

---

[6] See Don R. Pember, *Privacy and the Press: The Law, the Mass Media, and the First Amendment* (Seattle, 1972), pp. 23–5 for an account of the circumstances that led to the publication of the Warren and Brandeis article.

[7] My own abbreviated account of the legal history of the right to privacy has been guided by Schoeman's illuminating introduction to this thorny subject ('Privacy').

of the distinctiveness of the right to privacy claimed by Brandeis and Warren. Bloustein discerns in all of the manifold transgressions against the right to privacy 'an interference with individuality, an interference with the right of the individual to do what he will'. His portrait of the person deprived of privacy, moreover, is chilling: 'such a being, although sentient, is fungible; he is not an individual'.[8]

How did we come to possess the privacy that the Warrens and Jacqueline Onassis felt was being violated, the privacy that Warren and Brandeis and their followers would protect with the law? In *Home: A Short History of an Idea*, Witold Rybczynski has traced the outline of the history of privacy in the West, and as an architect himself, Rybczynski highlights the connection between privacy and physical space. The seventeenth century, especially in the Protestant bourgeois culture of Holland, marks the appearance of 'privacies', 'rooms to which the individual could retreat from public view'; before that, 'houses were full of people, ... and privacy was unknown'.[9] Citing the work of John Lukacs on 'The Bourgeois Interior', Rybczynski links this shift in the design of domestic space to 'the emergence of something new in the human consciousness: the appearance of the internal world of the individual, of the self, and of the family' (p. 35).[10]

Are these concepts of privacy and the individual peculiar to Western culture? Certainly Rybczynski's analysis suggests that they are by-products of a bourgeois capitalist society in which it has seemed natural to associate person and privacy with the notion of property. We do not need to look far, moreover, to find large-scale twentieth-century counter-examples, totalitarian societies whose state apparatuses of gulags and secret police are specifically designed to destroy the individual's 'right to an inviolate personality'; the very term *brainwashing*, which we instinctively associate with the Orwellian state, captures perfectly the antithesis of the ideal Warren and Brandeis sought to defend. Some anthropologists, however, taking the longer view, regard

---

8 Edward J. Bloustein 'Privacy as an Aspect of Human Dignity: An Answer to Dean Prosser' in Schoeman, *Philosophical Dimensions*, p. 188.

9 Witold Rybczynski, *Home: A Short History of an Idea* (New York, 1986), p. 18.

10 For further discussion of the emergence of the modern concept of the self, see Charles Taylor, *Sources of the Self: The Making of Modern Identity* (Cambridge, Mass., 1991) and Lionel Trilling, *Society and Authenticity* (Cambridge, Mass., 1972).

the need for privacy and the physical space required to achieve it as transcultural universals of human behaviour. Thus, concluding his analysis of the veil as a 'distance setting mechanism' among Tuareg males, Robert F. Murphy writes:

I have argued, following [Georg] Simmel, that social distance pervades all social relationships though it may be found in varying degrees in different relationships and in different societies ... The privacy and with-drawal of the social person is a quality of life in society. That he withholds himself while communicating and communicates through removal is not a contradiction in terms but a quality of all social interaction.[11]

Confirming Murphy's views, law professor Alan Westin traces the origins of the human need for privacy back to the territorial imperative that Robert Ardrey posits as a governing principle of animal behaviour. While Westin acknowledges that 'modern in-dustrial societies ... provide greater situations of physical and psychological privacy'[12] than do so-called 'primitive' cultures, he proceeds nevertheless to formulate the key features of privacy 'which apply to men living together in virtually every society that has been systematically examined' (p. 61).

Having considered privacy briefly from legal, sociological, and anthropological perspectives, I want to return to Reiman's hy-pothesis that privacy is 'a precondition of personhood' and ask this question: how can the practice of life writing be said to infringe on the individual's 'right to an inviolate personality'? In order to answer this question, however, we need to answer an-other one first, asking with Robert C. Post, 'What does it mean to violate personality'?[13] Post observes that when Warren and Bran-deis describe 'the space that is supposed to buffer personality from the world, the language is less that of empirical distance than of moral characterization ... So conceived, privacy does not refer to an objective physical space of secrecy, solitude, or anonymity, but rather to the forms of respect that we owe to each other as members of a common community' (p. 651). In distinguishing this 'normative' model of privacy from a 'descriptive' one, Post pro-

---

[11] Robert F. Murphy, 'Social Distance and the Veil' in Schoeman, *Philosophical Dimensions*, p. 51.

[12] Alan Westin, 'The Originals of Modern Claims to Privacy' in Schoeman, *Philosophical Dimensions*, pp. 56–74; p. 69.

[13] Robert C. Post, 'Rereading Warren and Brandeis: Privacy, Property, and Appro-priation', *Case Western Law Review*, 41 (1991), pp. 647–80, p. 650.

vides an important clue to the ethical problems posed by life writing in particular communities: 'Normative privacy ... lends itself to a straightforward account of why a person socialized to certain forms of respect would experience harm when those forms of respect are disregarded' (p. 653).[14]

Post offers further clarification of the ethical dimensions of privacy when he probes Brandeis and Warren's determination to found privacy 'within a regime of personal rather than property rights' ('Rereading', p. 667). In much of the thinking about copyright and publicity, the person is commodified as data or information, whereas 'the personal right of privacy advocated by Warren and Brandeis ... attaches personality firmly to the actual identity of a living individual' (p. 668).[15] The distinction between person and property strikes me as crucial, for the extent to which integrity of person rather than security of property is at stake in a given situation would provide a basis for assessing the comparative gravity of an ethical violation; moreover, to flout the distinction altogether, to treat the person *as* property, would carry denial of privacy to an absolute degree. Following Post, then, the ethical questions would be these: Is the life writer guilty of a fundamental lack of respect for the other? Has the life writer transformed the other 'into a *thing* or an object' (Post, 'Rereading', p. 667)?

Note, however, that there is a persistent and troubling ambiguity – an ambiguity, moreover, with important ethical conse-

---

[14] See Robert C. Post, 'The Social Foundations of Privavy: Community and Self in the Common Law Tort', *California Law Review*, 77 (1989), pp. 957–1010, for an illuminating account of privacy which balances 'the interests of individuals against the demands of community' (p. 959). Especially striking is his invocation of the work of Erving Goffman on 'The Nature of Deference and Demeanor'. Goffman's articulation of the rules governing social interrelations posits a model of the person that is established through a dynamic of mutual recognition:

> Each individual is responsible for the demeanor image of himself and the deference image of others, so that for a complete man to be expressed, individuals must hold hands in a chain of ceremony, each giving deferentially with proper demeanor to the one on the right what will be received deferentially from the one on the left. While it may be true that the individual has a unique self all his own, evidence of this possession is thoroughly a product of joint ceremonial labor, the part expressed through the individual's demeanor being no more significant than the part conveyed by others through their deferential behavior toward him. (quoted in Post, 'Social Foundations', p. 963)

[15] See J. Coombe 'Author/izing the Celebrity: Publicity, Rights, Postmodern Politics, and Unauthorized Genders' in Martha Woodmansee and Peter Jazi, eds., *The Construction of Authorship: Textual Appropriation in Law and Literature* (Durham, N.C., 1994) on the 'infinite' possibilities for commodification of 'the human persona' (p. 103).

Paul John Eakin

quences for the life writer – about the distinction between person and property, for many of the formulations of privacy, person, and autonomy are couched precisely in the language of property. Thus Reiman writes that 'to be a person ... presupposes that [the individual] believes that the concrete reality which he is, and through which his destiny is realized, belongs to him in a moral sense' (p. 310), and Brandeis and Warren construe 'the right of property in its widest sense' as the only possible basis for 'the right to an inviolate personality' (p. 85).[16]

Nevertheless, in placing person ('the actual identity of a living individual') rather than property (various alienable possessions – data, information) at the centre of their thinking about privacy, Warren and Brandeis, Reiman, and Bloustein suggest the potential gravity of infractions of privacy. As a measure of the harm that lack of respect or commodification can visit upon the 'inviolate personality', consider the consequences of the total deprivation of privacy. Positing privacy as 'a condition of the original and continuing creation of "selves" or "persons"' (p. 310), Reiman cites Erving Goffman's work on asylums as evidence that the programmatic elimination of the inmate's privacy can lead to 'destruction of the self' – can 'literally ... kill it off' (p. 311). James Rachels and William Ruddick take Reiman's hypothesis a step further, making liberty itself a precondition of personhood.[17] Distinguishing between *'being alive'* (a 'biological notion') and *'having a life'* (a 'notion of biography'),[18] they hold that 'only persons have lives' (p. 228). To the person they attribute what I would characterise as a distinctly *autobiographical* consciousness, a set of 'self-referring attitudes' that 'presuppose a sense of oneself as having an existence spread over past and future time' (p. 227). Paralleling Reiman's testing of privacy by evoking its deprivation, Rachels and Ruddick consider the consequences of the deprivation of liberty for the distinguishing mark of the person – 'having a life' – and conclude that 'victims of dire poverty, illness, and slavery' 'might

16 Historians of Western individualism trace its 'possessive' element back to seventeenth-century political theory which posits the individual 'as an owner of himself' (C. B. Macpherson, *The Political Theory of Possessive Individualism* (Oxford, 1962), p. 3).
17 Brandeis eventually linked the right to privacy to the pursuit of happiness (Edward J. Bloustein, 'Privacy as an Aspect of Human Dignity', pp. 186–7).
18 See especially their discussion of the question, 'Can a Slave Have a Biography?' in James Rachels and William Ruddick, 'Lives and Liberty' in Christmas, *Inner Citadel*, p. 226; emphasis in original.

retain the capacity for social responses and yet have none of the intentions, plans, and other features of will and action that define a life' (p. 228).

While Rachels and Ruddick's concern is with liberty rather than privacy, I introduce it here because of the suggestiveness of their concept of 'having a life' for any attempt to formulate the ethics of life writing. When it comes to texts, to life stories, the law tends to adopt a commodified notion of personality, gravitating to questions of ownership and copyright, but if we regard the possession of 'a life' – and, by extension, 'having' a life story – as a defining attribute of the individual, then – again – violations of privacy could be construed as committed against person rather than property. The conclusion from this style of reasoning – in Post, in Reiman, in Rachels and Ruddick – is clear: life writing that constitutes a violation of privacy has the potential to harm the very self of the other.

Before turning to the practice of life writing to test these findings, I want to repeat that all of the preceding discussion assumes an autonomous, discrete model of identity which makes it possible to distinguish clearly between one self and the next, between the boundaries of your life and mine. Much of this discussion also assumes that autonomous individuals in their status as persons stand free of questions of property. But what if individual identity is relational rather than autonomous in formation? What if individual agency is limited by the function of the person as property?

Carolyn Kay Steedman's *Landscape for a Good Woman: A Story of Two Lives* (1986) illustrates the problems posed by a relational model of identity for a privacy-based ethics of life writing. In writing her autobiography, Steedman tells the story of two lives because she believes that her mother's self and story provide the key to her own. 'Children are always episodes in someone else's narrative,' she affirms, 'not their own people, but rather brought into being for particular purposes' (p. 122). Steedman argues that her dawning recognition of the circumstances of her conception – her realisation that she was neither a wanted nor a legitimate child – determined the very structure of her personality. *Landscape for a Good Woman*, then, is a *relational life* in which the story and self of the author are shown to be intimately and inextricably linked to the story and self of another person. The illusory nature of autonomy is brought home to Steedman as a girl when she lingers one day after school to audition for a part in a radio programme. Arriving home late, she finds her mother 'waiting on the doorstep':

I withered, there was nothing I could say. She'd wanted me to go down the road to fetch a bunch of watercress for tea, and I ought to have known she couldn't go, couldn't leave my sister... In this way, you come to know that you are not quite yourself, but someone else: someone else has paid the price for you, and you have to pay it back.   (p. 105)

From a relational perspective, then, the boundaries between self and other are hard to determine, and, as the economic figure Steedman employs here suggests, the boundaries between person and property as well. In Steedman's view, women especially function in both registers simultaneously, operating willy-nilly in an intricate web of agency and commodity that challenges the simplifying vision of the law. Thus she portrays her working-class mother as 'both bargain and bargainer' (p. 69) in a patriarchal system of exchange, an individual who sought to exploit her status as a commodity for purposes of her own: 'Under particular social circumstances, people may come to understand that whilst they do not possess any*thing*, they possess themselves, and may possibly be able to exchange themselves for something else' (p. 68, emphasis in original). Steedman's 'story of two lives', then, makes us ask another question: in what way can the relational self be said to 'have' a life – and a life story – in Rachels' sense? As Lejeune reminds us, 'private life is almost always a co-property' (*Moi aussi*, p. 55, my translation).

II   Relational autobiography: 'she had taken over, or been taken over by, the voice I had created for her'

I began by delineating an ethics of privacy centred on the sanctity of the 'inviolate personality', which turns precisely on the notion of boundaries that may not be transgressed with impunity. Yet even Warren and Brandeis properly recognise the necessity of limiting the 'right to an inviolate personality', conceding, among other limitations, that protection of privacy must be balanced against the public's right to be informed about persons who 'have assumed a position which makes their doings legitimate matters of public investigation' ('Right to Privacy', p. 88). In turning to consider the ethics of relational autobiography, I want to ask whether there is not also a private good, even a private necessity, to be weighed against the other's right to privacy. If we assume a relational model of identity, as Steedman does when she speaks of children as 'episodes in someone else's narrative', then other people's selves and lives may become our business just as, reciprocally, ours becomes theirs. In these cases of what I call the *proximate* other – a parent, a child, a sibling, an intimate – it is difficult not only to determine the boundaries of the other's privacy but indeed to delimit the very otherness of the other's identity.

In proximate collaborative autobiography, the story of the self is constructed through the story told *of* and *by* someone else. These texts feature two first-person speakers, the 'I' of the proximate other's story and the 'I' of what I term *the story of the story*, the narrative of the self's recording of the other's story. Because identity is conceived as relational in these instances, such narratives defy the distinctions we try to establish between genres, for they are autobiographies that offer not only the autobiography of the self but the biography *and* the autobiography of the other. This indeterminacy of form points to the psychological ambiguity of the collaborative situation and the narratives it generates, for the identity of the self who writes and signs as author includes and is included in the identity of the other whose story she presents. The signature reflects the necessarily unequal distribution of power in situations of this kind; once the narrative has been published, whatever the terms of the collaboration may have been, an act of appropriation has occurred, and the self who signs may well be led to reflect on the ethical responsibilities involved.

Art Spiegelman's *Maus: A Survivor's Tale*, published in two volumes in 1986 and 1991, offers a peculiarly instructive example of proximate collaboration because the graphic medium of the text prompts us to visualise the collaborative process involved in its creation.[19] We see cartoonist Spiegelman recording and translating into comic-strip form his father Vladek's astonishing tale of his survival at Auschwitz. Troubled by the success of the first volume,

[19] Art Spiegelman, *Maus*, vol. I, *A Survivor's Tale: My Father Bleeds History* (New York, 1986), vol. II, *A Survivor's Tale: And Here My Troubles Begin* (New York, 1991).

Spiegelman opens the second chapter of the second volume with a disturbing self-portrait. The cartoonist depicts himself at his drawing board perched on a heap of bodies that we have been primed to recognise as the paramount symbol of those who perished in the Holocaust; shady entrepreneurs and reporters armed with microphones and video cameras are shown walking on the corpses as they bombard Spiegelman with questions and deals. Is the artist's representation of his father and his father's story somehow complicit, then, with his father's Nazi persecutors? Is he in effect trampling on his father's body, exploiting his life for gain?

Other images confirm this notion that the collaboration is somehow lethal, that the son's dogged determination to get his father to tell his story contributes to the father's death. Suffering from heart disease, Vladek is shown pedalling on his life-cycle as he tells his harrowing tale. The initial session of dictation begins with Vladek mounting his bike ('It's good for my heart, the pedaling' (I, p. 12)), and another ends, characteristically, with Vladek too exhausted to pedal and talk any more (I, p. 91). And in the final images Vladek calls a halt to all the talking ('Let's stop, please, your tape recorder' (II, p. 136)) and dies. The father's existence is, in the son's retelling, intimately linked to narration; the end of the one is the end of the other. Was telling his story life-sustaining, or did the collaboration finish him off? It is hard to say. In any case, *Maus* is particularly compelling in its unsparing evocation of the dark underside, the murderous impulses and guilts, of the son's attempt to restore an intimate bond with the father, a bond which may never have existed in the first place.

Collaborative autobiographies of this kind inevitably probe the self's responsibility to the proximate other. Is the act of writing about the other a violation of that responsibility? As its title suggests, this is the question that preoccupies novelist John Edgar Wideman as he attempts in *Brothers and Keepers* (1984)[20] to reconstruct the personal and family history that led to his brother Robby's life imprisonment for murder. As in Spiegelman's *Maus*, Wideman's rendering of the story of his story offers an elaborately detailed account of the collaborative process that leads him to question the ethics of his project. Focussing on the interpersonal dynamics of his visits to his brother in prison, visits during which

[20] John Edgar Wideman, *Brothers and Keepers* (New York, 1985), p. 77. Subsequent references will be given within the main text.

he gathers Robby's story, the novelist observes, 'I had to root my fiction-writing self out of our exchanges. I had to teach myself to listen ... tame the urge to take off with Robby's story and make it my own' (p. 77). Curiously, in Wideman's view, the 'fiction-writing self', despite its predatory nature, is drawn helplessly and irresistibly to inhabit the penal interior of the other – 'That boundless, incarcerating black hole is another person' (pp. 77–8). The imagination's out-of-the-body travel into the private territory of another's identity leaves the novelist feeling 'slightly embarrassed, guilty because I've been trespassing and don't know how long I've been gone or if anybody noticed me violating somebody else's turf' (p. 78).

Yet, listening to Robby and listening to himself listen, Wideman traces the origins of his brother's tangled history and his own to a family tradition of walled privacy that had kept them apart – 'He's been inside his privacy and I've been inside mine' (p. 80). Wideman's intricate, acutely self-conscious inquiry displays the ambiguities of privacy, at once the family's guarantee of Robby's integrity and autonomy yet implicated in his downfall because it fostered a dangerous, self-destructive isolation. Is the sanctuary of inviolate personality one more prison in this narrative of prisons and prisoners? Privacy may be a right, but is it a good? And is the act of representing the other and the other's story an exploitative invasion or a self-transcending attempt at empathy – as Wideman puts it, 'a way of seeing out of another person's eyes' (p. 78)?

It is one of the defining paradoxes of proximate collaborative autobiography that such narratives both confirm and resist the reality of relational identity. The very title of Kim Chernin's autobiography, *In My Mother's House: A Daughter's Story* (1983), attests to Chernin's belief – like Steedman's – that mothers and daughters are so intimately bound in the process of identity formation that to tell the story of the one is necessarily to tell the story of the other.[21] For Chernin, in fact, relational identity must be understood in generational perspective, for every mother has also been a daughter. Instinctively grasping the interconnectedness of her own life to her mother's, Kim Chernin initially resists when her mother Rose asks her to write the story of her tumultuous career as a tireless organiser for the Communist Party. To write her mother's

---

[21] Kim Chernin, *In My Mother's House: A Daughter's Story* (New York, 1994).

story, Kim fears, would be to lose herself 'back into the mother' (p. 12), reversing the quest for autonomy that had driven her to break away from her mother and especially from the Communist ideology that anchored her mother's identity. But Chernin persuades herself that in surrendering to her mother's wish she is initiating a therapeutic process that will heal the rift of the years between them.

In the foreword to the second edition of *In My Mother's House* (1994), Chernin traces the origin of the book and her own formation as a writer to the 'stories my mother told me when I was a small child' (p. vii). When she proceeds to comment on her representation of her mother's voice, however, Chernin inverts this reading of the source of her narrative and identity, presenting herself as the author of her mother in a very expansive sense. Readers of her narrative, she reports, have mistakenly assumed that she had merely 'recorded and transcribed my mother's stories, that her voice in my book was the voice in which she had told the stories to me' (p. ix). In fact, Chernin claims, in the interests of verisimilitude – 'to get my mother to sound like my mother on a page' – she was obliged to create a voice that had 'something of her in it but something of me as well' (p. x). But then this collaborative version of the book's creation gives way to a more distinctly imperialistic interpretation in which the domineering personality of the mother has been colonised by the resisting daughter. At a bookstore promotion the mother is presented as 'simultaneously the Rose Chernin she had always been, as well as, now, the central character of a book her daughter was proudly signing'. The shift in power relations between the two is completed when Kim overhears Rose telling one of her own stories *but in Kim's words*: 'after that, my mother never, to my knowledge, told her stories again in her own voice. From that moment in the bookstore she had taken over, *or been taken over by*, the voice I had created for her' (pp. xii–xiii, my emphasis).

In 'Sanctioning Voice: Quotation Marks, the Abolition of Torture, and the Fifth Amendment', Margreta de Grazia suggests the momentousness of such an appropriation of voice.[22] De Grazia's analysis of the Supreme Court's decision in the celebrated Jeffrey

---

[22] Margreta de Grazia, 'Sanctioning Voice: Quotation Marks, the Abolition of Torture, and the Fifth Amendment' in Woodmansee and Jazi, *Construction of Authorship*, pp. 281–302.

Masson–Janet Malcolm case (Masson v. *New Yorker Magazine*) argues that 'lurking behind the Court's dread of misquotation is ... a long history of the gruesome inquisitorial procedures deployed in Europe and England to exact self-incriminating testimonies' (p. 286) – the *peine forte et dure* prescribed to force speech from prisoners who refused to enter a plea before the bar (p. 295). Misquotation and torture, De Grazia concludes, 'produce the same effect: the takeover of another's voice' (p. 286), a takeover protected by the Fifth Amendment. But what, it is reasonable to ask, have torture and the Fifth Amendment to do with a mother–daughter story like Chernin's that is drenched in sentiment, that becomes, at the last, a veritable love fest? Namely this: legal protection of an individual's voice and words places them at the centre of the culture's definition of the integrity and liberty of the person; thus, in a culture centred on individualism, representation of the self and voice of the other acquires a special power. How that power is exercised becomes the central problem of the ethics of life writing, for there is no getting around the fact that ventriloquism, making the other talk, is by definition a central rhetorical phenomenon of these narratives. Proximate collaborative autobiography seems to embrace, conceptually, the reality of relational identity, the structuring bond between self and other, but the desire for autonomy, for mastery of one's origins, for authorship, persists. Children *may be* 'episodes in someone else's narrative', as Steedman proposes, whether they like it or not; when children turned adults become the authors of such a narrative, however, it is a different story, and the tables are turned. Rhetorically, Spiegelman, Wideman, and Chernin become self-determining and more: they make someone else into 'episodes' in their own narratives.[23] The ambivalences of these writers towards their projects express an unresolved tension between relational and autonomous modes of identity.

III   'Bury him naked': the legitimacy of life writing

Relational identity confounds our familiar literary and ethical categories; both need to be stretched to accommodate the fluidity

---

[23] Spiegelman gives a graphic representation of this split role – child/adult author – in numerous images in *Maus* (see especially vol. II, pp. 41–7), and both Spiegelman and Chernin stress the importance of the parent telling a story to the child as the prototype of the autobiographical acts they perform.

of selves and lives. The currency of hybrid forms in contemporary life writing points up the limitations of generic classifications focussed on individual selves and lives as discrete entities. An ethics of life writing founded on the inviolate personality becomes similarly problematic. How do we sort out the legitimacy of life writing, how can we specify its responsibilities, if we cannot say for sure where the 'I' begins and ends? The status of privacy is fraught with contradictions. Inviolate personality may be protected in the courts, but it is routinely violated in the practice of life writing – witness the scale and scope today of biographers, autobiographers, and their readers.

Lest I seem to have mounted a case against the propriety of writing lives, I want to conclude by considering Philip Roth's *Patrimony* (1991), a relational life modelling a relational concept of identity, which demonstrates that transgression of privacy is not incompatible with the most profound respect for the integrity of the person. Roth himself, however, seems to have had a bad conscience about his narrative of his father's last years and illness, for he ends the book with a harrowing dream in which the dead father reproaches his son for having buried him not in the business suit of his lifelong vocation but in a shroud. 'I had dressed him for eternity in the wrong clothes' (p. 237), Roth observes, whereas his instinct had been to say to the mortician, 'Bury him naked' (p. 234). He had, in effect, buried Herman Roth naked in a memoir of *apparently* total candour – this is the heart of the dream – and he interprets the father's 'rebuke' as an allusion to 'this book, which, in keeping with the unseemliness of my profession, I had been writing all the while he was ill and dying' (p. 237). *Patrimony* sets the son's 'unseemly' practice of life writing on a collision course with the father's right to privacy.[24]

The content of the memoir is as transgressive as its telling, and the figure of nakedness points, moreover, to the bodily nature of the boundary crossed between father and son.[25] Roth spares neither himself nor the reader the progressive intimacy with his

[24] The other's right to privacy is frequently assumed to terminate at death. It is worth noting that for Roth this is emphatically not the case – hence the disquieting dream.

[25] Nancy K. Miller, 'Autobiographical Deaths', *Massachusetts Review*, 33 (1992), pp. 19–47, notes the 'surprisingly permeable borders between ... fathers and sons' (p. 21) in *Maus*, and her comments on embodiment, on Roth's insistent preoccupation with the body of his father, are especially illuminating.

father's body that the circumstances of the father's debilitation require. In an early moment in the narrative Roth contemplates the MRI scan of the tumour in his father's brain ('I had seen my father's brain, and everything and nothing was revealed' (p. 17)); in a late episode, helping his father bathe, he studies his father's penis ('I don't believe I'd seen it since I was a small boy' (p. 177)). Gradually the taboo of the body of the other is eroded. 'Taking [his] dentures, slimy saliva and all, and dumping them in my pocket, I had, quite inadvertently, stepped across the divide of physical estrangement that, not so unnaturally, had opened up between us once I'd stopped being a boy' (p. 152).

In the most remarkable sequence in the narrative, an extended and detailed account of the father's exploding bowels after days of post-operative constipation, Roth explores every last crevice of a humiliating experience his father regards as the depth of shame and disgrace. '"I beshat myself"', he said' (p. 172). Cleaning up the befouled bathroom – 'the shit was everywhere . . . even on the tips of the bristles of my toothbrush . . . there was a little shit in my hair' (pp. 172–5), Roth is never closer to his father's body; mapping every inch of the interpersonal space they share, he works his way through to a stance of acceptance, coming into his own through the body of the other. 'So *that* was the patrimony . . . not the money, . . . but the shit' (p. 176). And as for privacy, that, too, is exploded with the shit. His father had pleaded with him never to tell anyone, whereas Roth pursues a policy of total disclosure – if he is holding anything back, what could it be?

This penetration of the territory of the other is not only physical but psychological as well. Roth recalls that if his college education deepened 'the mental divide' between him and his father, it also curiously involved a 'sense of merging' (p. 160) with him, and when Roth undergoes a quintuple bypass operation in the months just before the father's death, he recalls this experience of identification. 'Not since college . . . had our lives been, if not identical, so intermeshed and spookily interchangeable' (p. 225). This interchangeability extends to a reversal of roles between the two men, for 'the little son' displays a parental solicitude ('like a mother', 'like a father' (p. 181)) towards his father in his final dependency; indeed, in writing *Patrimony*, Roth proposes to father the father who had created him. Although we do not know exactly when Roth began this commemorative project, he dedicates himself to it solemnly when he helps his father bathe the night after the episode of the shit. Observing the size and surprising youth of his father's penis, the son vows 'to fix it in my memory for when he was dead': '"I must remember accurately," I told myself, "remember everything accurately so that when he is gone I can re-create the father who created me." *You must not forget anything'* (p. 177, emphasis in original).

Despite this display of filial piety, Roth's thoughts about his father in this scene and others are coloured by Oedipal conflict. Citing Freud's theory of 'the primal horde of sons who ... have it in them to nullify the father by force', Roth identifies himself as another kind of son, 'from the horde that can't throw a punch': 'When we lay waste, ... it isn't with raging fists ... but with our words' (p. 159). And his words, his weapons, Roth recognises, in a further twist of the Freudian paradigm, are part of his paternal legacy. 'He taught me the vernacular. He *was* the vernacular, unpoetic and expressive and point-blank, with all the vernacular's glaring limitations and all its durable force' (p. 181, emphasis in original).

The father is, then, the source of the son's creative power, yet this recognition does not seem to trigger a Bloom-style patricidal anxiety of influence. For all its unsparing display of his privacy, the portrait of Herman Roth reads not as an act of violation but of respect. Fearing an absolute autonomy – in the penultimate passage Roth dreams of himself as 'a small, fatherless evacuee' unwilling 'to be expelled' (p. 237) from the body of the dead father (the father displaces the mother in this fantasy birth) – the son presents his memoir in the final lines of the narrative as a restoration of filial relation in obedience to paternal law:

The dream [of having buried his father in the wrong clothes] was telling me that, if not in my books or in my life, at least in my dreams I would live perennially as his little son, with the conscience of a little son, just as he would remain alive there not only as my father but as *the* father, sitting in judgment on whatever I do.
    You must not forget anything.   (pp. 237–8, emphasis in original)

By repeating here the command he formulated earlier in the episode in which he observes his father's penis, Roth enhances its phallic authority: the son is under his father's orders to write this 'unseemly' book!

I want to return to the episode of the shit because it poses so starkly the ethical dilemmas of life writing. The father's position is absolutely clear: 'Don't tell the children', and the son replies, 'I won't tell anyone' (p. 176). Yet Roth not only persists in publishing these private things, but even seeks to put an obedient face on this act of disobedience. Thus for the paternal command – 'don't tell' – he substitutes another of his own design – 'You must not forget anything' – which he attributes ultimately to '*the* father, sitting in judgment on whatever I do' (p. 238). Which command should be observed? Should fidelity to the truth of the son's experience take precedence over the father's right to privacy?

To obey the father, to omit the episode of the shit, is to deny the son the climax of his story, by which I mean not only the rhetorical narrative he is writing but also the psychological narrative of identity formation it recounts. 'His story'? Is not there a legitimate sense, as *Patrimony* boldly asserts, in which the episode of the shit is inextricably relational, belonging at once to father and son alike? Or does the episode merely confirm our misgivings about life writing of any kind, prompting us to recognise that the confessional drive behind life writing that draws us to it – our desire to penetrate the mystery of another person – may also constitute its primary ethical flaw? Philippe Lejeune formulates the issue precisely when he observes, 'In confessing ourselves we inevitably confess those who have shared our life intimately . . . The attack on private life, which the law condemns, is the very basis of autobiographical writing' ('L'atteinte', p. 17). When Roth claims his father's shit as his 'patrimony', he calls on us, in effect, to acknowledge that the circumstances of relational identity challenge our familiar notions of privacy and ownership.

'Really, universally, relations stop nowhere', Henry James observed, 'and the exquisite problem of the artist is eternally but to draw, by a geometry of his own, the circle within which they shall happily *appear* to do so' (pp. 171–2, emphasis in original). James was referring to the problem of closure in the novel, but the comment applies with equal point to the dilemma of the ethicist who would draw the circle within which the individual is sacrosanct and may not be touched. If our identities and lives are more entangled with those of others than we tend to acknowledge in the culture of individualism, then existing models of privacy, personhood, and ethics may have to be revised. I would be the first to admit, however, that this is easier said than done, for in questioning the boundaries that secure the rights of individual subjects we may undermine the boundaries that define the moral responsibilities of those who write about them. I take heart, nonetheless, in Roth's brave negotiation of the difficulties posed by relational identity, in the seemliness of his practice of the 'unseemly' profession.

❖❖

8

The patient writes back
Bioethics and the illness narrative

❖❖

JOHN WILTSHIRE

About 1960, let us say, bioethics began to emerge as a specific intellectual practice; and from about the same time narratives by patients began to be published in increasing numbers. The argument of this chapter is that these narratives of illness, in which I include the writings of both patients and care-givers, expose some weaknesses of the discipline of bioethics as now usually understood; and furthermore that this genre of writing is a stronger domain of ethical thinking about medical experience than its officially sanctioned twin. The emergence of bioethics is commonly dated to the invention of the kidney dialysis machine, the problems of deciding access to this expensive technology that ensued, and the era of 'biomedicine' it initiated. The illness narrative, sometimes called the 'pathography',[1] a more or less

---

[1] The currency of the term 'pathography' probably originates with Oliver Sacks. In the preface to *The Man Who Mistook His Wife for a Hat* (1985), he writes that Hippocrates introduced the notion of disease as a historical or narrative event, 'the case history, a description, or depiction, of the natural history of disease – precisely expressed by the old word "pathography"' (p. ix). Anne Hunsaker Hawkins has extended the term to cover not just the history of a *disease*, but the history of an *illness* (the one being a medical diagnosis, the other the ill person's experience): *Reconstructing Illness: Studies in Pathography* (West Lafayette, 1993). Like Arthur Frank, who writes that 'to call people's stories "pathographies" places them under the authority of the medical gaze', I prefer the term 'illness narrative' (Arthur W. Frank, *The Wounded Storyteller: Body, Illness and Ethics* (Chicago and London, 1995), pp. 190–1). Sometimes here I use 'pathography' as shorthand for 'the narrative of illness experience written by a patient or care-giver'. For the illness/disease distinction, see Arthur Kleinman, *Social Origins of Distress and Disease, Depression, Neurasthenia and Pain in Modern China* (New

contemporaneous development – though examples before this era can certainly be found – results, I suggest, out of the same challenges. In both pathography and bioethics, argument and narrative intertwine, each dependent on the other.

For unlike traditional medical ethics, bioethics relies extensively upon storytelling. The typical biomedical handbook will display an array of case histories, different from the cases in the texts of earlier mainstream medicine in that they have a clearly definable plot and conflict, and even 'characters', the patient and his or her family.[2] The social status and religious belief of the protagonist may perhaps be indicated, the family constellation sketched; the doctor might be presented, the anxieties of his conscience briefly touched in. Almost certainly, the case will centre around a crisis of treatment and will pose a dilemma. Can a mentally retarded fourteen-year-old be asked to donate a kidney to his brilliant but dying sister? Should the doctor tell the patient about his malignant tumour, despite intense pressure to conceal the truth from the patient's wife? Should a bank manager who persists in claiming that he is dying of a brain cancer that all tests prove absent be removed without his consent to an insane asylum?:[3] and so on.

But if one's interest is caught by the subjects' predicaments in these often harrowing sketches, one is bound ultimately to be disappointed, for these stories are truncated, aborted at the point of crisis. One rarely learns the outcome of the case, or the sufferer's fate, and one realises that this is because these patient figures, though fashioned to arrest the reader's transient sympathy, are only there for the sake of the issues, the options for treatment that are the consequences of their plight. Distinguishing

Haven and London, 1986), pp. 144–8.
[2] For example, Tom L. Beauchamp and James F. Childress, *Principles of Medical Ethics*, 3rd edition (New York and Oxford, 1989), contains thirty-five case-studies (pp. 400–54) which are continually referred to throughout the text. Another standard handbook is Robert M. Veach, *Case Studies in Medical Ethics* (Cambridge, Mass., and London, 1977). A more 'popular' presentation, Ruth Macklin, *Mortal Choices, Bioethics in Today's World* (New York, 1987) argues throughout with case-narrative examples. An exception to my remarks about the patient's disappearance is Alastair V. Campbell and Roger Higgs, *In That Case, Medical Ethics in Everyday Practice* (London, 1982), which dramatises its central ethical contention of respect for the patient by presenting its (more than commonly convincing) narrative examples from the point of view of different healthcare professionals and then giving the patient's own voice and opinions.
[3] K. W. M. Fulford, *Medical History and Medical Practice* (Cambridge, 1989), pp. x–xi.

features, details, and idiosyncrasies that might impede these patients from functioning as representatives are strictly rationed. Whilst the function of these vignettes is to represent ethical dilemmas, they are always thus ultimately configured as dilemmas of treatment, so that in bioethics the site of ethical anxiety, and of true personhood, is the medical professional. These texts are commonly directed to a medical or medical-student audience, of course: but the fact remains that the narrative orientation is in conflict with biomedicine's avowed concern with what is often described as the patient's 'autonomy', the putative ascription to the patient of the power of choice and decision-making. A question to pose is whether such abstract narratives can ever function effectively as the teaching instrument of an ethics worthy of the name. Representations of complex and painful situations that, typically, minimise setting and ignore the constraints of time, may fit within a certain conception of ethical thought, but this conception may itself be impoverished.

At more or less the same historical moment when bioethics burgeoned, another form of medical narrative came into flower. Many hundreds of books have been published since the 1960s giving articulate, often finely wrought, accounts of medical and clinical experience from the client's point of view.[4] Like bioethics, this genre of narrative gives central status to the recipient of medical attention. A 'pathography' in the contemporary sense is an autobiographical narrative, sometimes written by the patient, and often by their nurse – husband, lover, wife or daughter. To extend the genre's range beyond the personal narrative of the individual patient is important. To do this is in part to recognise, as Eric Cassell puts it, that 'the boundaries of illness are poorly defined'.[5] Sickness tends to draw in others, the designated patient's care-givers and family, and to have destructive effects on their bodies and lives. To include narratives by care-givers as authentic contributions to the understanding of illness experience

[4] I use the word 'client' here as a useful shorthand for 'patient and his or her relatives and care-givers'. In general, the term *client*, as Michael Taussig argues, 'serves to mystify relations of inequality within the medical encounter, preserving professional dominance whilst at the same time producing a fiction of patient autonomy' (Robert Barrett, *The Psychiatric Team and the Social Definition of Schizophrenia* (Cambridge, 1996), p. 60, footnote, referring to M. T. Taussig, 'Reification and the Consciousness of the Patient', *Social Science and Medicine*, 14 (1980), section B, pp. 3–13.

[5] Eric Cassell, *The Healer's Art* (1976; Cambridge, Mass., 1985), p. 37.

is also to set up a alternative model of the biomedical, for it puts into question one of the cardinal principles of clinical practice – the focus on a single diseased organism.

The illness narrative, unlike the biomedical narrative, is reflective, situational, emotional, detailed (often to the point of extreme and saga-like length). Based on the diary or journal, it takes the form of a memoir and is dedicated to the inscription and celebration of one unique human life. Pathography is not devoted to ethics as a distinct professional practice, but, as I shall argue, it necessarily confronts ethical – or perhaps it would be better to say moral – questions. As Robert and Peggy Stinson write in their important *The Long Dying of Baby Andrew* (1983), 'We present the ethical problems which concern us as part of an unfolding personal story, not because we welcome the abandonment of our own privacy, but because that is where the ethical dilemmas occur: inextricably embedded in the lives of real people.'[6] The illness narrative poses ethical questions in a guise that makes them a valuable resource for the pondering of those issues that are, typically, specified, isolated, and addressed in abstract form in bioethical debate.[7] 'Inextricably embedded' ethical delemmas may be: but it is the amalgam of participation with observation and detachment that gives the patient narrative its edge.

Modern pathographers often seek to criticise or scrutinise their encounters with medical professionals (as in such a well-known example as Oliver Sacks's *A Leg to Stand On* (1984)) and simultaneously to explore those aspects of 'patienthood' and the body about which medicine itself is silent. Gillian Rose, whose surgery, as she declares, has been practised for centuries, finds no depiction of it from the patient's point of view, and therefore needs 'to invent colostomy ethnography'.[8] The illness narrative always contains some measure of critique: it relates the patient's or care-giver's experience, but it also compares this with modern medicine's modes of understanding. Barbara Creaturo's *Courage*

---

[6] Robert W. Stinson and Peggy Stinson, *The Long Dying of Baby Andrew* (Boston, Toronto, 1983), p. xiii.

[7] Paul A. Komesaroff, 'From Bioethics to Microethics: Ethical Debate and Clinical Medicine' in Paul A. Komesaroff, ed., *Troubled Bodies: Critical Perspectives on Postmodernism, Medical Ethics and the Body* (Ithaca, 1995), pp. 62–86. I am indebted to Dr. Komesaroff's thinking throughout this chapter.

[8] Gillian Rose, *Love's Work* (London, 1995), pp. 86–7.

(1991) for example, subtitled 'the testimony of a cancer patient', is an account of the impact upon one individual searching for treatment of the ethics and protocols surrounding the randomised control trial.[9] Part of Creaturo's story concerns the devastating recognition that the priorities of medical researchers are very different from her own. *The Long Dying of Baby Andrew* focusses more explicitly on the ethics of decision-making: in this case whether to withhold or 'aggressively' carry out treatment on a very premature infant. The flood of AIDS narratives more recently deals inevitably with the incursions of public health into the recesses of private life, as also with questions of personal loyalty and betrayal.[10] These are clear-cut examples: but it can be more generally suggested that the illness narrative, by the nature of its material, is, like bioethics, constrained to deal with moral issues.

So, after 1960,[11] these two new narrative forms emerge. Both pathography and bioethics centre, at least nominally, on the patient, the sufferer, the recipient of medical care. Both, it seems reasonable to suppose, owe their circulation to new conditions in the medical world, to the technologisation of medicine, that objectifying of the body commonly referred to as 'the medical gaze',[12] as well as the constraints imposed on the clinical interaction by governmentality and law. One might say that bioethics has come into being through the need for the older medical ethics, in which the leading belief was in the doctor's benevolent duty to care for and protect his patient ('do no harm'), to be reconciled with a newer injunction, legally mediated and enforced in many instances, for patients' rights as democratic subjects to be respected. Much bioethical discussion in fact is concerned with the struggle between these two principles or 'models' of the patient/physician

---

[9] Barbara Creaturo, *Courage: The Testimony of a Cancer Patient* (New York, 1991), p. 211.

[10] Examples are Paul Monette, *Borrowed Time* (New York, 1988), John Foster, *Take Me to Paris, Johnny* (Melbourne, 1993), and Christopher Coe, *Such Times* (London, 1993).

[11] I emphasise this is a schematic date: one might rather trace a gradual increase in the number of such publications, including, for example, Denton Welch's posthumous *A Voice Through A Cloud* (1950) and Grace Stuart's *A Private World of Pain* (1953), through to the present.

[12] See, for example, David Armstrong, *The Political Economy of the Body: Medical Knowledge in Britain in the Twentieth Century* (Cambridge, 1983), and David Silverman, *Communication and Medical Practice: Social Relations in the Clinic* (London, 1987).

relationship, beneficence and autonomy, or paternalism and agency, and with the conflicting courses of action that adherence to different principles seem to require.

A leading authority on bioethics, Tristram Engelhardt, defines its overall project as 'an endeavor to look at reasons and to determine what reasons should be credited by impartial, unprejudiced, nonculturally biased reasoners, whose only interests are in the consistency and force of rational argument'. Engelhardt adds that such a goal cannot, of course, be fully achieved, but that bioethics 'can at least make progress by providing some tentative answers, and by suggesting why some resolutions of moral questions are better than others in terms of consistency, scope, and strength of possible rational justification'.[13] I cannot make here a comprehensive critique of bioethics, which, in any case, takes many different forms and comes to a great range of conclusions,[14] but this broad conception of ethical inquiry, with its emphasis on a rationality closely linked to impartiality and the absence of bias, its segregation of reason from feeling and intuition, and its pursuit of consistency, is open to a range of criticisms that have emerged in recent years from ethical philosophers, and notably from Martha Nussbaum.

In *Love's Knowledge* (1990),[15] Nussbaum has offered sustained arguments about the limitations of 'rational' solutions to problems of moral choice, and an explication of an alternative, Aristotelian conception of the moral enterprise. Nussbaum argues that values are not qualitatively homogeneous, and are indeed incommensurate one with another, that particular instances are conceptually prior to general rules, and that the emotions are crucial instruments of ethical response and perception. Paraphrasing Aristotle's remark that 'the judgment rests with perception', she adds that 'the subtleties of a complex ethical situation must be seized in a confrontation with the situation itself, by a faculty that is suited to address it as a complex whole' (p. 69). Nussbaum turns to literature, and particularly the novel, for instantiation of these contentions. 'The content of rational choice must be supplied by

[13] Tristram Engelhardt, *Foundations of Bioethics* (New York, 1986), p. 10.
[14] See Roslyn Diprose, 'Biomedical Ethics and Lived, Sexed Bodies' in *The Bodies of Women: Ethics, Embodiment and Sexual Difference* (London and New York, 1995), pp. 102–30.
[15] Martha Nussbaum, *Love's Knowledge: Essays on Philosophy and Literature* (New York and Oxford, 1990). Subsequent references will be given in the main text.

nothing less messy than experience and stories of experience', she declares (p. 74).[16] She makes not the weak claim, that novels illustrate ethical issues, or demonstrate situations of moral choice, but the strong claim that 'novels and their style . . . are an ineliminable part of moral philosophy' (p. 49).

I take my lead from Nussbaum. As novels to formal philosophy in her argument, so pathography to bioethics in mine. In part this is to suggest that the body of work I have been describing is an immense untapped resource for the pondering of medical ethics.[17] Illness narratives do not merely describe the experiences of patients and those who, as care-givers, are intimately involved with their histories; nor do they merely involve the reader emotionally in the experiences they present, offering an exercise in moral choice by proxy. They instantiate and develop an ethics that is, in most respects, more complex, more adequate to the real dilemmas of choice as they are experienced within the turbulent and demanding conditions of medical crisis than do bioethical case-studies. Many illness narratives offer strong arguments for what Bernard Williams has called 'a reason beyond reason', for non-'rational' ways of deciding ethical issues 'as both genuinely rational and superior in richness and value'.[18] These arguments are commonly implicit, since they are not to be made apart from the particular situations, settings, and personal relations that constitute their provocation, but quite often they rise to explicitness, and they touch on all the main issues isolated by, and subject to technical discussion, in bioethics. By their necessary focus on the patient, pathographies enact what bioethics merely claims to do: give substance to notions of the patient's independence and autonomy.

[16] The word 'messy' recalls Bakhtin, whom Nussbaum never mentions. In general her commentary on the novel's presentation of moral issues has much in common with the ethical side of Bakhtin's account of the novel's superiority as a mode of representation. M. M. Bakhtin, *The Dialogic Imagination*, ed. Michael Holquist (Austin, 1981).

[17] Rita Charon, 'Narrative Contributions to Medical Ethics, Recognition, Formulation, Interpretation, and Validation in the Practice of the Ethicist' in Edwin R. DuBose, Ronald P. Hamel and Laurence J. O'Connell, eds., *A Matter of Principles? Ferment in US Bioethics* (Valley Forge, 1994), pp. 260–83. Charon shows how narrative knowledge and practice on the medical professional's behalf can contribute to 'the search for the meanings of singular human situations' (p. 260). Narrative can contribute 'substantially to the trustworthiness of biomedical ethics' (p. 278), an ethicist with narrative competence may transform the medical gaze (p. 279), but the narratives of patients are not specifically considered.

[18] Nussbaum, *Love's Knowledge*, p. 60.

More importantly, since the pathographer is entrammelled in a predicament, and, like the novelist, is devoted to the particular, he or she is able to give substance to the full complexity of moral choice. So my argument is that some pathographies are essential works of bioethics; and it parallels Nussbaum's claim that 'certain novels are, irreplaceably, works of moral philosophy' (p. 148).

Bioethics, then, isolates and simplifies situations in order to pursue its (non-Aristotelian) notion of 'rational' choice. Devoted to the establishment of rules to govern conduct and to alleviate the anxieties of professionals faced with intractable situations, it seeks to isolate principles as a guidance for action. In order for this to work, and for its cases to give sufficient lodgment to the broad issues that it develops, its narratives must be sufficiently broad, open and non-particularised. Its specification of the material itself dictates the form of the possible outcome.[19] Within the pathography, on the other hand, particular settings – personal and family relations, religious and cultural affiliation, geographical and spatial confines – always exert considerable pressure. Bioethics routinely alters setting and culture, supposing that this leaves the 'essential' aspects of the case untouched. 'Details have been changed to protect the anonymity of the patient': this disclaimer, so common in this form of writing, discloses bioethics' unawareness of how apparently incidental detail may actually structure, or provide the key, to a patient's experience. Imagine, for example, what a difference would be made if the subject of Philip Roth's illness narrative, *Patrimony* (1991), his father, became – to safeguard the patient's privacy – a Presbyterian rather than a Jew.

'Pathographies' are not novels, though many of the most instructive are written by novelists (in citing *Patrimony* I want to suggest one can throw the net wide). Yet it can be argued that some at least of the value Nussbaum finds in 'literature' and something of that mode of illumination that novelists may bring to bear on the moral life can be discovered in works that are less inclusive in their form, more hampered by responsibility, than works of imaginative fiction. Few illness narratives have the 'complex and mysterious construction, full of indefiniteness and obliquity, periphrasis and indirection' that Nussbaum discerns in *The Golden Bowl*, and that sometimes seems for her to be the only

---

[19] Komesaroff, 'From Bioethics to Microethics' p. 65.

adequate vehicle for a fully Aristotelian moral consciousness. Moreover, they are bound by their acceptance of the autobiographical pact.[20] But they certainly contain some elements that approximate to, or perform equivalent roles to, the novelist's complexity of description. Often, for example, they include material that suggests plurality of viewpoints, radically distinct conceptualisations of the illness condition, and play off their narrator's thoughts against constructions of his or her situation from other, principally medical, sources.[21] Both the autobiographical form of pathography and its occasional recourse to heteroglossia make it distinct from the formal expositional structures common to ethical discourse. Accepting the contraints of 'authenticity', many pathographies, I suggest, achieve not only ethically pertinent discussion, but a critique of bioethics itself.

'Death', to recall Samuel Johnson's phrase, 'concentrates the mind wonderfully.' Most illness narratives are written under the pressure of moral dilemmas and personal anguish. Caught within a situation, and often within events that move too quickly for meditation or considered decision-making, the pathographer attempts, in his or her journal, or retrospectively, to rescue the semblance of moral being. He or she strives to see what really happened, what it would have been right to do, what attitude it was proper to take up towards themselves or the sick person, in circumstances that scarcely permitted balance or detachment, and in which all courses would have been, in some measure, wrong. They realise how disconcertingly sickness transforms the self, and how crisis cascading into crisis can take from one all sense of power. How then can one believe oneself a person capable of choice? This sense of being immersed, if not drowned, in a situation in which loyalties and love are tested to the utmost is definitive of the pathography, and it is this perhaps that most sharply marks it off from the bioethical narrative. Time becomes crucial: both structurated by events beyond one's control, and moving with a roller-coaster dizziness.[22]

---

[20] Philippe Lejeune, *On Autobiography* (1975) foreword by Paul John Eakin, trans. Katherine Leary (Minneapolis, 1989), ch. 1, 'The Autobiographical Pact'.
[21] John Wiltshire, 'Beyond the Ouija Board: Dialogue and Heteroglossia in the Medical Narrative', *Literature and Medicine*, 13.2 (1994), pp. 211–28.
[22] Ronald Frankenberg, '"Your Time or Mine?" An Anthropological View of the Tragic Temporal Contradictions of Biomedical Practice', *International Journal of Health Service*, 18.1 (1988), pp. 11–34, pp. 21–2.

The writer of the illness narrative's immersion in the dilemmas of medical experience, the pressure of circumstances, is one source of the genre's ethical power. Yet it might well be countered that there are obviously limitations to this from a philosophical perspective. Immersion and helplessness might just as well give rise to distortion and hysteria, rather than the tempered balance, the thoughtful search after justice that we may have a right to expect from ethically enlightening texts. Certainly there are pathographies, even considerable ones, that are full of caricatured medical personnel, despair, and unreflective rage.[23] I can illustrate my claim about the genre's moral authority by considering two pathographies that combine representation of crisis with reflection and critique – one, a little-known illness narrative, the other a classic text. Both, as it happens, are written not by ill persons, but by their wives, which does mean that their agenda is different from the patient-authored text. Such writers are a kind of participant-observer of the illness experience, standing with the physician outside the illness and yet (through identification) sharing with the patient. The patient's own illness narrative will present issues differently, yet these two texts will serve to demonstrate what some of them are.

Gerda Lerner's *A Death of One's Own* (1979),[24] widely read on its publication, now almost forgotten, has many other features that make it typical of the genre, not least its heteroglossaic play between journal entries and poems written at the time of the events, and retrospective, reflective commentary. It is the record of a pact that in practice is impossible to carry out. It thus subjects ethical reasoning to the test of contingency. Like Simone de Beauvoir's *A Very Easy Death* (1963), which I shall consider in turn, it records how ideas formulated in the obliviousness of good health are challenged by the disintegrating body and the consciousness of imminent death. It is deeply preoccupied with one issue that has historically been an urgent one in medical ethics: one commentator speaks of it as 'what is quaintly called "telling the truth"'.[25] Both

---

[23] Two striking examples are Martha Weinman Lear, *Heartsounds: The Story of a Love and Loss*, (New York, 1980), and Bryce Courtenay, *April Fool's Day: A Modern Tragedy* (Melbourne, 1993).

[24] Gerda Lerner, *A Death of One's Own* (New York, 1979). Subsequent page references will be given in the main text.

[25] L. G. Henderson, quoted in Beauchamp and Childress, *Principles of Medical Ethics*, p. 213.

books are concerned with the inflection of that issue brought about by the advent of new therapies and techniques: how far does one embark on these strategies for the preservation of life that may be, after all, unavailing? How far is being persuaded by the opportunities of medical technology a surrender of one's most ethical being?

Lerner and her husband, a successful film editor, have discussed death and dying many times, and vowed that they will never allow either one of them to be reduced to the condition of patients they have seen in a hospital intensive care unit, kept alive on machines. When Carl Lerner is diagnosed with an inoperable brain tumour, his wife resolves, too, that they will not allow the illness to separate them: her husband will be cared for and nursed at home. But after surgery, when the tumour is discovered, husband and wife are already divided: 'We battled on separate battlefields, each very much alone. Mine: to prepare myself for his death, to help him die a good death. His: to live' (p. 49). Carl radiates confidence and strength, charming the staff with his wit and verve, but his wife has been told that he probably has no more than six months to live. He refuses to look her in the face.

The issue of 'telling the truth' is canvassed serially in a set of encounters with medical staff – a supervisor who urges it, doctors who advise against it, an old friend, a surgeon, who counsels that patients need hope above all, a psychoanalyst who advises just to wait. The presentation might not be out of place in a bioethics textbook, with its clear depiction of a range of options. Finally Lerner decides not to carry out the strict terms of their pact but to hold off until some prompting or question comes from her husband that intimates that he is ready for the news. This does not happen for months. Meanwhile she feels burdened by doing what she believes to be wrong. 'An enormous load of anger and bitterness began to build up inside of me. I felt I had to stand up to all the knowing experts. I had to stand alone, or almost alone, and take all the responsibility upon myself. It took me a few weeks to realise that that was exactly what was required of me. I would have to take the full responsibility for everything from here on out' (p. 56).

Eventually Carl reads the prognosis on an insurance form and accuses her of betraying him. It is a terrible moment. 'Why should I have to ask?' he says quietly (p. 143). But Lerner discovers that she has constructed the issue and the dilemma from the wrong perspective, from the point of view of the living. What can 'knowing' that you are dying mean? She reflects profoundly on this:

As long as we look at death from the shore of the living, it seems indeed, that such a fact – a man learns he is dying – should be final. For months I had thought that way about it: the problem was how to tell him, when to tell him. Once he knew, everything would change. I never asked myself how it would change. I had no experience to guide me. Once he knew, I had thought vaguely, we would be in this together and it would be easier. Like all the living, I was concerned with lessening my own pain.

In truth, there is no equality with the dying, no sharing. A man learns he will die and that moment separates him from the living. There is no way to bridge that. Yes, for the last time, he and I were sharing pain, but he would be dead and I would be alive and whatever that meant was what the next months were about. As I see it now, that 'big moment', that 'big question', was only a way-stop in the slow process of dying. That process is not yet over for me, even as these words are being written. He is dead, and I am still trying to come to terms with this fact within myself so that I can survive as a living person, not as a ghost. As would happen many times when there were decisive shifts from one stage to another, the 'decisive moment' turned out not to have been so significant after all. Carl undoubtedly 'knew' before I told him and certainly many times refused to 'know' after I told him. He was already deeply caught up in the process of dying and conscious knowledge was only a minor aspect of it. Just so it is with me now: the fact of his death, his absence, is incontrovertible. I 'know' it in many different ways and with many different modes of perception. Yet, to this day, I still do not 'know' it the way I know other facts. It shifts; it wavers – sometimes it is as true as a rock; sometimes it is as true as a bad dream. I imagine it must be that way for the dying until that final stage when they really 'know' – then they let go.   (p. 145)

This is surely an example of what Nussbaum terms 'practical wisdom': a concentrated intensity of thought, alert to qualifications, limitations, and paradoxes, yet focussed always upon the testing issue of how one ought to act, of how, indeed, to 'live'. The examination of what it means to 'know', in particular, undermines the premise upon which so much bioethics depends – that a point of view outside, and detached from, a crisis is both attainable and ethically sound.

Both the Lerners' own ethics, and the text itself, are influenced by existentialist thought. De Beauvoir's *A Very Easy Death*[26] is a

---

[26] Simone de Beauvoir, *Une Mort Très Douce*, trans. Patrick O'Brian as *A Very Easy Death* (Paris, 1983). Subsequent page references to the translation will be given in the main text.

pathography in which a rationalist philosopher and ethicist herself confronts the contingencies of the sick and dying body. Published after her mother's death in 1963, de Beauvoir's narrative is both in effect a confession that her own ethics are inadequate, and the descriptive ground upon which, perhaps, a more adequate ethics might be founded.

Françoise de Beauvoir collapses and is taken to a private hospital in Paris. Her daughter is not unduly disturbed. She remarks at the opening of the text with impeccable sang-froid: 'In spite of her frailty my mother was tough. And after all, she was of an age to die' (p. 12). And de Beauvoir does not particularly care for her mother whose conventionality, self-deception and inability to face the truth, as her daughter sees it, grate upon her nerves. When de Beauvoir sees her mother's body, naked, vulnerable, and suffering, though, all this changes. Her habitual conception, or image, of her mother has not prepared her for the violent distress that now overwhelms her. X-rays are taken and disclose cancer of the intestine. Maman is vomiting continually, and things seem to be moving swiftly towards her death.

The 'resuscitation expert', Dr N – one of the earliest appearances in the pathography of the doctor as technician – brooks no interference with his intention to prolong Maman's life at any cost:

Dr N had been working on Maman: he was going to put a tube into her nose to clean out her stomach. 'But what's the good of tormenting her, if she's dying? Let her die in peace,' said Poupette [the younger sister] in tears ... Dr N passed by me; I stopped him. White coat, white cap: a young man with an unresponsive face. 'Why this tube? Why torture Maman, since there's no hope?' He gave me a withering look. 'I am doing what has to be done.'   (p. 25)

In this, the first of several confrontations with him, de Beauvoir meets Dr N as an equal, for she has a programme, a belief, a conviction to confront his: that the relief of suffering should take precedence over the preservation of life. So far, so good: a clearcut debate, a confrontation conformable to the discourse of ethics. The doctor, here and elsewhere, shades a little into caricature.

Simone's confidence in her own beliefs is sapped by the unexpected strength of her responses to her mother's suffering body, but it is also undermined by the pressing circumstances, the 'stream of uncontrollable events'[27] and unwanted consequences, that so many patients report as their experience of the contemporary medical world. She is rung up early in the morning by her sister. The surgeon wants to try the operation since there is a chance that her mother's condition may be peritonitis, not cancer. Despite her instinctive resistance, Simone finds herself agreeing. There is no time for anything else, and no rational ground on which she can make a decision. 'At the first trial', she later comments, 'I had given in; beaten by the ethics of society, I had abjured my own. "No," Sartre said to me, "You were beaten by technique: and that was fatal"' (p. 50). But this is altogether too simple: de Beauvoir is 'beaten' by hope, and by her unadmitted and unconscious bonds.

The figure of Sartre in the background, giving advice, makes clear the underlying theoretical narrative. The operation has been performed; a huge cancer has been discovered, Maman is still alive and Dr N is triumphant:

Maman was sleeping, lying flat on her back, her face the colour of wax, her nose pinched, her mouth open . . . I went home. I talked to Sartre. We played some Bartók. Suddenly, at eleven, an outburst of tears that almost degenerated into hysteria.

Amazement. When my father died I did not cry at all. I had said to my sister, 'It will be the same for Maman.' I had understood all my sorrows until that night: even when they flowed over my head I recognised myself in them. This time my despair escaped from my control: someone other than myself was weeping in me [*d'autre chose que moi pleurait en moi*]. I talked to Sartre about my mother's mouth as I had seen it that morning and about everything I had interpreted in it – greediness refused, an almost servile humility, hope, distress, loneliness – the loneliness of her life and of her death – that did not want to admit its existence. And he told me that my own mouth was not obeying me any more: I had put Maman's mouth on my own face and in spite of myself, I copied its movements. Her whole person, her whole being, was concentrated there, and compassion wrung my heart. (pp. 27–8)

The incoherent syntax, at one moment ascribing will, at another passivity, to the speaking subject, reproduces that ossilation between merging and separation that is the troubled position of the participant observer. This is a resonant moment, a personal but also an epistemological crisis. Alistair MacIntyre writes, 'To say to

---

[27] Stinson and Stinson, *The Long Dying of Baby Andrew*, p. 211.

oneself or to someone else "Doubt all your beliefs here and now" without reference to historical or autobiographical context is not meaningless; but it is an invitation not to philosophy, but to mental breakdown, or rather to philosophy as a means of mental breakdown. Descartes concealed from himself ... an unacknowledged background of beliefs that rendered what he was doing sane and intelligible to himself and to others. But suppose he had put that background in question too – what would have happened to him then?' MacIntyre goes on to illustrate what he means by complete epistemological breakdown with a passage that he describes as 'Hume's cry of pain',[28] in which Hume writes, 'I ... begin to fancy myself in the most deplorable condition imaginable, inviron'd with the deepest darkness and utterly deprived of the use of every member and faculty.'

De Beauvoir's collapse, as represented and mediated by her text, can more accurately than Hume's be described as 'a cry of pain'. Its significance is signalled by the presence of the man with whom she has, as a philosopher, fashioned her life's work, and whose philosophy, above all others, is based on freedom, and lauds the power of the individual, the autonomous, subject to shape and determine her own life. In Mary Warnock's paraphrase of Sartre's thought: 'It is certainly true that I cannot choose entirely what I am or who my parents were or how strong I am. What I can choose is my reaction to my facticity.'[29] At this moment in de Beauvoir's life it is just this claim that is annulled: her 'facticity' prohibits any choice. Cassell writes, 'The intensity of ties to the family cannot be over-emphasised; people often behave as though they were physical extensions of their parents.'[30] In Simone's response to her mother, the body speaks, and that entails the overthrow of the premises on which she has founded her understanding of herself, for it was the immanent body that she sought always to subdue. It is not simply a crisis of physiology, since here physiology forces entry into the symbolic order, and hysteria becomes a signifying medium. This, then, is not a dialectical but a dialogic critique of existentialist ethics – one that forces one form

---

28 Alasdair MacIntyre, 'Epistemological Crises, Dramatic Narrative, and the Philosophy of Science' in Stanley G. Clarke and Evan Simpson, eds., *Anti-Theory in Ethics and Moral Conservativism* (New York, 1989), pp. 241–61, pp. 250–1.

29 Mary Warnock, *Existentialism*, (Oxford, 1970), p. 123.

30 Eric Cassell, 'The Nature of Suffering and the Goals of Medicine', *New England Journal of Medicine* (1982).

of knowledge against another.[31] It is the epistemological crisis that puts not the beliefs but the whole 'background' of beliefs into question. It challenges not only her specific beliefs, but that rationality upon which those beliefs are founded.

The doctors lie to Françoise de Beauvoir about her condition, as 80 per cent of doctors do (or did),[32] and the daughters are caught up in the deception. Maman is persuaded to believe she has peritonitis:

She raised one finger, and, with a certain pride, whispered. 'Not appendicitis. Pe-re-ton-it-is.' She added. 'What luck ... be here.'
'You are glad that I am here?'
'No. Me.' Peritonitis; and her being in this clinic had saved her! The betrayal was beginning. 'Glad not to have that tube! So glad.' (p. 40)

Who is being 'betrayed'? Maman: for she is being deluded, persuaded that she can get well again; Simone, for she has abandoned her own convictions by not allowing her mother knowledge of her impending death. Once again, the confusion of pronouns marks both merging and separation. 'Despairingly, I suffered a transgression that was mine without my being responsible for it and one that I could never expiate' (p. 51): the unequivocally theological language is only one indication of the strain this experience is putting on Simone's explicit philosophy, and the moral desolation this entails. In defiance of Sartre's advice, she finds that she must do things that are meaningless. 'Why attribute such importance to a moment since there would be no memory?' he asks with innocently rational brutality. 'There would not be any atonement either' (p. 55).

One increasingly needs to have recourse to some notion like Merleau-Ponty's 'intercorporeality' to understand what is being represented. For it seems that Simone rediscovers herself in her mother and expresses, speaks, both for herself and for her mother. Like Michael Ignatieff's more recent *Scar Tissue* (1994), in which a philosopher addresses his own fears of the loss of memory amidst his mother's decline into Alzheimer's disease, this memoir is an exemplar. It suggests how an illness experience breaks up the hard autonomous shell of the subject: the human person is more than a rational transcendent being, and de

---

[31] Bakhtin, *The Dialogic Imagination, passim.*
[32] Veach, *Case Studies in Medical Ethics*, pp. 144, 444.

Beauvoir's denial of this returns to afflict her. It also shows how a pathographic narrative may undermine the assumptions of bioethics. *A Very Easy Death* not only displays this process of undermining, descriptively, phenomenologically, but also, since the subject is a philosopher, entails an accompanying critique of a philosophy based upon the essential liberty of the agent. 'In general', writes Engelhardt, 'physicians and patients meet as free individuals.'[33] On the contrary, as these illness narratives suggest, being a care-giver or relative, as well as a patient, is to be in a state of impaired, and contingent, subjectivity. Only in the ideal and empty space of bioethics, de Beauvoir's text suggests, does this freedom exist.

A Very Easy Death is not consciously a critique of that ethics, of course, which as an institutional practice hardly existed at that period. Nor does de Beauvoir abandon either ethics or philosophy. Her text is itself a work of ethical reflection – as well as one of mourning. And if one were to bring 'pathography' to bear upon bioethical debate, one would have to admit that such narratives are, and always must be, anecodotal evidence. This would also be precisely the point: in the realm of ethics, as the narrative reliance of bioethics seems to glimpse, there never can be any other evidence. W. D. Ross in *The Right and the Good* writes that the 'sense of our particular duty in particular circumstances, preceded and informed by the fullest reflection we can bestow on the act in all its bearings, is highly fallible, but it is the only guide we have to our duty' and he quotes that aphorism of Aristotle of which Nussbaum is also so fond: 'the decision rests with perception'.[34] Perhaps, then, illness narratives give us access to that micro-ethical domain of patient experience, that end-point of ethical rumination at which only perception can decide. Can we think indeed about bioethical issues with any pertinence without thinking as intently as possible of real persons in specific situations? What might follow from this is that the enhancement of bioethics depends upon the enhancement of the narrative tools upon which its discourse depends.

Pathography might also be thought of as a means of furthering the programme of a phenomenologically orientated critique of biomedicine, presented, for example, by Drew Leder – a critique consonant with feminist 're-readings' that affirm the previously

[33] Engelhardt, *Foundations of Bioethics*, p. 278.   [34] (Oxford, 1930), p. 42.

pathologised to be culturally produced.[35] But a phenomenological approach to 'the body' shares with the Cartesian medical assumptions which it attacks a tendency to focus on the body in its singleness. Despite its nominal attention to the life-world, this version of phenomenology obeys the imperatives of the wider philosophical tradition in which it is articulated, and is constantly drawn towards framing the experience of 'the body' as if it were only the experience of one, monadic, body. Pathography, because it usually tells a story, and has a plot, however simple, is concerned also inevitably with relations between patients, caregivers, and doctors, and between the sufferer and the wider medical, healthcare, and cultural world. Moreover, narrative is the only discursive form that can adequately represent those contingencies of time that play such a crucial role in all of the crises and dilemmas of illness experience. This focus, both upon the lived body and upon the lived body's relatedness in time, defines the new genre of pathography, and distinguishes it from the new bioethical narratives of biomedicine.

[35] Drew Leder, 'A Tale of Two Bodies: The Cartesian Corpse and the Lived Body' in Drew Leder, ed., *The Body in Medical Thought and Practice* (Dordrecht), pp. 17–35.

PART III

Politics and ethics

❖❖

9

Literature, power, and the recovery of philosophical ethics

❖❖

C. A. J. COADY AND SEUMAS MILLER

One of the striking features of contemporary literary theory, and indeed cultural studies more generally, is what might be termed its socio-politicisation of the ethical. Literary texts, traditionally viewed as repositories of moral and aesthetic insight or challenge, tend now to be seen as predominantly ideological constructions, or sites of power struggles between social forces of various kinds. Individuals and individual actions are treated as wholly explicable in terms of impersonal social forces locked in political conflict. We are urged to see ourselves as 'docile bodies', and to view 'creative' literary output as simply evidential of impersonal social power struggles.

In what follows we will not directly concern ourselves with literature but with certain understandings of the social and political domains. Our aim is first of all to clarify the nature of social and political action and thereby to free it from some of the confusions to which its interpretation can be prone (this will be the primary task of Miller's section of the chapter) and second, to illustrate, in Coady's section, the complexities of ethical thinking about social and political realites by examining two relatively unexplored 'moral situations', those of compromise and extrication, each of which shows some of the ways in which moral reasoning and practical necessity can and should complement each other.

Socio-political action: a theoretical framework
(Seumas Miller)

Much of the theoretical – as opposed to political – impetus for the process of the socio-politicisation of the ethical in the writings of literary and cultural theorists derives from two tendencies. Firstly, there is the tendency to operate with an insufficiently differentiated notion of social action. All action is seen as social, indeed, all action tends to be viewed as constituted by social realities. This tendency derives from the abandonment of substantive notions of the self; the self is conceived simply as a social construction. Thus Roger Fowler asserts that 'a real person can be seen, as the social psychologist sees him, as a construction of roles acquired through the process of socialisation'.[1]

Secondly, there is the tendency to become fixated with the power dimension of social action; social action is taken to be principally action driven by socio-political forces. Again this tendency derives from the rejection of the substantive self. Thus Foucault: 'The individual which power has constituted is at the same time its vehicle.'[2]

The net result of these two tendencies is that human action is understood only in terms of power struggles. Socio-political power turns out not simply to be one dimension of human action, but rather to be wholly constitutive of it.

This result ought to be rejected, and the twin tendencies that lead to it, strongly resisted. I have argued against these tendencies elsewhere.[3] Here I will present a replacement conception. By contrast with the tendency to conceive of all action as social, there is a need for (a) distinctions to be made between social action and other sorts of action of a non-social sort, and (b) clarification of the concept of social action itself.

Regarding (a), I will briefly characterise non-social – in the sense of not necessarily social – action types under the following headings: (a) individual; (b) natural; and (c) interpersonal. I do not pretend to offer adequate accounts of each of these action types. My concern is merely to draw attention to distinctions that will

[1] Roger Fowler, *Linguistics and the Novel* (London, 1977), p. 128.
[2] Michel Foucault, 'Two Lectures' in *Power/Knowledge: Selected Interviews and Other Writings, 1972–1977*, ed. C. Gordon (Brighton, 1980), p. 98.
[3] Seumas Miller and Richard Freadman, *Re-thinking Theory: A Critique of Contemporary Literary Theory and an Alternative Account* (Cambridge, 1992).

serve my purposes in this chapter. Moreover, an action may fall under more than one heading.

An individual action is one performed by an individual and such that it involves no essential reference to other persons, and is therefore non-social. Thus going for a walk for exercise, taking a shower to cool down on a hot day, are instances of non-social individual actions.

A natural action is that which one performs in virtue simply of needs and dispositions one has in virtue of being a member of the human species as distinct from, say, some social group. Examples of such actions would be eating and drinking.

An interpersonal action is an action directed to some other person *qua* particular person – as opposed to *qua* member of some social group or *qua* physical obstruction. Typically acts of friendship would be interpersonal acts in this sense, but institutional acts of conferring degrees, or conforming to conventions of dress, would not be.

None of the above categories – individual, natural and interpersonal – is reducible to social action. Accordingly, and contrary to much contemporary literary theorising, human action is not necessarily social action. This claim is entirely consistent with the fact that there are very few actions which are not *in some sense* social. There is a distinction to be made between actions that are *constitutively* social, and actions which are social in some other senses. Roughly speaking, the notion of a constitutively social action is the notion of an action the social dimension of which makes it the action that it is; its social properties *wholly* define it. It is a matter of controversy whether there are in fact any actions which are constitutively social in this sense. Candidates for being constitutively social would be actions performed in highly formalised settings such as wedding ceremonies, débutante balls, law courts and trophy presentations. My point here is simply that, even if there is a category of constitutively social action, it is not nearly as important a category as the writings of postmodernist theorists (including Foucault) make out.

Firstly, not all actions are social. Secondly, of those that are social, most are not constitutively social. Obviously the above-mentioned non-social action types are not constitutively social. However most concrete actions of these types are social in some other way. What other way might this be? For example, most actions of eating, drinking, and having sex are in fact social in some sense, although eating, drinking and having sex are natural actions.

The most important sense in which an action might be social is that it is permeated by the social. An action which is social in this sense is not (wholly) constituted by its social dimension. Rather in the case of an action permeated by the social, a non-social action takes on a social dimension. Thus chewing food with one's mouth closed because of the convention to keep one's mouth closed is a case of permeation. The basic and prior action of eating is not social. However the action of eating with one's mouth closed is social in the sense that the way of performing it is governed by a convention. Again, two members of a particular society having sex is a case of social permeation. The basic instinctual action of having sex is not in itself social; rather it is natural. (It is also interpersonal rather than individual. It is interpersonal in virtue of being directed at another person.) However when two members of a particular society have sex their action is typically regulated and structured in various ways by the conventions and taboos in force in that particular society. Most actions are social, and of the actions that are social, most are social in the sense that they are permeated by the social dimension.

On this conception, firstly, most actions are in fact social, but individual, natural, and interpersonal actions are logically prior to social actions. The social dimension principally consists in the *regulation*, but not the *constitution*, of prior individual, natural, and interpersonal actions.

Secondly, the social regulation, adjustment, and structuring of prior non-social individual, natural, and interpersonal actions, enables the possibility of higher level individual, natural, and interpersonal actions. Individual humans have a prior capacity to think and act in rudimentary ways in accordance with natural inclinations, and on the basis of their initial interpersonal contact with other individuals. However it is their induction into the social world of conventions and institutions that enables the possibility of any higher level thought or activity, including, in particular, literary activity.

Social phenomena, such as language and literary genres, are conventional enabling mechanisms. Language is a conventional system which enables high-level communication. The genres of fictional literature, for example, are conventional mechanisms which enable, among other things, the communication of ethical content by the construction of imaginary worlds.[4] Crucially, in the case of language and literature, the conventions do not fully determine the content of the communicative actions performed in accordance with them. New sentences expressing new thoughts are uttered every day yet without violating any conventions. Again, entirely original novels are often written largely in conformity to, rather than in contravention of, existing conventions, though it is also a significant feature of artistic performance that conventions may be changed, modified, or abandoned by creative writers and performers.

The second above-mentioned tendency in contemporary literary theory is to become fixated with the power dimension of social action. My strategy here is not to deny this power dimension – its importance has been a matter of common knowledge throughout the course of human history – but rather to *reaffirm* a different, but nevertheless very fundamental, feature of social action, namely, social co-operation. This dimension is ignored, and in effect denied, in the writings of most contemporary literary theorists.

Having, as it were, resurrected the co-operative dimension of *social* action, I will go on to locate the power dimension, and thereby arrive at a general model of *socio-political* action. This will disclose key elements of the *ethical* dimension of socio-political action.[5]

There are a number of basic types of social actions. There are certain kinds of joint action, such as playing in an orchestra or building a house.[6] There are institutional actions of various types, for example governmental action, getting married, and so on. There are actions performed *qua* member of social groups other than institutions, such as professions. There are actions performed in accordance with social rules such as conventions and norms. And there is at least one other basic category of social action which I will term 'socially directed' action. I will explain this term in due course.

[4] See ibid., ch. 7 and Seumas Miller, 'Truth and Reference in Fictional Discourse', *South African Journal of Philosophy*, 11.1 (1992).
[5] Note that my concern in what follows is with the social actions of individual human persons, as opposed to the actions of corporate entities, such as nations or universities.
[6] For a detailed account of joint actions see Seumas Miller, 'Joint Action', *Philosophical Papers*, 21.3 (1992).

In respect of joint action it is easy to detect interdependence of action and co-operation to secure collective ends. Moreover, joint action is ubiquitous. Consider economic activity such as building houses. The completion of the house is dependent on the work of the carpenter as well as the bricklayer, the roofer and the architect. The completed house is the collective end of all these activities. Moreover, the activities of the one tradesman are dependent on the activities of the others. The roof must be placed where the walls have been built, and the wall built where the roof is to be placed. If the house is to be built, and many, many houses are built, there will have to be co-operation, interdependence of action, and collective ends.

Consideration of another pervasive form of social action, namely, convention following, also reveals the existence of interdependence of action, co-operation, and collective ends.[7] Take the conventions of language. Without conventional connections between sounds and meanings, there could hardly be communication. Language is primarily an enabling mechanism; it enables individuals to secure the collective end of communication. Individual members of a linguistic community use a particular set of words on condition others deploy those words; they co-operate to secure the collective end of communication.

Now consider institutions and institutional roles. Take the education system. This system has as a collective end the provision of a range of intellectual skills and the acquisition of certain kinds of knowledge. Children learn to read, write, and count, and they acquire a body of knowledge. So an education system serves the collective end of education. Moreover, the education system relies on interdependence of action and hence co-operation. The pupils work at learning on condition the teacher works at teaching and vice versa.

Finally, let us consider a literary phenomenon such as a novel. As I said above, fictional literature is a conventional enabling mechanism. As such it requires the co-operation of author and reader; both must know and conform to the linguistic and literary conventions in force if communication is to be achieved. This remains true notwithstanding (a) the fact that what is communicated is often propagandist in character, either overtly or

[7] For a detailed account of conventions see Seumas Miller, 'On Convention', *Australasian Journal of Philosophy*, 70.4 (1992).

implicitly, and (b) particular conventions can be, and sometimes ought to be, scrutinised, and even rejected, by the author and the reader. Enough has been said to demonstrate, what is in fact rather obvious, namely, that social action involves a great deal of interdependence of action and co-operation in the service of collective ends.

However my recourse to joint actions, conventions, and institutions is designed to underpin a much stronger claim, namely, that interdependence of action and co-operation in the service of collective ends is fundamental to social action, and, therefore, to most human action, and certainly to human action at any level beyond the very rudimentary. Co-operation in the service of collective ends is not simply the co-option and coercion of individuals in the course of prior socio-political power struggles. Rather interdependence of action and co-operation in the service of collective ends are the defining features of joint enterprises, conventions and institutions, and joint enterprises, conventions, and institutions provide the framework within which most human action takes place.

On this conception an individual entering the social world finds him- or herself in a complex web of co-operative action, none of which in the first instance is of his or her own making. Since this complex web – this network of conventions and structure of institutions – constitutes the background and medium in which s/he acts, it makes no sense to speak of the individual rejecting or transforming the web in its entirety. This is really a logical point. Change or rejection of any particular convention or institution is possible at any one time, but not the social fabric in its entirety.

Kant provides the image of a bird to make this kind of point. 'The light dove cleaving in free flight the thin air, whose resistance it feels, might imagine that her movements would be far more free and rapid in airless space.'[8] In their preoccupation, indeed obsession, with the repressive nature of conventions and other social forms, many contemporary literary theorists make the mistake of Kant's dove. They fail to understand that without, for example, the conventions of language and of literature, there would be no communication and no literature. Just as air is necessary for flight, so conventions are necessary for poetry.

[8] Immanuel Kant, *Critique of Pure Reason*, trans. J. Meiklejohn (New York, 1943), p. 6.

Notwithstanding appearances, this co-operation model of social action accommodates the contrasting dimension of social action, namely, conflict and power. The social world thus modelled is a *socio-political* world. Individuals, classes, and factions spend a great deal of time and energy engaging in competition and conflict. In the course of these power struggles some individuals and groups amass considerable power, wealth, and status. Moreover, they often do so at the expense of other individuals and groups, and in part by ideological manipulation. However the fact remains that these power struggles take place within a framework of institutions and conventions between individuals and groups, exploiters and exploited, at many different levels, including the communicative level of language and literature. Nor is this framework simply a device by means of which the powerful can rule the weak. Without this framework of conventions and institutions there is no longer a society, and no longer the possibility of other than very rudimentary forms of life.

The fact that a framework of conventions and institutions constitutes a set of enabling mechanisms for communication, education and so on, is entirely consistent with the sometimes widespread use, or rather abuse, of such conventions and institutions to repress or coerce. My claim, that language and literature are fundamentally conventional mechanisms for enabling communication, is not undermined by the fact that these same mechanisms are also deployed in order to propagandise and manipulate.

Nor is this model inimical to fundamental social change. Rather the point is that fundamental change cannot be brought about by one agent acting alone; it can only be brought about by agents acting collectively. A single agent cannot change conventions, or transform institutions all by him/herself. Not even a very powerful political figure can transform the system of linguistic conventions overnight, and even if s/he can do so over time, s/he can do so only in co-operation with his/her political supporters. Finally, from the fact that individual persons are inducted into a particular framework of conventions and other social forms, and therefore exhibit the characteristic features and orientations of members of the social group in question, it does not follow that those individuals are not autonomous agents, or that they are to any significant extent coerced.

In participating in such a network of co-operative action, the individual adopts the ends that in part define those conventions, norms, and roles. Indeed it is inevitable that at least some of these socially given ends will end up being in part constitutive of the selfhood of the participating agents. However the conventions and institutions definitive of some social group may function chiefly as mechanisms that enable individuals to achieve high levels of individual autonomy, and enable interpersonal relationships to flourish in ways that far outrun the dictates of conventions, norms, or roles.

Naturally many of the conventions and institutions in some other society may be profoundly coercive and repressive. Whether or not there are high levels of coercion or conflict in some social group, or whether or not some particular convention or institution is fundamentally repressive, is something that has to be looked at on a case-by-case basis. It is an empirical question to be settled on the basis of the evidence, not an a priori truth to be assumed by investigators and interpreters, whether they be literary theorists or others.

Having provided a model of socio-political action, we are positioned to explore the ethical dimension of socio-political action. I must begin with a couple of deflationary points.

Firstly, there is a tendency to believe that the existence of co-operation of itself signals the presence of ethical value, and, conversely, conflict the absence of it. This no doubt in part explains the tendency to jettison the ethical upon embracing the ubiquity of political struggle. But from the fact that social action is fundamentally co-operative action, it does not follow that social action is good. An enterprise, for example, bringing the Third Reich into existence, may be a joint enterprise yet essentially evil. The value of, for example, a convention is to be determined principally not by the fact that it involves co-operation and realises a collective end, but rather by the value of the particular collective end that it realises. Perhaps the convention of opening doors for women serves a reprehensible end, namely, the suppression of women.

Secondly, the agents participating in such an array of collective enterprises and practices will not only have at least some shared interests and beliefs, they will also have some shared values, in the sense of things they all believe to be good. But a believed value is not necessarily a value worth having. Female circumcision may be a shared 'value' in some societies, but nonetheless it is an evil practice.

Co-operating agents will have to have some genuine values such as trust and honesty, but they can probably maintain these at relatively low levels. If everyone lies all the time, no one will believe anyone, and the system of communication will collapse. But, as the world of advertising demonstrates, a fairly high level of deceit can be maintained without the system of communication collapsing.

Notwithstanding these deflationary points, it is an important feature of social action that it is consistent with, and indeed partially explanatory of, individual autonomy. If conventions and institutions are enabling mechanisms, then far from being inconsistent with individual autonomy, they are preconditions for its existence. Thus, to take one example, it is only the possessors of a language – beings who can reflect on their circumstances and provide reasons for their actions – who could possibly have individual autonomy.

This point is important here, because our concern is with ethics, and ethical problems only exist for autonomous agents. If human beings are simply the constructions and playthings of socio-political forces then there is simply no point or substance to ethical deliberation. The rejection of individual autonomy has been a persistent tendency in contemporary literary theory, and the issue of individual autonomy has been to the forefront in discussions such as those concerning the alleged death of the author, the ideological constructedness of texts, and so on. Our model of socio-political action re-establishes the possibility of individual autonomy, and thereby makes room for the ethical dimension of socio-political action.

The ethical dimension of any given form of socio-political action is pervasive and multifaceted. Take institutions. It can be asked whether the collective end of an institution is a good end. It depends on whether its collective end has been subverted – perhaps the end of a particular education system is no longer education but propaganda. There are questions concerning the justice of the distribution of benefits and burdens within an institution. Does our current economic system reward shareholders at the expense of workers? Do workers in powerful unions receive too much money relative to workers in less powerful unions? There are also questions about the powers attaching to the constitutive roles of an institution, and about the exercise of those powers. Perhaps an institution has too hierarchical a structure of roles. Do presidents and vice-chancellors of universities have too much power? And perhaps certain individuals are exceeding the bounds of their legitimate powers.

So the ethical dimension of any particular category of social action is multifaceted. However there are a number of typical kinds of ethically problematic situations that arise in a large number of social action contexts. These situations include ones that give rise to the ethical problems of compromise, extrication, and moral isolation. These are the focus of the next section. I will close this section with some points about the relation between the social and the ethical dimension of literature. Literature constitutes at one and the same time a form of social action, namely, socially directed action, and an activity with an ethical dimension. Socially directed action is essentially a form of communicative social action, and is perhaps best captured by somewhat exaggerated examples such as the following. Suppose a black man and a white woman are going out together to a large social function in a racially segregated society. The function is organised and attended by white people only, and the couple know that what they are doing is socially unacceptable. The white woman is intentionally resisting the social pressure of the social group to which she belongs. She is doing so by a social action which constitutes a public rejection of the attitudes of the group to which she belongs.

Now the above example is somewhat exceptional; no doubt most cases of what I am calling socially directed action are a good deal more mundane. However my hope is that this example will serve to highlight the kind of action I have in mind.

The first point to be noted is that these actions are in a certain sense individualistic actions. They are not actions that are performed in accordance with a convention or norm or social or institutional role. Indeed they fly in the face of convention. But on the other hand they are not individual or interpersonal actions. To see this consider the following fairly typical case of an interpersonal action. I am communicating with my friend. In order to convey my communicative intentions, I make use of various linguistic conventions. Nevertheless my utterance, though conventionally governed, may well express an entirely new thought.

Here the conventions simply function as a means by which I perform my interpersonal action. In such cases conventions function as enabling mechanisms. They enable, but do not determine, certain kinds of interpersonal and individual action.

The social, as opposed to the individual or interpersonal, dimension to the action illustrated in my example involving the white woman lies in the object of its directedness. The action of the woman is directed at the social group, or at least, individuals *qua* members of some social group, as opposed to being directed at individuals *qua* individuals or *qua* friends.

Now I suggest that the communicative content of literature is in fact socially directed action. It is social, but it is not determined by convention or ideology; rather – at least in the case of good literature – it is individualistic, and sometimes profoundly original. In fact its social character is twofold. Firstly, it relies on social forms such as conventions; they enable its very possibility (but do not determine its specific content). Secondly, it is social in that it is socially directed. It seeks to communicate to individuals *qua* members of a social group, whether that social group consists of those people who speak a certain language, or those that belong to the so-called educated public or those that read neo-formalist poetry.

Since literature is a form of communication, albeit one that typically communicates what it communicates *implicitly*, the question arises as to what it communicates, and indeed, what it ought to communicate. The question as to what literature *ought* to communicate is an ethical question. Perhaps it ought to communicate whatever it wants to, or what someone might be interested in hearing. Perhaps literary communicators have responsibilities beyond entertainment. This kind of issue reveals one of the levels at which ethics connects with literature.

As it happens, many literary works do have ethical content. They are concerned to communicate to an audience, and to communicate matter which has an ethical aspect. Their ethical content can be scrutinised, evaluated, appreciated, and indeed absorbed. Here is another level at which ethics connects with literature. So literature is not only social action, it is social action with a multilevel ethical dimension. This dimension is surely one that stands in need of much further and deeper exploration than has thus far been undertaken by contemporary literary theorists. At any rate my specific aim here has simply been to try to locate the ethical dimension of literature within a general model of socio-political action. Having identified and elaborated the co-operative character of social action, and having resurrected individual autonomy, and thereby the possibility of ethics, we are now positioned to explore some of the ethical problems that arise in socio-political contexts.

The socio-political and the ethical (C. A. J. Coady)

I shall provide a sketch of the difficulties raised by two perfectly general moral 'situations', those of compromise and extrication.[9] Part of my purpose is to show that an ethical concern with politics need not be the simplistic matter that so many post-structuralist theorists implicitly, and sometimes explicitly, take it to be. Writers influenced by Foucault, in particular, often seem to think that morality, especially humanist morality, must always be a matter of irrelevant abstraction, 'absolutist' principle, or 'transcendent' values. If ethical concern was entirely of this type then it would indeed have little to offer politics or literature. But moral perspectives arise from within various practices and activities rather than being wholly imposed from above, and this is something that most moral philosophers have always, in their different ways, acknowledged. It is true that moral thinking cannot be entirely immune to abstract considerations or to integration into wider perspectives than the practices themselves provide, but moral thought and imagination need to be rooted in an attentive perception of the messy particularities of life, with all their uncertainties and complexities in full view. Moral thinking can, and must, strive for objectivity, but this does not entail a mindless and insensitive application of a grid of rules and formulae to whatever situation arises. Such mechanical apriorism is what many contemporary literary theorists imagine morality to be, and, not surprisingly, they reject it. But what they are rejecting is moralism not

---

[9] For a good deal of what follows I draw upon other work of mine, most notably, 'Messy Morality and the Art of the Possible', *Proceedings of the Aristotelian Society*, supplementary volume LXIV (1990). In that paper I consider a third situation involving what I call 'moral isolation'. This is concerned with what happens to moral thinking in contexts where the normal expectation of co-operation that underpins many moral interactions breaks down significantly. The situation was of primary interest to the great 'realist' thinkers about political morality, such as Machiavelli and Hobbes.

morality. Moreover, the rejection is often more verbal than real, since many of their own critical and political reactions are highly moralistic. Who needs reminding of the litany of condemnatory abstractions, 'phallocentrism', 'totalism', 'elitism' and the like, that obstruct serious moral discussion in so much postmodernist writing?

Moralism is a distortion of morality, and it is a vice in politics as elsewhere, but morality is essential to a serious politics, as my discussion will, I hope, illustrate. It should also illustrate some of the ways in which power is important in political and social contexts but not all-important. In politics, to paraphrase Kant, power without morality is blind and morality without power is empty (or at least ineffectual).

The morality of my two 'situations' is relatively unexplored but it is noteworthy that they have a particular cutting edge in the context of the kind of co-operative actions discussed by Miller in the previous section. Such co-operative action can itself be joint action or it can be action which is part of some joint enterprise or action the full significance of which presupposes some co-operative context, be it institutional, conventional, or some other. In any case, without, for the present, further exploration, I will suggest that political action, in particular, is very commonly co-operative in one or other of these senses.

The problem of compromise

Compromises occur in every area of life, but have some claim to be at the centre of political existence just because co-operative or perhaps collaborative activities are so constitutive of them. Interests, desires, or policies can come into conflict within a person who cannot find a way to satisfy them all, and then we may speak of his/her resolution of the conflict as a kind of compromise within him/herself, but, if so, it is by analogy with what can happen amongst groups. It is more natural to speak of compromise as one of the ways out of a conflict of interests, desires or policies within a group of persons. But, in either the individual or group case, compromise offers only one way out of the impasse. There are others. The conflicted child or adult can throw a tantrum or the group can resort to internecine war, but such recourses have their disadvantages. A compromise is often less risky and more rational. It is a kind of bargain in which (ignoring the single-person case) several people who see advantages in co-operative endeavours of some sort agree to proceed in a way that requires each of them to surrender (temporarily or permanently) some of their interests, ends, or policies in order to satisfy others.[10]

Although compromise may be rational, and may well secure certain goods, it often has an element of coercion, or at least pressure, about it. It is common to speak of being 'forced to compromise'. Certainly, the path of compromise is not one that would be taken were it not for the pressures produced by the context of joint actions and the necessities they create. Nonetheless the element of pressure is not enough to make the actions that constitute the compromise unfree. This is an important point about a wide range of social interactions, and it is a point too often neglected in discussions of such notions as autonomy, liberty, and the like. Hobbes no doubt overdoes the point in his insistence that fear and liberty are *always* consistent.[11] On the contrary, there are certain kinds of fear and threat that can make actions unfree, but it is still true that our choices may be constrained and restricted in a variety of ways by circumstances, feared outcomes, and social contexts and yet they remain free and we remain responsible.

Although there is nothing immoral in the procedure of compromise *per se*, it is not surprising that the word *compromise* has some negative overtones and that there is indeed an application of it which has an essentially derogatory meaning. This occurs when we talk of a person's or an institution's being compromised. This is a very interesting use of the verb and suggests that there are some deals which involve not just the trading of desire fulfilment, but of basic principle. Such deals go beyond the denial of an interest; they require the undermining of self and integrity. The one compromised has done deals which amount to abandoning (enough of) those basic principles which are partly constitutive of his or her identity. The practice of compromise contains inherent

[10] For recent philosophical discussions of compromise see J. P. Day, 'Compromise', *Philosophy* (1990) and Martin Benjamin, *Splitting the Difference: Compromise and Integrity in Ethics and Politics* (Kansas, 1990).

[11] Thomas Hobbes, *Leviathan*, ed. Michael Oakeshott, intro. R. S. Peters (New York, 1971), ch. 21, pp. 159–60. Day tends to the other extreme of denying that there can be any element of coercion in compromise. See Day, 'Compromise', pp. 47–8.

dangers of this, but most compromises do not involve this sort of damage, though, by definition, all involve some sort of loss. Often, in politics, the loss will be a postponement of opportunities to implement changes that one sees as morally significant, but usually this will not amount to the betrayal of principle unless, as certainly happens, the postponement becomes permanent and accepted in one's heart as permanent, whatever the overt protestations one continues to make. Certainly, someone who cannot compromise on any of his/her goals or policies, no matter how temporarily, is out of place in any form of political action.

The elusive notion of principle thrown up by the discussion of compromise deserves more attention in discussions of political morality. The sense of the term which seems relevant here is that which goes not with universality but with depth. When something is a matter of principle for a person, it is fundamental and not up for negotiation. Inevitably, it has a moral flavour about it, but it need not be a moral principle in the way that a basic prohibition or a negative duty is. These should figure amongst a person's principles, but there may be other principles of a more particular and personal kind: 'It was a matter of principle with her to help struggling young artists', 'It was a principle of his never to forget his parents' birthdays', 'On principle, he never picked up hitchhikers.' Principles are indeed open to criticism; they can be more or less sound or healthy, they can be bad or cruel, but there is also room for a reasonable divergence in what is acceptable. What is a matter of principle for one person may not figure at all in the moral make-up of another, without this being a ground for criticism of either. Nor may relativist conclusions be drawn from such facts, since the values embodied in a principle may be acknowledged as reasonable by those who do not hold it as a principle themselves. You may see the good in struggling artists receiving help, and approve of people who make such a principle their own, without having it as a principle shaping your life. Principles are important in the structuring of moral personality. So are certain other things, such as powerful emotions like compassion (or, on the darker side, hatred), but principles are more reflective, more a matter of reasoning to or settling upon.

In the matter of politics, as elsewhere, it is a damaging criticism that a person is unprincipled and when it comes to compromise, principles are not to be compromised. Moreover, some 'values' or maxims commonly encountered in politics are un-suited to the role of principle, even where they exert a powerful or even dominant influence upon an agent's behaviour. The Vicar of Bray was not a man of principle (nor are his numerous contemporary descendants). Indeed, he is the paradigm of the unprincipled politician, even though he ran his life by the basic 'creed' that 'whatsoever king may reign I'll still be the Vicar of Bray'. Short of being a mere time-server like the unworthy vicar, one must pay some attention to the needs, dangers, and exigencies of the times and the possibilities they allow. Without com-promising principles, one may have nonetheless to compromise on valuable objectives or commitments, or on the expression of principle at a certain time or place. This may involve distressing decisions such as appointing less worthy but politically accept-able people to positions of influence, being less candid with your friends than you would like to be, postponing or abandoning the implementation of valuable projects because, for instance, if you go ahead with them you will not receive co-operation on other projects which also matter a lot, and so on. Such problems lie predominantly in the area of moral discomforts rather than crimes or misdemeanours.

We should not leave the matter of compromise without noting that if compromise can involve moral dangers and loss, it can also be a locus for moral growth. People who are engaged in a com-mon enterprise, be it a marriage, an educational project, or a business undertaking, may find that the path of compromise provides ways of advancing their mutual trust, affection or friendship, as well as the goals they have in common. There are benefits to compromise amongst adversaries, but also amongst friends. A spirit of compromise and the process of compromise need not then be seen as solely oriented to cutting one's own losses, for it may be collectively valuable for the community to which one belongs and the good of which one values.

The problem of extrication

In any sphere of activity one's own past decisions and the deci-sions of others (as well as non-personal factors) will have shaped the physical and moral possibilities open to one. This is relevant to the centrality of compromise in political life, but it is also relevant to the two remaining moral 'situations' that I want to discuss. I call these 'extrication' and 'moral isolation'.

An extrication situation exists, at its simplest, when an agent has embarked upon a course of immoral actions or instituted an abiding immoral state of affairs, but now repents of it and asks how s/he can and should extricate him/herself from the mess. Even more significant, for politics, is the related case in which some political actor inherits an immoral situation for which s/he must now take responsibility. Believing it to be seriously immoral, s/he must surely try to change it, but just stopping the immoral actions which make it up may sometimes cause greater harm than some temporary persistence in the evil with a view to extrication from it. Whether s/he stops or persists, it seems the agent is responsible for the harm s/he causes by continuing or the harm s/he causes by stopping at once. Moreover, these are plausibly seen as wrongs he or she does and not only evils consequent upon his/her actions. It is not the sort of problem that is posed by utilitarian and other consequentialist outlooks for *any* agent who refuses to do something morally forbidden or disgraceful, that is that s/he will be morally responsible for the evils that follow upon his/her refusal. We may well query the value of such wholesale attributions of negative responsibility, but in the extrication situation we seem forced to accept the responsibility. A non-political example would be that of a woman who is engaged in an adulterous affair with a man who is suicidally dependent on the relationship.[12] She has come to regard the affair as seriously immoral, but she reasons that it would be less bad to continue the relationship for a time rather than end it abruptly, her hope being to ease out of the situation without a disaster. In politics, you may be personally blameless for some evil that your party has brought about, say, an unjust war. We may suppose that you opposed it in the party council rooms while in a junior position, though you did not resign because there were other good things the party stood for and you hoped to reverse the bad policy in due course. Indeed, you eventually inherit the leadership and the policy of unjust killing. Immediate cessation of the war may well be the best extrication policy, but it is at least possible that another route is

---

[12] Barrie Paskins discusses a similar example in 'Deep Cuts are Morally Imperative' in Geoffrey Goodwin, ed., *Ethics and Nuclear Deterrence* (London, 1982), pp. 99–100.

better, though still aimed at ending the immoral involvement. Suppose you know that an immediate cessation order would lead to widespread disobedience by your own generals and troops, who would slaughter enemy civilians and overthrow you to install someone who will continue to prosecute and even escalate the war. It may then be better to ease out of the war, even if this involved tolerating, and even authorising more unjust killing. You are damned if you do and damned if you don't, but one route can still make more moral sense than the other.

The political example given is not one in which you are personally responsible for creating the evil, but it has been created by those with whom you are identified. In this case the bond is one of free association, but there are others which also seem to carry some degree of responsibility with them, such as family or national membership, which are certainly not chosen, though they may be disavowed. Someone engaged in political activities is particularly likely to find him/herself implicated in or inheriting wrongdoing, but this does not mean that political reasons override moral reasons *tout court*, but that the moral verdict on the wrongdoing may need to be implemented, for morally relevant reasons, in ways which involve temporary persistence in the immorality. The moral verdict remains dominant because the agent is guided by it in seeking extrication.

What I say about extrication may give rise to several different sorts of misgivings. The first is one with which I have considerable sympathy: it is the worry that appeals to prudent disengagement can lead to temporising with evil so that extrication becomes an ever-receding horizon. This problem is likely to be particularly acute in politics and, such is the power of evil, that we should be especially wary of the idea that temporary persistence in it can be a way of escape from it. I agree that we should be wary; very often, the best thing is just to stop, or to resign from the position of responsibility. My claim, however, is that sometimes this is not so, and, in any event, for the cases I am interested in, just stopping or resigning will itself *be* a form of wrong-doing.

This claim itself may be contested as too concessive to a consequentialist ethic. The harmful consequences of the agent's abandoning immoral behaviour (it may be urged) should not count in his/her decision no matter how sorry s/he may feel about them. The choice to act on the judgment of serious immorality simply is the choice to stop at once, and a non-consequentialist should have no truck with consequences here. Against this, I would argue that a concern for consequences cannot be dismissed so lightly where they are the consequences of an agent's own evil acts or intentions. The non-consequentialist stance itself seems to dictate that there is an asymmetry between moral responsibility for the harmful consequences of bad and good actions. You may plausibly disavow moral responsibility for the harms consequent upon refusal to do some disgraceful act where another is threatening to do something dreadful if you do not comply. By contrast, an agent's original commitment to some evil will often carry responsibility for many of the harmful consequences of the evil, and of perseverance in it. My claim is that such responsibility extends even to some of the harmful consequences of ceasing the bad actions. It is, after all, the agent's evil will, not just the vagaries of life and history or the malevolence of others, that has brought about the situation in which acting to abandon evil will (let us say) harm innocent people. The agent cannot say that it is none of his/her doing when such harm results, as s/he might more plausibly say when others structure the situation in which his/her refusal to do wrong results in harm.

The interest of extrication situations for a discussion of the dirty hands problem is that the hands are getting dirty in the interests of getting clean. The agent is faced with a moral tangle, more or less of his/her own making, but it is explicable in moral terms and it does not require the abandonment of the idea that moral reasons are dominant. It might, however, be argued against this relatively comforting perspective that some immoral situations are inextricable. They are so, not in the sense that the agent lacks the power to disengage (as s/he might be unable to make restitution because the victim and all his/her relatives are dead) but in the sense that it would be wrong to do so. All too briefly, let me say three things. First, the existence of such situations would not mean that others amenable to prudent disengagement were lacking in theoretical interest or relevance to problems of political dirty hands. Second, it may be that, even if inextricability situations are possible, the agent should not think of his/her own predicaments in terms of them. The moral life is part of the practical life and so has essential reference to action, challenge, and problem-solving. Having it in mind that there may be no way out of one's moral predicament is liable to blunt imagination and resource. There are parallels here with the sportsperson who can only win if s/he does not entertain the truth that s/he is likely to lose. Third, if there is room for the idea of an inextricably immoral situation, it is likely to be at the tragic limit of moral consciousness rather than somewhere near the centre. After all, the idea is not that of an isolated act of wrong-doing, but of the persistence in such wrong-doing without the possibility of rightful extrication, and, whatever we think of the degree of coherence required of a moral outlook, it is hard to make sense of the idea that such situations could be a relatively standard ingredient of a way of life. It is thus unlikely that inextricability can figure significantly in the elucidation of what is distinctive of political morality.[13]

My hope has not been to settle the debate about 'dirty hands' in politics or related issues in political ethics but to shift its emphases. The shift involves changing focus from the local necessity of some particular immorality to the probable mutability of the wider social context which gives rise to it, and the consequent re-establishment of the importance of moral judgment in such contexts with a view to eliminating or reducing the necessities. It also involves attention to the continuity of the political and other areas of life and a less ready acceptance of the claims of large-scale political values to dominate practical reasoning.

[13] For more discussion of this issue and a closer treatment of different types of example, see my 'Escaping from the Bomb' in Henry Shue, ed., *Nuclear Deterrence and Moral Restraint* (Cambridge, 1989), especially pp. 195–216.

10

The literary imagination in public life

MARTHA C. NUSSBAUM

'Bitzer,' said Thomas Gradgrind. 'Your definition of a horse.' 'Quadruped. Graminivorous. Forty teeth, namely twenty-four grinders, four eye-
teeth, and twelve incisive. Sheds coat in the spring; in marshy countries,
sheds hoofs, too. Hoofs hard, but requiring to be shod with iron. Age
known by marks in mouth.' Thus (and much more) Bitzer.

(Charles Dickens, *Hard Times*)

A child said *What is the grass?* fetching it to me with full hands,
How could I answer the child? I do not know what it is any more than he.

I guess it must be the flag of my disposition, out of hopeful green stuff
    woven.

Or I guess it is the handkerchief of the Lord,
A scented gift and remembrancer designedly dropt,
Bearing the owner's name someway in the corners, that we may see and
    remark, and say *Whose?*

Or I guess the grass is itself a child, the produced babe of the vegetation.

Or I guess it is a uniform hieroglyphic;
And it means, Sprouting alike in broad zones and narrow zones,
Growing among black folks as among white,
Kanuck, Tuckahoe, Congressman, Cuff, I give them the same, I receive
    them the same.

And now it seems to me the beautiful uncut hair of graves.

Tenderly will I use you curling grass,
It may be you transpire from the breasts of young men,
It may be if I had known them I would have

loved them,
It may be you are from old people, or from offspring taken soon out of
  their mothers' laps,
And here you are the mothers' laps.

This grass is very dark to be from the white heads of old mothers,
Darker than the colorless beards of old men,
Dark to come from under the faint red roofs of mouths.

(Walt Whitman, *Song of Myself*)

Noting in his children a strange and unsavoury exuberance of imagination, an unwholesome flowering of sentiment – in short, a lapse from that perfect scientific rationality on which both private and public life, when well managed, depend – Mr Gradgrind – political economist, public man, and educator – inquires into the cause:

'Whether,' said Mr Gradgrind, pondering with his hands in his pockets, and his cavernous eyes on the fire, 'whether any instructor or servant can have suggested anything? Whether Louisa or Thomas can have been reading anything? Whether, in spite of all precautions, any idle story-book can have got into the house? Because, in minds that have been practically formed by rule and line, from the cradle upwards, this is so curious, so incomprehensible.'   (p. 63)[1]

Mr Gradgrind knows that storybooks are not simply decor-ative, not simply amusing – though this already would be enough to cause him to doubt their utility. Literature, he sees, is subvers-ive. It is the enemy of political economy, as Mr Gradgrind knows that science. It expresses, in its structures and its ways of speak-ing, a sense of life that is incompatible with the vision of the world embodied in the texts of political economy; and engage-ment with it forms the imagination and the desires in a manner that subverts that science's norm of rationality. It is with good reason, from his point of view, that Mr Gradgrind lapses into depression about the nation's future when he considers the citi-zens who, flocking to the public libraries of Coketown, 'took Defoe to their bosoms, instead of Euclid, and seemed to be on the whole more comforted by Goldsmith than by Cocker' (p. 90).

---

[1] All citations from *Hard Times* are taken from the Penguin edition (Harmondsworth, 1969), edited by David Craig; hereafter cited in main text. The studies of the novel from which I have learned most are Raymond Williams, *Culture and Society* (London, 1958), part 1, ch. 5; Craig's excellent introduction to the Penguin edition; and F. R. Leavis, *The Great Tradition* (New York, 1948).

When idle storybooks get into the house, political economy is at risk. The world is seen in a new way, and uneconomical activities of fancying and feeling are both represented and, worse still, enacted.

I shall argue that Mr Gradgrind is right: literature, and the literary imagination, are subversive. Literary thought is, in certain ways that remain to be specified, the enemy of a certain sort of economic thought. We are accustomed by now to think of literature as optional: as great, valuable, entertaining, excellent, but something that exists off to one side of political and economic and legal thought, in another university department, ancillary rather than competitive. The segmentation of the modern academy – along with narrowly hedonist theories of literary value – has caused us to lose hold of the insight that Mr Gradgrind securely grasped: that the novel (for from now on I shall focus on the novel) is a morally controversial form, expressing in its very shape and style, in its modes of interaction with its readers, a normative sense of life. It tells its readers to notice this and not this, to be active in these and not these ways; it leads them into certain postures of the mind and heart and not others. And, as Mr Gradgrind all too clearly perceived, these are the wrong ways, and highly dangerous postures, from the point of view of the narrow conception of economic rationality that is, in his view, normative for both public and private thought.

But if literature is dangerous from the political economist's viewpoint, this implies as well that it has the potential to make a distinctive contribution to our public life. And if one should have some doubts about the texts of political economy – as to their adequacy, as visions of humanity, expressions of a complete sense of human social life – one might then see in the very zeal of Mr Gradgrind's repudiation a reason to invite idle storybooks into the house to plead their cause. And if they should plead their cause successfully, we might have compelling reasons to invite them to stay: not only in our homes and schools, shaping the perceptions of our children, but also in our schools of public policy, and government offices, and courts, and even law schools – wherever the public imagination is shaped and nourished – as centrepieces of an education for public rationality.

I shall focus, then, on the characteristics of the literary imagination as a public imagination, an imagination that will steer judges in their judging, legislators in their legislating, policy-makers in measuring the quality of life of people both near and far. Elsewhere I have argued the case for the novel as an inelimin-able part of personal deliberation; I have also made a beginning on the task of commending it in the public sphere.[2] This task is difficult, since many people who think of literature as illumina-ting concerning the workings of the personal life and the private imagination believe that it is idle and unhelpful when the larger concerns of classes and nations are at issue. Here, it is felt, we need something more reliably scientific, more detached, more sternly rational. But I shall now argue that here, all the more, literary forms have a distinctively valuable, and ineliminable, contribu-tion to make. I shall make this case by focussing on the novel above all, and, in particular, on Dickens's *Hard Times*, which takes as its explicit theme the contribution of the novel to the moral and political life, both representing and enacting the novel's triumph over other ways of imagining the world. The antagonist through-out will not be sophisticated philosophical forms of utilitarianism, and not the political economy of the greatest philosophical politi-cal economists – such as Adam Smith – but the cruder form of economic utilitarianism that is actually used in many areas of public policy-making, and is commended as a norm for still others. (Later I shall exemplify this with cases drawn from quality of life measurement in development economics.) I shall focus above all on the issue of measuring the wellbeing of a population, which happens to be a central theme of *Hard Times*, as well as an excellent place to see the contrast between the economic and the literary at work; and I shall be asking what activities of the personality are best for this task, what thoughts, what sentiments, what ways of perceiving. This will lead naturally to the question, what texts represent these desired activities, and call them into being?

My question, then, will be not just about what the novel repre-sents, what goes on inside it. I want to ask, as well, what sense of life its form itself embodies: not only how the characters feel and imagine, but what sort of feeling and imagining is enacted in the telling of the story itself, in the shape and texture of the sentences,

[2] See Martha C. Nussbaum, *Love's Knowledge: Essays on Philosophy and Literature* (New York, 1990), especially 'The Discernment of Perception', pp. 54–105, and 'Perception and Revolution', pp. 195–219.

the pattern of the narrative, the sense of life that animates the text as a whole. And I shall ask as well, and inevitably, what sort of feeling and imagining is called into being by the shape of the text as it addresses its imagined reader, what sort of readerly activity is built into its form.[3] I shall ask, then, not only about the opposition within the story of *Hard Times* between Gradgrind and M'Choakumchild on the one hand, Sissy Jupe and the circus on the other, but also about the ways in which the sentences and chapters of the novel itself, and the activity of reading it, triumphantly enact their exuberant rebellion against political economy,[4] and against the 'blue books' in which its view of the human world is encoded.

I   Nothing but facts

Dickens's *Hard Times* contains a normative vision of a scientific political economy and of the scientific political imagination. It presents this norm, to be sure, as a target of withering satirical attack. But since the attack is a deep attack, the satirical target itself is described with insight, as the novel both depicts and shows the deeper significance of what is still today very often taught as normative in public policy-making, in welfare and development economics – and, recently, even in the law. What makes this norm appear so odd to the reader of the novel is that it is taken seriously all the way down, so to speak: understood not just as a way of writing up reports or of doing economics, but as a way of dealing with people in daily encounters. But since this norm does in fact claim to be a norm of rationality, and not just a handy professional tool, and since, if it is really a norm, it seems fair to ask people to abide by it consistently, it seems perfectly fair to ask what people who really and thoroughly saw the world in this way would be like, and whether such a vision really a complete one. (It seems reasonable, too, to suppose that the personal

[3] Compare the account of the reader's activity in Wayne Booth, *The Company We Keep: An Ethics of Fiction* (Berkeley, 1988); the account of the ways in which narratives embody forms of desire in Peter Brooks, *Reading for the Plot* (New York, 1984); and the account of the reader's acknowledgment in Stanley Cavell, *The Claim of Reason* (New York, 1979), part IV.

[4] Today 'political economy' is a term used (in self-description) primarily by the most critical and philosophical of economists, for example Amartya Sen; so what I am criticising here is not what would be so described in contemporary economics.

vision and conduct of committed social scientists is actually influenced, at least to some extent, by the content of the norm their
science upholds, by the habits of perception and recognition it
encourages. So in examining it this way we can expect to learn
something about what we do *to* people by holding it up as a norm,
and what we can expect *from* people so treated.)

It is part of the novel's design that the economist's way of
thinking, seen in the full context of daily life, should look extremely strange, and the opposing way natural. However, the
economic opponent is not a straw man: it is a conception that
even now dominates much of our public life, in a form not very
different from the form presented in this novel. Once, focussing
on the subtle modifications of utilitarianism that one finds in
recent philosophy,[5] I felt that the satire of *Hard Times* was unfair.
But now that I have spent time in the world of economics (see
section IV), reading the prose and following the arguments, I am
convinced that the criticisms in the novel are both fair and urgent.
The simple utilitarian idea of what rational choice consists in
dominates not only economic thought and practice, but also –
given the prestige of economics within the social sciences – a
great deal of writing in other social sciences as well, where 'rational choice theory' is taken to be equivalent to utilitarian rational choice theory as practised in neoclassical economics. Public
policy-makers turn to these norms to find a principled, orderly
way of making decisions. And the allure of the theory's elegant
simplicity is so great that it is having an increasing influence even
in the law, which has traditionally reasoned in a very different
way, using a different norm of the rational.[6] Recently the theory
has even made its way into literary studies, where the prestige of
neoclassical economics, Chicago style, is evoked in defence of a
broad application of its behavioural theory to all areas of human
life.[7]

---

[5] For example, see James Griffin, *Well-Being* (Oxford, 1986), and Richard B. Brandt,
A Theory of the Good and Right (Oxford, 1979).
[6] See above all the writings of Richard Posner, including *Economic Analysis of Law*
(Boston, Mass., 1977), *The Economics of Justice* (Cambridge, Mass., 1981), and *Law
and Literature: A Misunderstood Relation* (Cambridge, Mass., 1988). In *The Problems
of Jurisprudence* (Cambridge, Mass., 1990) Posner has modified his approach,
espousing a kind of 'pragmatism'. For a good general critique of economic
reasoning in public life generally, see the introduction to *Utilitarianism and
Beyond*, ed. Amartya Sen and Bernard Williams (Cambridge, 1988).
[7] See Barbara Herrnstein Smith, *Contingencies of Value* (Cambridge, Mass., 1988).

'"In this life, we want nothing but Facts, sir; nothing but Facts"' (p. 47). This famous demand, announced in the Gradgrind school-room in the opening chapter of the novel (a chapter entitled 'The One Thing Needful'), states the essence of the Gradgrind philosophy. And the novel shortly characterises it further, speaking for Mr Gradgrind in the hard, blunt, confrontational sentences that seem well suited to express the quality of his mind:

Thomas Gradgrind, sir – A man of realities. A man of fact and calculations. A man who proceeds upon the principle that two and two are four, and nothing over, and who is not to be talked into allowing for anything over. Thomas Gradgrind, sir – peremptorily Thomas – Thomas Gradgrind. With a rule and a pair of scales, and the multiplication table always in his pocket, sir, ready to weigh and measure any parcel of human nature, and tell you exactly what it comes to. It is a mere question of figures, a case of simple arithmetic. (p. 48)

Gradgrind's political economy claims to be a science, to offer facts in place of idle fancy, objectivity in place of mere subjective impressions, the precision of mathematical calculation instead of the intractable elusiveness of qualitative distinctions. 'The reason is (as you know),' he remarks to Bounderby, 'the only faculty to which education should be addressed' (p. 62). And Gradgrind economics claims proudly to approach the world with reason rather than sentiment – and with the detached theoretical and calculative power of the mathematical intellect, rather than any more qualitative type of reasoned deliberation.

In this brief description, we see four aspects of the economic–utilitarian mind, neatly encapsulated.[8] First, it reduces qualitative differences to quantitative differences. Instead of Louisa, Tom, Stephen, Rachael, in all of their complex qualitative diversity, their historical particularity, we have simply so and so many quantifiable 'parcels of human nature'. This effacement of qualitative difference is accomplished, we see, by a process of abstraction from all in people that is not easily funnelled into mathematical formulae; so this mind, in order to measure what it measures, attends only to an abstract and highly general version of the

---

[8] Some of these criticisms do apply, as well, to philosophical utilitarians, many of whom do treat values as commensurable by a single quantitative standard. See, for example, James Griffin, 'Are There Incommensurable Values?', *Philosophy and Public Affairs*, 7 (1977), pp. 34–59, criticised in Nussbaum, 'The Discernment of Perception'.

human being, rather than to the diverse concreteness with which the novel confronts us.

Second, the Gradgrind mind, bent on calculation, is determined to aggregate the data gained about and from individual lives, arriving at a picture of total or average utility that effaces personal separateness as well as qualitative difference.[9] The individual is not even as distinct as a distinct countable insect; for in Mr Gradgrind's calculation it becomes simply an input into a complex mathematical operation that treats the social unit as a single large system in which the preferences and satisfactions of all are combined and melded. Thus, in Louisa's education, the working classes become:

[s]omething to be worked so much and paid so much, and there ended; something to be infallibly settled by laws of supply and demand; something that blundered against those laws, and floundered into difficulty; something that was a little pinched when wheat was dear, and over-ate itself when wheat was cheap; something that increased at such a rate of percentage, and yielded such another percentage of crime, and such another percentage of pauperism; something wholesale, of which vast fortunes were made; something that occasionally rose like the sea, and did some harm and waste (chiefly to itself), and fell again; this she knew the Coketown hands to be. But, she had scarcely thought more of separating them into units, than of separating the sea itself into its component drops. (pp. 187–8)

Mr Gradgrind does not achieve this goal perfectly in his school, where students retain their distinct levels of performance, their abilities to think and speak as separate centres of choice, and even some measure of qualitative distinctness. He does not achieve this goal perfectly, we are bound to observe, in his relation to himself: for his internal rhetoric insists on the separateness and the qualitative difference of his own mind from those of others: 'You might hope to get some other nonsensical belief into the head of George Gradgrind, or Augustus Gradgrind, or John Gradgrind, or Joseph Gradgrind (all suppositious, non-existent persons), but into the head of Thomas Gradgrind – no sir!' (p. 48). It is a subtle point in the novel that the measure of personal autonomy and self-respect that Mr Gradgrind wishes to claim for himself requires him to view himself with a distinctness denied in

---

[9] See the good account of this feature in Sen and Williams, introduction to *Utilitarianism and Beyond*.

his calculations – and even to indulge in a rare bit of (however crude) fiction-making.

But within his immediate family, he does manage, most of the time, to perceive his own children in more or less the way that political economy recommends.[10] When Louisa, in agony about her impending marriage to Bounderby, bursts out: '"Father, I have often thought that life is very short,"' her baffled father replies:

'It is short, no doubt, my dear. Still, the average duration of human life is proved to have increased of late years. The calculations of various life assurance and annuity offices, among other figures which cannot go wrong, have established the fact.'
'I speak of my own life, father.'
'O indeed? Still,' said Mr Gradgrind, 'I need not point out to you, Louisa, that it is governed by the laws which govern lives in the aggregate.'

(p. 135)[11]

And in one of the novel's most chilling and brilliant moments, we see what it can be like to see one's own self through the eyes of political economy. Mrs Gradgrind, subservient and with an always fragile sense both of her own qualitative distinctness and of her separate boundaries, her separate agency, lies on what will soon be her deathbed. '"Are you in pain, dear mother?"' asks Louisa. The answer comes back. '"I think there's a pain somewhere in the room," said Mrs Gradgrind, "but I couldn't positively say that I have got it"' (p. 224). Political economy sees only pains and satisfactions and their general location: it does not see persons as distinctly bounded centres of satisfaction, far less as agents whose active planning is essential to the humanness of whatever satisfaction they will achieve. Mrs Gradgrind has learned her lesson well.

The initial description of Mr Gradgrind reveals a third feature of the political–economical mind: its determination to find a clear and precise solution for any human problem.[12] Mr Gradgrind, we

10 That this is no mere fiction can be confirmed by reading Becker's *A Treatise on the Family* (Cambridge, Mass., 1981).
11 Contrast p. 241, where Louisa now sees that her marriage failed because of 'all those causes of disparity which arise out of our two individual natures, and which no general laws shall ever rule or state for me, father, until they shall be able to direct the anatomist where to strike his knife into the secrets of my soul'.
12 This lies very deep in the motivation behind utilitarianism in general, and inspires some of its deliberate departures from ordinary belief. Henry Sidgwick, for example, conceding that to adopt a single metric of choice is to depart from

recall, is prepared 'to weigh and measure any parcel of human nature, and tell you exactly what it comes to' (p. 48). And his study, later on, is described as a 'charmed apartment' in which 'the most complicated social questions were cast up, got into exact totals, and finally settled' (pp. 131–2). The economic mind finds it easy to view the lives of human beings as a problem in (relatively elementary) mathematics that has a definite solution – ignoring the mystery and complexity that are within each life, in its puzzlement and pain about its choices, in its tangled loves, in its attempt to grapple with the mysterious and awful fact of its own mortality.[13] In one of the most striking incursions of a first-person voice into this novel this habit of mind is described and criticised:

So many hundred Hands in this Mill; so many hundred horse Steam Power. It is known, to the force of a single pound weight, what the engine will do; but, not all the calculators of the National Debt can tell me the capacity for good or evil, for love or hatred, for patriotism or discontent, for the decomposition of virtue into vice, or the reverse, at any single moment in the soul of one of these its quiet servants, with the composed faces and the regulated actions. There is no mystery in it; there is an unfathomable mystery in the meanest of them, for ever. – Supposing we were to reserve our arithmetic for material objects, and to govern these awful unknown quantities by other means! (p. 108)

If political economy does not include the complexities of the moral life of each human being, if it does not distinguish in its descriptions between a human life and a machine, then we should regard with suspicion its claim to govern a nation of human beings; and we should ask ourselves whether it might not be capable of treating us with a certain lack of tenderness.

And this brings us directly to the fourth characteristic of economic rationality with which the novel acquaints us. Seeing human beings as counters in a mathematical game, and refusing to see their mysterious inner world, the Gradgrind philosophy is able to adopt a theory of human motivation that is elegant and simple, well suited for the game of calculation, but whose relation to the

ordinary belief, writes, 'If we are not to systematize human activities by taking Universal Happiness as their common end, on what other principles are we to systematize them?' – and remarks that such departures are always found when a science is born (*Methods of Ethics*, 7th edition (London, 1907), pp. 401, 406, 425).

[13] Just before we hear of the 'leaden books', the narrator himself describes the people of Coketown as 'walking against time towards the infinite world' (p. 90).

more complicated laws that govern the inner world of a human being should be viewed with scepticism. In accordance with Gradgrind's view of himself as a down-to-earth realistic man, a man of cold, hard fact rather than airy fancy, the theory has an air of hard-nosed realism about it, suggesting the unmasking of pleasant but airy fictions. Human beings, this unsentimental view teaches, are all motivated by self-interest in all of their actions.[14] The all-too-perfect Gradgrind pupil Bitzer, at the novel's end, reveals the principle on which he was raised. As the chastened Mr Gradgrind attempts to appeal to his gratitude and love, Bitzer cuts in:

'I beg your pardon for interrupting you, sir,' returned Bitzer; 'but I am sure you know that the whole social system is a question of self-interest. What you must always appeal to, is a person's self-interest. It's your only hold. We are so constituted. I was brought up in that catechism when I was very young, sir, as you are aware.'   (p. 303)

Bitzer, the perfect product of political economy, refuses to acknowledge even those residual motivations of love and altruism that now grip the heart of Mr Gradgrind himself.

In short, the claim of political economy to present all and only the facts of human life needs to be viewed with scepticism, if by 'facts' we mean 'truths'. And its claim to stand for 'reason' must also be viewed with scepticism, if by 'reason' we mean a faculty that is self-critical and committed to truth. For the 'facts' of political economy are actually reductive and incomplete perceptions, and its reason is a dogmatic operation of intellect that looks, frequently, both incomplete and unreliable.[15] Gradgrind's very sentences express a commitment to be detached, and realistic, and unbiased – in their blunt square shape, their syntactical plainness, their hard sound and rhythm.

But, the novel shows, in its determination to see only what can enter into utilitarian calculations, the economic mind is blind: blind, above all, to the fact that human life is something mysterious and not altogether fathomable, something that demands to be

---

[14] For a trenchant documentation and critique of these behavioural assumptions, see Amartya Sen, 'Rational Fools', *Philosophy and Public Affairs*, 6 (1976–7), pp. 317–44.

[15] Indeed, if we bear in mind that one of utilitarianism's central claims on its own behalf is that it can take seriously the pain of the poor, we see the novel as offering, in addition, a devastating *internal* critique. I develop this argument further in *Poetic Justice: The Literary Imagination and Public Life* (Boston, 1996).

approached with faculties of mind and resources of language that are suited to the expression of that complexity.

II   Mere fables about men and women

How does Dickens's novel differ from the texts in political economy that Mr Gradgrind reads, with their 'tabular statements' measuring social welfare? In considering this, we might focus on our relationship, as readers, to Mr Gradgrind. If Mr Gradgrind wrote an economics book, placing himself in it as an agent in a way consistent with his system, what would be interesting and salient about the Gradgrind character? How would it address the reader's imagination? Only through the fact that his life was governed by the laws that govern lives in the aggregate, and through the fact that he exemplifies the so-called rationality of the economic bargainer. Only under these descriptions could Mr Gradgrind appear in his own book. The 'story' of such a book would be the story of transactions; and its reader would be held to it not by love or fear, but by a mixture of intellectual exhilaration and rational self-interest.

How different our own relation to Mr Gradgrind here. Part of what makes Mr Gradgrind an interesting and ultimately a moving character, in a way that Bitzer and Bounderby are not, is his failure to be a consistent utilitarian. As Dickens reveals early on, Gradgrind is motivated by love, commitment, and plain decency in ways that do not find expression in his philosophy. He refuses to endorse Bounderby's crude dismissal of Sissy's father. We are aware of high-minded humanitarian motives in his preference for reason over fancy. Above all, we notice a degree of love for his daughter, a hesitation in his implementation of his schemes for her, that makes us think 'So this man has a soul.'

If from Gradgrind's viewpoint novels are bad economics, lacking in mathematical refinement, from the novel's viewpoint sophisticated economics is a bad novel – crude in its powers of representation and depiction, falsely detached toward the situations of fellow human beings, impoverished in the range of sentiments it recognises and inspires. This fact can hardly, it claims, be politically irrelevant. For what one can do to ants and beetles is, morally, altogether different from what one can do to a being whom one sees as invested with the dignity and mystery of humanness. Dehumanise the worker in thought, and it is far easier to deny him or her the respect that human life calls forth.

A further distinguishing feature of this novel is its capacity to give pleasure. Its moral operations are not independent of its aesthetic excellence. A tedious novel would not have had the same moral power; or, rather, the precision of attention that makes for interest is itself a moral feature. This is no incidental aspect of *Hard Times*, but one that it prominently stresses in its self-referential manner. The moral antitype of Gradgrind's school is Sleary's circus, whose capacity to please is closely linked to its moral superiority. And if we ask once again our question about differences between this work and a text in political economy, we surely must answer that one of the greatest is that this book is fun to read. Like the circus, it contains humour and adventure, grotesqueness and surprise, rhythm, and motion. Its language is lyrical and full of poetic figures. Its plot is dramatically compelling; its characters inspire our trust and sympathy, or excite our laughter, or frighten us, or generate anger and disdain – or some complex combination of several of these. Its pleasure is more complexly critical, richly moral, than the pleasure of the circus; and it depicts the circus as intellectually incomplete, insisting on a complex mixture of storytelling and social criticism that the novel as genre is well equipped to offer. And by forming with the reader a relationship rich in pleasure, as well as in moral reflection, it shows the reader a style of human relating in which deliberation is nourished by the exuberance of fancy, and moral attitudes are made more generous by the play of the imagination. Unlike Louisa, the reader of this novel 'com(es) upon Reason through the tender light of Fancy' (p. 223); this colours reason, making it, the novel claims, both more lively and more humane.

III Fancy and wonder

But we must now try to say more about the fiction-making imagination itself, as the novel both represents and exemplifies it: above all, about *fancy*. For it is this activity of the mind that the Gradgrind school above all abhors and seeks to extirpate; and it is this capacity that the novel most centrally defends as necessary for good life, and triumphantly, exuberantly exemplifies in its every chapter.

Fancy is the novel's name for the ability to see one thing as another, to see one thing in another. We might therefore also call it the metaphorical imagination. It begins simply, as an almost instinctual reflex of mind (only Bitzer and Mrs Gradgrind lack it totally). Even Louisa, forbidden its cultivation, sees shapes in the fire, endows perceived patterns with a significance that is not present in the bare sense perception itself.[16] Things look like other things; or, more precisely, the other things are *seen in* the immediate things, as Louisa is aware at one and the same time both of the conjured images and of the fact that they are not present realities.[17] Seeing a perception, then, as pointing to something beyond itself – seeing in the things that are perceptible and at hand other things that are not before one's eyes: this is fancy, and this is why Mr Gradgrind disapproves of it.

In childhood, the novel reminds us, this ability is usually cultivated in countless ways – by games, stories, nursery rhymes – all of which are forbidden in the Gradgrind scheme for education:

No little Gradgrind had ever seen a face in the moon ... No little Gradgrind had ever learnt the silly jingle, Twinkle, twinkle, little star; how I wonder what you are! No little Gradgrind had ever known to wonder on the subject, each little Gradgrind having at five years old dissected the Great Bear like a professor Owen, and driven Charles's Wain like a locomotive engine driver. No little Gradgrind had ever associated a cow in a field with that famous cow with the crumpled horn who tossed the dog who worried the cat who killed the rat who ate the malt, or with that yet more famous cow who swallowed Tom Thumb: it had never heard of those celebrities, and had only been introduced to a cow as a graminivorous ruminating quadruped with several stomachs.   (p. 54)

From the Gradgrind viewpoint, this is the omission of useless frills, leaving more time for the real stuff of education. But the novel announces and shows in its portrayal of Thomas and Louisa that it is the omission of a morally crucial ability, one without which both personal and social relations are impoverished.

Neither, as [Louisa] approached her old home now, did any of the best influences of old home descend upon her. The dreams of childhood – its airy fables; its graceful, beautiful, humane, impossible adornments of the

---

[16] See p. 240, where Louisa contrasts the perception of 'the shapes and surfaces of things' with the exercise of fancy.

[17] On this, see Richard Wollheim, 'Seeing-In and Seeing-As', in *Art and its Objects*, 2nd edition (Cambridge, 1980), and *Painting as an Art* (Princeton, 1987), ch. 2.

world beyond: so good to be believed in once, so good to be remembered when outgrown, for then the least among them rises to the stature of a great Charity in the heart, suffering little children to come into the midst of it, and to keep with their pure hands a garden in the stony ways of this world, wherein it were better for all the children of Adam that they should oftener sun themselves, simple and trustful, and not worldly-wise – what had she to do with these? Remembrances of how she had journeyed to the little that she knew, by the enchanted roads of what she and millions of innocent creatures had hoped and imagined; of how, first coming upon Reason through the tender light of Fancy, she had seen it a beneficent god, deferring to gods as great as itself: not a grim Idol, cruel and cold, with its victims bound hand to foot, and its big dumb shape set up with a sightless stare, never to be moved by anything but so many calculated tons of leverage – what had she to do with these?   (p. 223)

Here the novel makes some complicated connections, which the narrative as a whole has prepared us to see. How, exactly, is Fancy connected with charity and generosity, with general human sympathy and a beneficent use of reason? The man in the moon, the cow with the crumpled horn, the little star – in all these cases the child fancies that a form, which perception presents to it as a simple physical object, has a complex inner life, in some ways mysterious, in some ways analogous to its own. To see moon craters as a face, to speak to a star, to tell a story about a cow – these are things that the factual detached imagination of economic science is unwilling to do. But there is, as the novel shows, a charity in this willingness to go beyond the evidence. And this charity is a preparation for greater charities in life.

Consider, now, what it is to see a human being. Perception represents a physical object, possibly in motion. It has a certain shape, rather like the one we ascribe to ourselves. Well, how do we really know what sort of physical object this is, and how to behave toward it? Do we ever have unimpeachable evidence that it is not a sophisticated robot or automaton? That it does indeed have a complex inner world of the sort that novels depict? How do we *know*, really, that this is a face before us – and not, say, a complex mechanical object with craters, a fiendishly clever machine? Where could such evidence ever be obtained? In this sense, Dickens suggests, all of human life is a going beyond the facts, an acceptance of generous fancies, a projection of our own sentiments and inner activities on to the forms we perceive about us (*and* a reception from this interaction of images of ourselves, our own inner world). We are all of us, insofar as we interact morally and politically, fanciful projectors, makers of and believers in fictions and metaphors.[18] But the point then is that the 'fact' school – which denies life to cows and horses, humanity to workers – engages in fiction-making as much as do the novel readers and fanciers, in its adamant denials of life and humanity, which go, like the other's assertions, beyond the limits of the evidence. We never know for sure the contents of this perceived shape's heart; we have a choice, only, between a generous construction and a mean-spirited construction.[19] Seeing-in or Fancy, the great Charity in the heart, nourishes a generous construal of the world. This construal is not only, as the novel suggests, more adequate as an explanation of the totality of human behaviour as we experience it,[20] but also a cause of better ways of living.

We see the difference, for example, in the contrasting ways of regarding workers: Bounderby seeing only self-interest, the novel seeing a complex variety of motives. We see it in the ways of contemplating possibilities for political change – for even when the ways of the world are 'stony', Fancy can imagine a garden growing there. We see it too in the contrasting attitudes of the circus and of Tom Gradgrind towards the appetites of the body. The circus people are passionate in a romantic and tender manner, always seeing in one another a complex life, and delighting in that. Of Tom, the novel remarks, with heavy irony, 'It was altogether unaccountable that a young gentleman whose imagination had been strangled in his cradle, should be still inconvenienced by its ghost in the form of grovelling sensualities' (p. 165). Seeing bodies only as physical objects in motion produces an impoverished sexual life. It is by no means accidental that the utilitarians are depicted throughout with language at once phallic and military, as hard aggressive weapons conducting a pitiless assault on all that is tender. Mr Gradgrind is a 'cannon loaded to the muzzle with facts', a 'galvanizing apparatus', directed against 'the tender young imaginations that were to be stormed away' (p. 48). By

---

[18] See the wonderful account of this in Cavell, *The Claim of Reason*, part IV.

[19] See p. 77, where the circus people are said to be 'deserving' of both 'respect' and 'generous construction'; and also Sleary's famous injunction to 'Make the betht of uth: not the wurtht!' (p. 83).

[20] For it is part of the novel's claim that the simple economic model does not really reliably predict how people will behave: its formulae are not even in that sense useful. See Sen, 'Rational Fools'.

contrast, the approach of Fancy is depicted as delicately, tenderly sensuous, as delighting in the dexterity, of speech and gesture, the intricate rhythm and texture of words themselves. Gradgrind language sounds hard, intrusive, its cadences fierce and abrupt. As language, its body moves itself with a pitiless directness, combining aggressiveness with self-righteous complacency. By contrast, the speech of Fancy has, so to speak, a supple and acrobatic circus body, a surprising exuberant variety. It loves the physical texture of language, and plays with it, teasing and caressing the reader. Even when it speaks about its adversaries, it cannot long restrain itself from treating them playfully and almost tenderly, as partners in a game of words, in which delight is taken for its own sake.

Imagine language as a way of touching a human body, Dickens suggests – and you have a good way of scrutinising the claims of political economy to stand for us in the fullness of our selves.

(Dickens has sometimes been represented as repressing sexuality, especially female sexuality. I believe that this reading cannot stand up to a close scrutiny of this novel's depiction of the ways in which tongue and mind approach a human form. It is not only that a crude aggressiveness is condemned while a gentler, more varied, and more playful sensuality is celebrated; it is also plain that this sensuous play is linked repeatedly with the influence of the female. What I have elsewhere argued about Dickens's feminisation of the author-narrator in erotic contexts fits well here: the susceptible, playful side of life, the side lost, David Copperfield says, by most adult males, is the side out of which novels are generated.[21] This one is no exception, clearly.)

And with this mention of play, we come to a further element in Fancy, which we must now explore to complete our account of its social role. When a child learns to fancy, it is learning something useless. This is the Gradgrind school's main objection to it: storybooks are 'idle'. Facts are what we need, 'the one thing needful'; and what use has anyone ever gotten from the man in the moon? But the child who takes delight in stories and nursery

---

[21] See 'Steerforth's Arm' in Nussbaum, *Love's Knowledge*. This, of course, does not imply that Dickens is altogether free of contradiction on this point, as the harsh treatment of Emily shows. But in this novel it is noteworthy that the representative of the artistic imagination, Sissy Jupe, is also the only character to achieve a happy and loving marriage.

rhymes is getting the idea that not everything in human life *has* a use. It is learning a mode of engagement with the world that does not focus exclusively on the idea of use, but is capable, too, of cherishing things for their own sake. And this too it takes into its relations with other human beings. It is not only the ability to endow a form with life that makes the metaphorical imagination morally valuable; it is the ability to view what one has construc- ted in fancy as serving no end beyond itself, as good and delight- ful for itself alone. Play and amusement are thus not simply adjuncts or supplements to human life, but also exemplary in a crucial way about how to view life's central elements. In this sense, the reader's delight in this novel has yet a further moral dimension, and is a preparation for moral activities of many kinds in life.[22]

We can perhaps sum all this up by examining the two contrast- ing scenes of education presented in the two epigraphs to this chapter. Both are scenes in which a request for a definition or account, of something has been made. In the first, we have the orthodox Gradgrind answer given by the pupil Bitzer. The second passage is from Walt Whitman's *Song of Myself*.

Bitzer has never loved a horse, and has no interest in thinking what it might be like to be one. With an air of finality and certainty he recites the detached external description. The horse emerges as a useful machine, no more. How different is Whitman's speaker. First of all, he is motivated not by a mechanical urge to complete enumeration, but by the child's real curiosity, and by the sight and touch of the grass of which, lying in the grass, he speaks. His first response is to acknowledge that he does not finally know – to acknowledge, that is, a mystery in nature. All his ensuing answers are presented as *guesses*. He speaks first of his inner life, his hope; next, whimsically and not at all dogmatically, of a child's idea of god; then he tells the child that the grass is sort of like him, a young bit of vegetation – he asks the child to see it as like himself. He then shows the child that it can have, as well, a social signifi- cance: for one can see in it the equal vitality and dignity of all Americans, their equal rights and privileges across racial and ethnic differences. Then, turning in, we imagine, on himself, the speaker sees in the grass a darker set of significances, pondering

---

[22] In *Poetic Justice* I explore the reader's moral operations further, focussing on the connection between fancy and the emotions of love and gratitude.

in and through it about the beauty of dead men. He endows even their corpses beneath the earth with beauty, and speaks of them with a profoundly erotic reverence and tenderness – but in a way that does not exclude further thoughts of the grass as from elderly parents, or prematurely dead children. And yet, in its darkness – too dark to come from old mothers, or even from the mouths of those he has or might have loved – he sees an image of his own death.

Here we see all the abilities of fancy, woven together: its ability to endow a perceived form with rich and complex significance; its generous construction of the seen; its preference for wonder over pat solutions; its playful and surprising movements, delightful for their own sake; its tenderness, its eroticism, its awe before the fact of human mortality. It is Dickens's view, as it is also Whitman's, that this imagination is the necessary basis for good government of a country of equal and free citizens. For, as Whitman elsewhere writes, the literary artist 'sees eternity' in men and women, he does not see men and women as dreams or dots.[23] With it, Reason is beneficent, steered by a generous view of its objects; without its charity, Reason is cold and cruel.[24]

We can now understand that the persistent exuberant meta-phoricity of the language of *Hard Times* is no mere game, no stylistic diversion; it goes to the heart of the novel's moral theme. Even while the novel portrays the Gradgrind schoolroom, it cannot help comparing one thing to another, seeing one thing in another: two dark caves, in Mr Gradgrind's eyes; a plantation of firs in his hair; the crust of a plum pie in the bald surface of the top of his head (p. 47). Even while it depicts the monotony and soul-crushing dreariness of the Coketown factory, it triumphs over it in language, comparing the coils of steam to serpents, the moving

[23] Walt Whitman, 'By Blue Ontario's Shore' line 153, in *Walt Whitman: The Complete Poems*, ed. Francis Murphy (Harmondsworth, 1975), p. 369.

[24] One might naturally ask, but can one not use Fancy to hate? I say more about this in *Poetic Justice*, where I talk about the range of sentiments the reader is and is not invited, by the novel's form, to have; I connect this with Adam Smith's account of ideal emotional spectatorship. *Hard Times* urges us, further, to consider the non-judgmental participation of the novel in each and every life, its recognition that each life does have its own story, its invitation to see each life from the person's own point of view. Here, I think, we see what Dickens means by 'the great Charity in the heart': the novel, even while permitting and even suggesting certain criticisms of its characters, promotes mercy through its invitations to empathetic understanding.

machine parts to 'melancholy-mad elephants' – showing in these ways the human meaning of the inhuman. The novel cannot describe its opposition without doing battle with it, approaching it through Fancy and playfully surmounting it.[25]

In this novel – and in my own view – there is no disparagement of reason or of the scientific search for truth. What I am criticising is a pseudo-science that claims to stand for truth and for reason. It fails to stand for truth insofar as it dogmatically misrepresents the complexity of human beings and human life. It fails to stand for reason when it uncritically trusts half-baked perceptions and crude psychological theories in order not to complicate its elegant models. The novel speaks not of dismissing reason, but of coming upon it in a way illuminated by fancy, which is here seen as a faculty at once both creative and veridical. The alternative I am proposing is not Sleary's circus. The circus offers the reader essential metaphors of art, discipline, play, and love; but even within the novel its attitudes are shown as politically incomplete, too ill-educated and whimsical to govern a nation. The novel offers us an alternative: itself, its complex combination of qualitatively rich description with critical social reflection. And it indicates that political and economic treatises of a more abstract and mathematical sort would be perfectly consistent with its purpose – so long as the view of the human being underlying the treatises was the richer view available in the novel; so long as they do not lose sight of what they are, for efficiency, omitting. Government cannot investigate the life story of every citizen in the way a novel does with its characters; it can, however, know *that* each citizen has a complex history of this sort, and it can remain aware that the norm in principle would be to acknowledge the separateness and qualitative difference of each in the manner of the novel.

In one particular way the novel, as genre, is strongly in league with a certain norm of rationality: namely, in its insistence on the fundamental role, in its own construction, of a general notion of the *human being*. The description of the Coketown library speaks of 'human nature, human passions, human hopes and fears', as the subject matter of the novel. In so doing it reminds us that the novel does not purchase its attention to social context and to individual variety at the price of jettisoning a sense of human

---

[25] Compare Mr Gradgrind on pp. 242 and 244, where he is able to see a fire in Louisa's eyes, and begins to use metaphorical speech.

community. It forges a complex relationship with its reader in which, on the one hand, the reader is urged to care about concrete features of circumstance and history, and to see these as relevant for social choice; but is, on the other hand, urged always to recognise that human beings in different spheres do have common passions, hopes, and fears, the need to confront the mystery of death, the desire for learning, the deep bonds of the family. Its hypothetical reader is explicitly addressed as one whose sphere of life is different from that of the author – with different concrete choices and possibilities. And yet it is assumed that the reader can still identify with the characters and events of the novel as with possibilities for human life in general, and think how 'such things' can be instantiated in his or her own concrete life.[26] This complex movement of imagination and reason, from the concrete to the general back to the concrete, through both sympathy and identification, is built into the genre, as *Hard Times* correctly states. And in real life one does find that works of imaginative literature are frequently far more supple and versatile deliberative agents across cultural boundaries than are philosophical treatises, with their time-bound and culture-bound terms of art, their frequent lack of engagement with common hopes and fears.

In its engagement with a general notion of the human being, this novel (like many novels) is, I think, while particularistic, not relativistic. That is, it recognises human needs that transcend boundaries of time, place, class, religion, and ethnicity, and it makes the focus of its moral deliberation the question of their adequate fulfilment. Its criticism of concrete political and social situations relies on a notion of what it is for a human being to flourish, and this notion itself, while extremely general and in need of further specification, is neither local nor sectarian. On the other hand, part of the content of the idea of flourishing is a deep respect for qualitative difference – so the norm enjoins that governments, wherever they are, should attend to citizens in all their

---

[26] For more on this, see Martha C. Nussbaum, 'Aristotelian Social Democracy' in *Liberalism and the Good*, ed. R. Bruce Douglass, Gerald M. Mara, and Henry S. Richardson (New York, 1990), pp. 203–52; 'Aristotle on Human Nature and the Foundations of Ethics' in *World, Mind and Ethics: Essays on the Ethical Philosophy of Bernard Williams*, ed. Ross Harrison and J. E. J. Altham (Cambridge, 1995), pp. 86–131; and 'Human Functioning and Social Justice: In Defense of Aristotelian Essentialism', read at the Institute for Humanities at the University of Chicago (*Political Theory*, 20.2 (1992), pp. 202–46).

concreteness and variety, and should respond in a sensitive way to particular historical and personal contingencies. But the point is, that is itself a universal injunction, and part of a universal picture of humanness. And it is by relying on this universal ideal that the novel, so different from a guidebook or even an anthropological field report, makes the reader a participant in the lives of people very different from herself and also a critic of the class distinctions that give people similarly constructed an unequal access to flourishing.[27] Thus the novel, in its structure and aspiration, is, I think, a defender of enlightenment ideals of the equality and dignity of all human life, not of traditionalism or parochialism. It is opposed to the perversion of that ideal in the name of the pseudo-science of economics, and also to its insensitive application with insufficient respect for stories told within a concrete historical context – not to the ideal itself.

IV Sissy Jupe's political economy lesson – and ours

What does all of this mean for political economy? I shall conclude by telling the story of my own instruction in that science, in which I am no better a pupil than Sissy Jupe. For some years I have been affiliated with the World Institute for Development Economics Research, a research institute connected with the United Nations University, whose aim is to explore broader interdisciplinary approaches to the economic problems of the developing world. I have been a research advisor in a project that discusses how one should measure the 'quality of life' of developing countries.[28] This is in fact the topic of Sissy Jupe's first lesson in political economy. And my interest in Dickens's novel was very much increased by the fact that it corresponds still, even in its broad satirical elements, to much of the practice of development economics, and to public policy as influenced by it.

This is how the Gradgrind school, then as now, proceeds (Sissy narrating to Louisa):

And he said, 'Now, this schoolroom is a Nation. And in this nation, there

---

[27] See Amartya Sen, *Choice, Welfare, and Measurement* (Oxford, 1982); *Resources, Value, and Development* (Oxford, 1984); *Commodities and Capabilities* (North-Holland, 1985); *The Standard of Living* (Cambridge, 1987).
[28] See *The Quality of Life*, ed. Martha Nussbaum and Amartya Sen (Oxford, 1991).

are fifty millions of money. Isn't this a prosperous nation? Girl number twenty, isn't this a prosperous nation, and a'n't you in a thriving state?' 'What did you say?' asked Louisa.
'Miss Louisa, I said I didn't know. I thought I couldn't know whether it was a prosperous nation or not, and whether I was in a thriving state or not, unless I knew who had got the money, and whether any of it was mine. But that had nothing to do with it. It was not in the figures at all,' said Sissy, wiping her eyes.
'That was a great mistake of yours,' observed Louisa.   (p. 97)

Today, in fact, when the prosperity of developing countries is compared in 'tabular form', by far the most common strategy is simply to enumerate GNP per capita. This crude measure, of course, as Sissy immediately recognises, does not even tell us about the distribution of wealth and income. Far less does such an approach, focussing exclusively on the monetary, tell us about how the human beings who have not or do not have the money are functioning, with respect to various activities that might be thought to be important for human life. It does not even tell us about life expectancy and infant mortality – far less about health, education, political functioning, the quality of ethnic and racial and gender relations.

A slightly more sophisticated approach measures, as Gradgrind would wish, the total or average utility of the population, amalgamating satisfactions. This at least has the advantage of looking at how resources work *for people*, in promoting human aims of various sorts. But it has a disadvantage that the novel makes all too plain: it ignores the fact that desires and satisfactions are highly malleable, and that people who are especially miserable can adapt to the circumstances in which they live – that one of the worst parts about deep deprivation is that it robs people of the aspirations and *dissatisfactions* connected with a robust sense of what is due to their dignity.[29]

Such criticisms of utility as a measure – together with the other points I have mentioned about aggregation and qualitative differences, which have been much stressed in recent philosophical critiques of economics – have led a group of economists and philosophers, of which I am part, to defend an approach to quality of life measurement based on a notion of human functioning and human capability, rather than on either opulence or utility. (This

---

[29] See Sen, *Choice, Welfare, and Measurement* and *The Standard of Living*.

approach was pioneered within economics by Amartya Sen, who is also a philosopher; and it has more adherents to date within philosophy than within economics.) The idea is to ask how well people are doing, by asking how well their form of life has enabled them to function in a variety of distinct areas, including, but not limited to, health, mobility, education, political participation, and social relations. This approach refuses to come up with a single number, reducing quality to quantity. And it insists on asking about the actual functional capabilities of each distinct and qualitatively different individual, rather than simply about how much in terms of resources an individual commands. This is so because the approach recognises that individuals need varying amounts of resources in order to arrive at the same level of functioning: the handicapped person needs more resources to be mobile than the person of ordinary mobility, the large and active person more food than the small and sedentary person, and so forth.[30] Nonetheless, the approach does actually permit modelling and measurement: as when one studies the access that mobility-impaired people do and do not have to functions of various sorts in a given society; as when one studies the different food needs of people of different sizes, ages, and occupations; as when one studies the ways in which class distinctions impede access to political participation. The governments of Finland and Sweden actually use such plural quality-based measures to study inequalities in their populations – proving, by doing so, that it is possible to measure in this way.[31] Such measures will indeed be plural and not single, qualitatively diverse rather than homogeneous. This, we argue, makes them better, not worse.

What I now wish to claim is that a novel such as *Hard Times* is a paradigm of such assessment. Presenting the life of a population with a rich variety of qualitative distinctions, and complex individual descriptions of functioning and impediments to functioning, using a general notion of human need and human functioning in a highly concrete context, it provides the sort of information such an assessment requires, and involves its reader in the task of making the assessment. Thus it displays a kind of imaginative

---

[30] See Sen, *Choice, Welfare, and Measurement*; *The Standard of Living*, and his chapter 'Capabilities and Well-Being' in Nussbaum and Sen, *The Quality of Life*.
[31] See the chapters by Robert Erikson and Erik Allardt in Nussbaum and Sen, *The Quality of Life*.

paradigm for public work in this sphere, to which any more quantitative and simplified model should be responsible.

Hard Times ends by invoking one of its most central characters: 'Dear reader! It rests with you and me, whether, in our two fields of action, similar things shall be or not. Let them be! We shall sit with lighter bosoms on the hearth, to see the ashes of our fires turn gray and cold' (p. 314). Addressing the reader as a friend and fellow agent, though in a different sphere of life, the authorial voice turns this reader's sympathetic wonder at the fates of the characters back on him or herself, reminding her that she too is on the way to death, that she too has but this one chance to see in the fire the shapes of fancy, and the prospects these suggest for the improvement of human life. The novel is right: it does rest with us whether such things shall be or not. I claim, with it, that it is not as economic utilitarians but as readers of novels that we should approach the social choices before us, trying, before our death, to consider our fellow citizens, our fellow human beings, with the wonder and the generosity that this imagination promotes.

11

Ethics in many different voices

ANNETTE C. BAIER

What difference is the increasing number of women philosophers making to the way ethics gets thought about in philosophy seminars, at philosophy conferences, in the philosophy books and articles now being published? It is making many differences. The new voices that are joining the debate are interestingly various. We should no more expect agreement in views, in method, and in style among women who write on ethics, than we expect to find agreement among male moral philosophers. There are as big and important disagreements between say, J. J. Thomson and Catharine MacKinnon, or Mary Daly and Simone Weil, as there are between Aquinas and Hobbes, or Hume and Kant. Some women moral philosophers dislike being perceived as *women* philosophers, while others glory in being so perceived; some call themselves 'feminist', some refuse that label, and some of us welcome it when others apply it, while having felt no need to proclaim it for ourselves.

It is dangerous to make suggestions about what difference women are making to the ethics getting done in philosophy departments, since any generalisation will be disputed by some women. Male observers down the centuries have seen women as a quarrelsome lot, given to mutual hair pulling and jealous spite, as well as to maternal solicitude and gentle soothing of the hurt feelings of others. We have shown ourselves capable of pandering to male fantasies as well as of having our own alternative fantasies. In philosophy seminars, as in the boudoir, some will prove protective of fragile male egos, others will fulfil the worst male nightmares of the castrating woman by putting some teeth into our philosophical grip on male moral theories. Some try gentleness where the style of debate had been aggressive cut-and-slash. Others try new modes of slashing, and yet others alternate their styles in disconcerting ways, or simply display that post-menopausal rise in assertiveness which should be no surprise, but often does disconcert those who suffer assaults from feisty old women who had been meeker and more diplomatic when younger. Some focus on women's issues, such as abortion, others avoid those, and prefer to rethink the issues that concern men as closely as they do women, issues such as environmental protection, healthcare, civil disobedience. Some do theory, some engage in anti-theory campaigns. Whatever else we are doing, we are helping to diversify the philosophical scene.

Some who undoubtedly altered the moral philosophy agenda include women whose academic home base was not philosophy, but literature, law, politics, theology. (The revolt of the nuns is a significant and still reverberating social event.) Mary Daly from theology, Catharine MacKinnon from law, Adrienne Rich from literature, Hannah Arendt, Judith Sklar, and Carole Pateman from political science, have voiced challenges that moral philosophers today can scarcely ignore. Women who were or are not academics – Virginia Woolf, Rebecca West, Doris Lessing, Nadine Gordimer, Alice Walker – are altering our sense of the moral issues, as are ex-academics such as Iris Murdoch. When we look beyond writing in English, at least to Europe (and I am not knowledgeable enough to look to Asia, South and Central America, or Africa), there is of course the voice of Simone de Beauvoir to be taken into account. *The Second Sex*[1] continues to provoke both men and women, and provokes many feminists. Other women writing in French, such as Hélène Cixous, Luce Irigaray and Julia Kristeva, are also increasingly impinging on our Anglo-American consciousness.

There are a few English-speaking and English-writing women philosophers whose writings have had great impact of a less agenda-altering sort on the Anglo-American philosophical profession. J. J. Thomson's article on abortion must be among the most frequently cited twentieth-century English-language publi-

---

[1] Simone de Beauvoir, *The Second Sex* (New York, 1974, 1952; New York, 1961).

cations in ethics. But, like most influential articles, it did not exactly change the agenda – rather it carried a certain style of thinking about this issue, one already popular among men who wrote about it, to its logical conclusion. Some regard it as a *reductio ad absurdum* of that approach, but there is no evidence that it was intended that way, and considerable evidence that it was not. Philippa Foot's work in ethics is very influential, especially among those favouring the 'virtues' approach to ethics, but of course this is a very old approach, one favoured by those notorious spokesmen for patriarchal values, Aristotle and Aquinas. (No feminist with any sense of etymology is likely to select the word 'virtue' for whatever sort of moral excellence she is endorsing, but we have not settled on a better word.) Susan Wolf's 'Moral Saints'[2] has become a classic, but there were earlier papers by men, such as Michael Stocker's 'The Schizophrenia of Modern Ethical Theories',[3] which had started the train of thought which Wolf developed so memorably.

There are very many self-styled feminist philosophers, exhibiting a great variety of approaches and opinions. Sandra Bartky, Seyla Benhabib, Claudia Card, Marilyn Friedman, Marilyn Frye, Virginia Held, Alison Jaggar, Maria Lugones, Linda Nicholson, Nel Noddings, Martha Nussbaum, Susan Moller Okin, Sara Ruddick, Elizabeth Spellman, Ids Young, and hearteningly many others, are doing ethics in a self-consciously feminist manner. These feminists do not all welcome the idea that the different voice with which they speak on ethical issues is one which puts more emphasis on 'care' than on 'justice'.

John Rawls's influential theory of justice has been criticised by some, in particular by Susan Moller Okin,[4] for ignoring the question of justice within the family, indeed for tacitly assuming that the institution of the family, as it now exists, is a just institution. Others[5] have criticised Rawls's account of the virtue of justice for

---

[2] Susan Wolf, 'Moral Saints', *Journal of Philosophy*, 79 (August 1982), pp. 419–39.
[3] Michael Stocker, 'The Schizophrenia of Modern Ethical Theories,' *Journal of Philosophy*, 73 (1976), pp. 453–66.
[4] Susan Moller Okin, *Justice, Gender and the Family* (New York, 1989).
[5] I made this criticism in 'What Do Women Want in a Moral Theory?', *Moral Prejudices: Essays on Ethics* (Cambridge, Mass., 1994), pp. 6–8, and in 'The Need for More than Justice', *Moral Prejudices*, p. 27 make a criticism more similar to Okin's. As Okin notes in 'Political Liberalism, Justice and Gender', *Ethics* (October 1994), p. 23, Jane English made this sort of criticism of Rawls in 1977. It has been repeated by many of us since then.

the loan apparently taken out on the virtue of parental love, especially in his discussion[6] of the way the sense of justice, needed for the stability of just institutions, develops in a child, when that child has loving parents, and comes to return their love. But Rawlsian justice seems insufficient to ensure that each child receives loving care, that all parents will be loving parents. Even if Rawls remedied the gap that Okin points to, and attended to justice within the family, the most that a fair division of home and parental duties between spouses would ensure would be that children were cared for by unexploited care-givers, not that they receive the love they need, to develop as moral beings with a sense of justice and a capacity to love. Some women are continuing the fight for justice for women, while others are seeing a need for more than justice. These different feminist lines of thought are best seen as complementary and mutually supportive, rather than mutually opposed. But there are some real disagreements among self-styled feminists when it comes to the details of what would count as justice within the family, and who should be socialised to be willing to take care of whom. The influence of traditional patriarchal religions is not automatically cancelled by the rise of a feminist consciousness, and so we should expect all degrees of radicalism among those who call themselves feminists, all degrees of determination to distance ourselves from the old oppressors, ranging from lesbian separatism, through resolute spinsterhood, and a rethinking and reform of the roles and priority of careers of wife and husband within a heterosexual marriage, to a willingness to continue as before to 'love, honour and obey' a male lord and master, as long as the service is voluntary, and as long as there is no male conspiracy to restrict all women to the role of devoted wife and mother. There are all sorts of feminists, of all sorts of political persuasion.

A question which would bear looking into is that of just when in their careers our more radical self-styled feminist moral philosophers began so styling themselves, when they began to make feminist philosophy their 'AOS'. I have here listed the women who made it to some security in our academic system, and I would not like to bet much on the chances of success of more than one or two of all the many bold young women philosophers who

---

[6] John Rawls, *A Theory of Justice* (Cambridge, Mass., 1971), ch. 8, 'The Sense of Justice', especially section 70.

are trying to get tenure by their explicitly feminist written work. For they are engaged in exposing the sexist bias of our society, our academic establishment, and so of most of those who will decide their own academic fate. They are bold; they may be rash. How many tenured women philosophers who write in provocatively feminist ways wrote this way before they had tenure? Or wrote mainly in this vein? Maybe I stand out as conspicuously cowardly, but I certainly did not. It was not until I had a secure base that I published anything about the position of women. As far as public statements went, I ignored that issue until it was relatively safe for me to speak about it. I admire the courage of my younger colleagues, but such courage will not topple a patriarchal academic establishment that can so easily evict them from its halls. It can easily do so, as long as the senior faculty who are making the tenure decisions can tell themselves, with perfect correctness, that they cannot judge the merits of this sort of philosophy (especially when it is co-operative), and that there is no one whose views they already respect who can judge it and who also judges the candidate's work to be of the quality required for tenure. As long as such a situation prevails, it will remain professionally suicidal for untenured women philosophers to specialise in feminist philosophy, and perhaps dangerous for them even to pursue their feminist interests openly. Unless some tenured philosophers make it their business to become knowledgeable about feminist philosophy, it will be a no-win situation for younger feminist philosophers.

One way that women are certainly changing the profession of ethics is by presenting the professions, including the profession of academic philosophy and ethics, with some acute problems of professional ethics. We are enlarging the subject matter for problem-oriented ethics. It is also pretty clear that there is a lot more attention being paid to the old topic of pornography, and that sexual harassment is joining rape on the normal agenda for applied ethics. Women's voices on those topics are obviously essential for informed debate. Yet they were just as essential for the debate on abortion, which for long enough proceeded contentedly without them, at both supreme court and philosophical levels. Even when women did join the philosophical debate, the ones whose voices were listened to most respectfully, on both sides, were those whose views chimed in best with men's way of reasoning on this topic. So we had good Catholic women arguing against abortion and good liberal women arguing for it, each lot saying just what their respective male teachers and lovers would want them to say. We are only recently getting the views of the independent-minded women philosophers who are mothers, the views of single mothers, of lesbians, and of others who are both experience-informed enough about pregnancy and its early termination, and liberated enough from male indoctrination, to have the best credentials for deliberation on this matter. The philosophical debate on abortion is just beginning to get really going, as it at last gets taken over by those who know what they are talking about.

As to what more general difference has been made by the different way that Anglo-American women philosophers have approached topics in ethics, before and after tenure decisions, probably there are at least as many different answers as the different women whose voices have been heard, and as many as the phases of their articulate philosophical lives. One fairly pervasive difference that I perceive is a greater realism, a reluctance to do 'ideal' ethical theory, an insistence on looking for a version of ethics that applies to us now, in the conditions we actually find ourselves in, oppressed or beginning to be liberated, few or increasingly many in the tenured ranks, on the hospital rounds, on the advisory boards and the policy-setting councils. We find this real-world emphasis in relatively theoretical writings, such as Virginia Held's *Rights and Goods*,[7] in Cora Diamond's essays on the 'realistic spirit' in philosophy,[8] and in the writings of the many women who are choosing to do 'applied ethics'.

Along with this realism goes a greater emphasis than before on what we could call the ethics of timing. J. J. Thomson's 'The Time of a Killing'[9] got considerable philosophical mileage from pressing a question that only lawyers (and Rod Chisholm) had seen fit to press earlier – namely the question of *when* exactly a killing happens, at the time that the marksman pulls the trigger, or when the victim dies perhaps half an hour later in a hospital emergency

---

[7] Virginia Held, *Rights and Goods: Justifying Social Action* (New York and London, 1984).

[8] Cora Diamond, *The Realistic Spirit: Wittgenstein, Philosophy, and the Mind* (Cambridge, Mass., 1991).

[9] Judith Jarvis Thomson, 'The Time of a Killing', *The Journal of Philosophy*, 68 (1971), pp. 115–32.

room. In chapter 14 of *The Realm of Rights*,[10] Thomson also has interesting discussions of when an invitation lapses, how long the right given in an accepted invitation can be taken to last. Is it fanciful to see it as typically a woman's preoccupation to care about timing and timeliness, indeed to be very interested in ways of dividing up and managing time? Women, because of the rhythm of their biological lives, have had to make themselves think about the precise timing of what they do and what they promise, and relate that appropriately to the timing of what their bodies do. They have to think about ways of undoing what was regrettably done, and of fixing the future so that regrets may be minimised.

I shall now turn to one woman philosopher whose thoughts about our attitudes to time present and time past had considerable impact on me – indeed reading her book, *The Human Condition*,[11] divides my philosophical past into its purely analytic early period and its more eclectic later period. I refer of course to Hannah Arendt. There was a woman who really knew what she was talking about when she spoke of resistance or non-resistance to evil regimes, when she spoke about civil disobedience, and about forgiveness. In *The Human Condition* she chooses two human actions as the quintessentially human ones: forgiving a past wrong (unfixing the fixed past), and promising a future benefit (fixing the unfixed future). Concern with past evils and future avoidance of evils is a common human concern, and it would be absurd to suggest that male moralists had not thought about forgiveness, or about ways of securing the future. But it took Arendt to couple contract, that favourite moral device of the secular male theorists, with forgiveness, which had been more or less left to the theologians. Arendt writes, 'The two faculties belong together insofar as one of them, forgiving, serves to undo the deeds of the past, whose "sins" hang like Damocles' sword over every new generation; and the other, binding oneself through promises, serves to set up in the ocean of uncertainty, which the future is by definition, islands of security without which not even continuity, let alone durability of any kind, would be possible in the relationships between men' (p. 237). She

[10] Judith Jarvis Thomson, *The Realm of Rights* (Cambridge, Mass., 1990).
[11] Hannah Arendt, *The Human Condition* (Chicago, Ill., 1958). Page references, unless otherwise indicated, are to this book.

means 'between human agents', of course, not 'between *men*', but part of what makes *The Human Condition* the interesting work that it is, is the odd mix of Arendt's originality and her deference to the ideas and the terminology of her teacher and lover, Heidegger,[12] of her teacher and friend, Jaspers, and of the sexist tradition of Hegel and Marx which she is transcending. Her book is about the active life, about various conditions of labouring, working, and acting together, about escape from 'the darkness of each man's lonely heart' (p. 237). There is little explicit discussion of women's hearts, or women's work, except in the early chapter on 'The Public and Private Realm', where (pp. 47–8, n. 38; pp. 72–3) it is noted that women's relegation to the private realm went with the belief that their task was 'to minister to the bodily needs of life with their bodies' (Aristotle, *Politics*, 1254b25). Arendt refers to 'the odd notion of a division of labor between the sexes, which is even considered by some writers to be the most original one. It presumed as its single subject man-kind, the human species, which has divided its labors among men and women' (p. 48, n. 38). Odd indeed, to take women to be a subdivision of 'man-kind', labouring for it, in or out of the home. But Arendt, after this subversive note, continues to speak of 'man' and 'men' as those whose powers of action she is analysing. Their redemptive action possibilities are located, however, in the combined miracles of forgiveness and promise, which come together in what Arendt terms 'natality'. 'The miracle that saves the world, the realm of human affairs, from its normal "natural" ruin is ultimately the fact of natality, in which the faculty of action is ultimately rooted … "a child has been born unto us"' (p. 247). Appropriating Nietzsche's Zarathustra as much as the New Testament's Jesus of Nazareth, Isak Dinesen as much as Dante, Arendt plunders the Western cultural tradition to get a version of human agency (*praxis*), in relation to human work (*poesis*) and human labour, a version that makes women's labour in childbirth the bringer of redemption, in the birth of a new person whose life story will be a fresh one, a bringer of hope. Action, Arendt believes (with Dante) discloses the agent, and is intended

---

[12] Arendt went at age nineteen to Marburg, studied philosophy, became Heidegger's lover, then at the end of one year, transferred to Freiburg to study with Husserl, then to Heidelberg. She wrote *Die Schatten* as a sort of record of their relationship, which continued intermittently during her student years.

to do so. Individual agents' lives are 'enacted stories', unique narratives, produced by action 'with or without intention as naturally as fabrication produces tangible things' (p. 184).[13] Arendt's self-disclosure in writing *The Human Condition* can be seen as an act of forgiveness to a tradition which had endorsed and enforced that odd notion that women's labour is for men. It is also a fulfilled promise of better thinking, an act of faith in the possibility of better conditions for women's action, and of less tragic narratives with women as heroines.

As far as I am aware, Arendt never called herself a feminist, and probably would not have wanted to be so called. From her youth in Germany she had opposed the separation of women's issues from more encompassing political concerns. (In 1931 she reviewed Alice Ruhle-Gerstel's *Das Frauen-problem der Gegenwart*.[14]) Her biographer, Elisabeth Young-Bruehl, writes that she urged younger women to independence, 'but always, always with a qualification: for women, her maxim was *Vive la petite différence*'.[15] In an interview which she gave at the time of her Christian Gauss Lectures at Princeton in 1953, she said, 'I am not disturbed at all about being a woman professor, because I am quite used to being a woman',[16] a rather splendid statement. She did not want to be seen as an 'exception woman', any more than as an 'exception Jew', but of course in 1953 the press were not in error in seeing it as exceptional for a woman to be a professor at Princeton. During a discussion of 'women's liberation', on the editorial board of the *American Scholar* in 1972, Arendt is reported to have written a note to Hiram Haydn commenting, 'The real question to ask is, what will we lose if we win?'[17] She clearly valued what she feared we might lose, and was not merely used to being a woman, but gloried in it, even in conditions of inequality where a married woman's options seemed to be as Ruhle-Gerstel saw them – becoming either housekeepers, princesses, or demonesses.[18] It seems to me now time for those of us who do call ourselves

---

13 See Seyla Benhabib, 'Hannah Arendt and the Redemptive Power of Narrative', *Social Research*, 57 (Spring 1990) for an exploration of Arendt's emphasis on narrative, not just in *The Human Condition*, but also in other works, especially *The Life of the Mind* (New York, 1978).

14 Alice Ruhle-Gerstel, *Das Frauen-problem der Gegenwart*, reviewed by Hannah Arendt, *Die Gesellschaft*, 10 (1932), pp. 177–9.

15 Elisabeth Young-Bruehl, *Hannah Arendt, For Love of the World* (New Haven, Conn., 1982), p. 238.

16 Ibid., p. 273.   17 Ibid., p. 513, n. 54.   18 Ibid., p. 96.

feminists to draw freely on whatever philosophical resources nourish our enterprises, to be feminist in a large and generously appropriative sense, not a narrow sectarian one. Now that we are winning, we can afford to disagree about what loss our win entailed, and whether it must be permanent.

Arendt's work certainly nourished my philosophical soul. She led me to re-read Hegel, to read Heidegger, and certainly to re-conceive what 'action-theory' might become. Among other twentieth-century books in that genre, hers cries out with the voice of a prophet. The term 'action-theory' itself invites reflection, but few of its analytic practitioners reflect, as Arendt does, on the exact links between theory and action, on how various sorts of thinking can transform action, on how thinking and theorising are themselves actions that are as self-disclosing as any other. As the current rage for 'applied ethics' in the health professions, in business, in engineering and in scientific research can be expected to revivify ethical theory, so attention to these various sorts of professional action would revivify our moribund analytical action theory, a field where things are still more or less where they were when I opted out twenty years ago, at best a matter of co-operative house painting, at worst of solitary agents vainly willing to move their missing limbs. Arendt-type action, such as civil disobedience, emigration, proclamation, let alone pardoning and forgiving wrongs, is still to make it into the discussions of the self-styled action theorists. (Even those who do ethics and social philosophy as well as action theory can choose, in their action-theoretical guise, to discuss house-cleaning, not voting or political protest. Anscombe had 'bringing down the regime' in her analysis, but her followers have tended to stick with the pumping.)

'There is a time for all things under the sun', but since Solomon's time not much has been said about the ethics of good timing. Nor is it easy to say anything general and more helpful than Solomon's pronouncements. Although Arendt's discussion of the twin miracle workers, forgiving and promising, forces our attention on the relation between our backward-looking surveys of action and efforts at wiping of our copybooks and our forward-looking agreements and solemn signings, she does not in *The Human Condition* discuss the question of how agents decide when is the time to give their word, or to forgive broken words and other wrongs.[19] But in her more political works we do get more such attention,[20] and it is a natural follow-up to an account of action which put such emphasis on these two cycle-breaking acts, forgiving and promising, without which 'we would be doomed to swing forever in the ever-recurring cycle of becoming' (p. 246). Forgiving is of definite past offences or debts, which are taken to have been as it were recorded in some doomsday book, complete with date and details. Their remission is also a definite dated act, as it were a crossing-out in the record book, signed and dated. A promise similarly is an act that fixes some aspect or aspects of a

---

[19] Did she forgive Heidegger when she met him again after the war? And for what exactly? In her letter to Jaspers shortly before that meeting, she sounds very condemnatory of his 'dishonesty'. After their meeting in Freiburg in 1950, she described his demeanour to a friend as like a 'begossener Pudel' (ibid., p. 246 and p. 514, n. 81). His tail was between his legs not for his Nazi activities, which had led to the break in their relationship in about 1930 (ibid., p. 69), but for wrongs against her personally, presumably at least the secrecy which he had imposed on their affair. At any rate, the form his penitence took was to make, to his wife Elfriede Heidegger-Petri, a belated declaration of the fact that Arendt had been the passion of his life and inspiration of his work. This news was not well received (ibid., p. 247, p. 514, n. 83). Jaspers's ironic words are apt: 'poor Heidegger'. Arendt had written to Jaspers, in the letter discussing Heidegger's habitual dishonesty (and his 'quite awful babbling lectures about Nietzsche'), that what Jaspers saw as Heidegger's 'impurity' she would call 'a lack of character ... At the same time he lives in depths and with a passionateness that one can't easily forget' (*Hannah Arendt and Karl Jaspers Correspondence*, ed. Lotte Kohler and Hans Saner (New York, San Diego, London, 1992), p. 142, letter 93, Hannah Arendt to Karl Jaspers, 29 September 1949). She did not forget him. Did she forgive him his cold reaction to her gift of *Vita Activa* (her German version of *The Human Condition*)? He had not acknowledged the gift, and when Arendt was in Freiburg in 1960, he not merely ignored her presence but pressured his disciple Eugen Fink to refuse an invitation to a reception given in her honour (*Correspondence*, p. 447, letter 293, Hannah Arendt to Karl and Gertrude Jaspers, 6 August 1961). Her explanation to Jaspers of his change of attitude to her, while it is generous in assuming some blame herself, is not notable for any forgiving note: 'Last winter I sent him one of my books, the *Vita Activa*, for the first time. I know that he finds it intolerable for my name to appear in public, that I write books, etc. All my life I've pulled the wool over his eyes, so to speak, always acted as if none of that existed and as if I couldn't count to three, unless it was in the interpretation of his own works. Then he was always very pleased when it turned out that I could count to three and sometimes even four. Then I suddenly felt that this deception was just too boring, and so I got a rap on the nose' (*Correspondence*, p. 457, letter 297, Hannah Arendt to Gertrude and Karl Jaspers, 1 November 1961). Jaspers replied that Heidegger must have been long aware that she had become a famous author, and that 'the only thing that is new is that he received a book directly from you – and what a reaction!' (*Correspondence*, pp. 459–60, letter 298, Karl Jaspers to Hannah Arendt, 6 November 1961).

[20] For a very comprehensive and helpful study of Arendt as a political philosopher, see Margaret Canovan, *Hannah Arendt: A Reinterpretation of Her Political Thought* (New York, 1992).

limited future, a time future to the time of the promise. Often we promise to do something by a certain day or hour, and even when we promise mutual devotion 'till death do us part', death does end the period that was fixed by the promise. Without calendars, there could be no promising of our normal sort, and where clocks are rare or rarely used, promises are interpreted more flexibly. In New Zealand we have the phrase 'Maori time', which means Pakeha (European) time, give or take an hour or so. ('We are to meet at noon, Maori time.') Without any rough measures of time, the 'pro' element in promising would become simply a future-tense marker, and promises would be indistinguishable from totally vague hopes or predictions. 'We will overcome' is not a promise, precisely because of its lack of temporal precision.

With forgiving, the need for time specifications is not so obvi-ous, given the religious near-monopoly on that concept and the promiscuous scope of Christian forgiveness. It is typically *all* one's sins, as an undifferentiated bunch, that get forgiven by divine pardoners (although there is that mysterious unforgivable sin, against the Holy Spirit, that has to be sifted out, so maybe some sin-by-sin count does actually have to go on). Human for-givers are selective – typically they forgive particular specifiable doings or omissions. To announce 'I forgive you for any wrongs you have done me, and forgive you in advance for any you may do me', is to debase the moral currency, just as senseless an act as to say 'I promise you that you could count on me, for all our past, and can count on me, in whatever way you wish, in the future.' Promises must be for the future, and must be selective as to what aspect of that future they purport to fix. Forgiveness must be of the past, and of selected wrongs within it. The selection is the hard bit. Arendt writes, 'the moment that promises lose their character as isolated islands of certainty in an ocean of uncertainty, that is when this faculty is misused to cover the whole ground of the future and to map out a path secured in all directions, they lose their binding power and the whole enterprise becomes self defeat-ing' (p. 244). Many of us who have inveighed against contractar-ianism in ethics have merely repeated Arendt's point, at greater length and with less eloquence.

It may reasonably be objected[21] that my claim that promises

---

[21] Walter Sinnott-Armstrong, in conversation, made this objection.

typically mention dates or time periods ignores promises of the form 'I will never do x again' – the sort of commitment given by those trying to turn away from bad habits, from excessive drinking, smoking, drug taking, or by those entering monasteries. Such promises, or vows, do seem to be for an open-ended future, and could be made by members of a pre-calendar culture. Vows of allegiance to superiors, vows of abstinence of various sorts, divide time simply into the pre-vow and the post-vow periods. But 'vow', not 'promise', is the right word for these acts. They are typically made to some higher-than-human power, to God, or one's country. Or one might 'sign the pledge', and then there seems to be no one in particular who plays any analogue of the role of promisee, of the one who is counting on one's doing, or not doing, a particular thing or type of thing. Vows are indeed taken and sometimes honoured. It was not vows that Arendt chose to focus on, but promises, which 'depend on plurality, on the presence and acting of others, for no-one … can feel bound by a promise made only to himself' (p. 237). It is an important fact about the human person that she can be multiple, play many roles, and play roles before her other personae, but Arendt is surely right that promises lose grip once the promisee is oneself, one's conscience, or the divine spokesman within. Our ability to talk to ourselves can be a redemptive power,[22] but the speech acts we can perform to ourselves do seem of a limited variety, compared to the ways in which we can speak to others. We can tell ourselves stories, ask and answer questions, propose courses of action then criticise and reject them, encourage, deceive, flatter, mock, and denigrate ourselves. But promising ourselves, like lying to ourselves, seems ruled out, except for those who are seen to suffer from multiple personality disorders, or who alter their status within the time between the promise and its expected performance.[23]

The biblical notion of a covenant between God and Israel, which

---

[22] I have only recently come to realise that part of what I like so much about New York City is the number of people a pedestrian encounters who are unabashedly talking aloud to themselves.

[23] An interesting case is where a promise is made by a person in some special capacity, say as provost, to a group, say a department of which the now ex-provost becomes chair. Then her successor in the provost's chair could break that promise, to herself as departmental representative, so the promise that one person made is broken to that very person, in another role. Thanks to Paul Benacerraf for alerting me to this real possibility.

might reasonably be taken to serve the identity-establishing function for a whole people rather well, was a very special sort of commitment, both in the open-ended time which it covered, and in the sort of parties it involved – a divine being and the father of a people. Arendt's discussion of the biblical covenant made by Abraham with God is distinctly ironical. 'Abraham, the man from Ur, whose whole story, as the Bible tells it, shows such a passionate drive towards making covenants that it is as though he departed from his country for no other reason than to try out the power of mutual promise in the wilderness of the word, until eventually God himself agreed to make a covenant with him' (pp. 243–4). Such a 'covenant' with God, until it acquires human witnesses and public recognition,[24] is no different, on Abraham's part, from cases of 'promising enacted in solitude or isolation', and so 'without reality . . . no more than a role played before one's self' (p. 237). The covenant as described in Genesis 17 is an 'everlasting' one, binding not just Abraham but his seed ('Thy seed after thee in their generations'). Ordinary promises are neither everlasting nor taken to bind the promisor's seed. (Hume relies heavily on this fact in his arguments against a social contract theory of political obligation.) A covenant of the sort that the nation of Israel took itself to have with its God can indeed serve to confer a distinctive identity both on nationals of that nation and on the God in question ('The God of Israel'), but 'promise' is the wrong term for the sort of identity-establishing tie for a whole people which the biblical covenant instituted.

Arendt claims that our identity over time is confirmed by those others who recognise the one who fulfils a promise as the same person who gave it, and that this confirmation of identity is needed, if we are not to 'be condemned to wander helplessly in the darkness of each man's lonely heart' (p. 237). This is a strong claim. One might think that a recorded lifetime resolve would be the simplest way to give direction to the aimless wanderer, pro-

[24] Spinoza in chapters 8 and 12 of his *Theological Political Treatise* discusses the renewals of the covenant made by Moses and Joshua, and implicitly raises questions about the criteria of identity for such a covenant, which apparently was interrupted by periods of idolatry and desecration of the Ark of the Covenant, an ark eventually lost track of. With mock innocence he writes, 'I find it strange that Scripture tells us nothing of what became of the Ark of the Covenant' (p. 207 in *Tractatus Theologico-Politicus*, trans. Samuel Shirley and E. J. Brill Leiden, Germany, New York, 1989).

viding at least as good an identity-marker as that conferred by a series of promises to different people to do differing things by a series of deadlines. (I often have felt torn into pieces by the different promises I have given.) Arendt's 'promise' may need overtones of an ongoing 'covenant' to do the job that she gives it, that is to structure a life over a long period.

In a television interview in 1964 Arendt told how, when as a child in Königsberg she encountered anti-Semitism in her play-mates and schoolmates, her mother instructed her to defend herself, and, if a schoolteacher made anti-Semitic remarks, 'to stand up immediately, to leave the class, go home'.[25] This policy of standing up and leaving anti-Semitic company seems to have been followed by Arendt throughout her life. She and her mother left Nazi Germany in 1933 (over the Erzegebirge mountains, into Czechoslovakia), and she eventually made her 'home' with other emigrants from Europe in New York. Her last years in Germany were spent working on her study of Rahel Varnhagen (born as Rahel Levin in 1771). She subtitled this book 'The Life of a Jewess', and referred to Rahel as 'my best friend, although she has been dead for some one hundred years'.[26] She also wrote a newspaper article on 'The Jewish Question', and publicly criticised those who (like Adorno and Heidegger) were co-operating with the Nazis. She certainly 'stood up' before 'walking out' of the country that had become 'nicht fur meiner Mutters Tochter'.[27] Such clear self-identification involved no covenants nor promises, simply a consistent line of action and proclamation. (Her 'Mutt', as she calls her mother in her letters to Jaspers, seems to have been a splendidly devoted and loyal mother. When both mother and daughter were arrested by the Nazis in 1933, and interrogated separately, Martha Arendt was asked what her daughter Hannah had been doing in her regular visits to the Prussian National Library, where she had in fact been researching anti-Semitic literature for the German Zionist Organisation. She replied that she did not know, but she knew that whatever it was, it was right for her daughter to do it, and she herself would have done the same. The Nazis released her after one day, having the sense to realise that she was interrogation-proof.[28])

Do we really need witnesses and records to give us reassurance of who we are? Do we need receipts to reassure us that we are the

---

[25] Young-Bruehl, *Hannah Arendt*, pp. 11–12. [26] Ibid., p. 56. [27] Ibid., p. xv.
[28] Ibid., p. 107.

same persons as the ones who entered into the sale as a buyer? Do we need some 'well done, good and faithful servant' to be sure that we are the same ones who entered into that service? Arendt, when she makes her claim about the role of promises, is writing about the active life, the life of labour, work, and action, about the bringing into existence of the means of subsistence, of artefacts, of narratives, of commitments, of meaningful lives such as her own. If our service is mere labour, which another labourer or a relay team of labourers could have done as well as one and the same person, then there may be no signature, as it were, left on the outcome of our labour, on the field that is ploughed, or the house that is cleaned. But if we have made something or built something – a pot, or a church – then we may leave our signature on the base of the pot, or our face carved into the door lintel. Even if we do not, the work may exhibit our distinctive personal style, so not be just what any other potter or architect (or team of them) could as easily have come up with. Our work is not fungible, in the way that our labour is. But the work of our hands and minds, like our labour, is alienable and can have a price put on it. What Arendt calls our actions, by contrast, are inalienable. Their distinctive style, if indeed they have that, results not in any saleable product, but in a unique life story, a succession of words and deeds bounded by birth and death, a sequence of commitments and refusals to commit oneself, of forgiving and refusals to forgive, and of words and deeds in reaction to others' actions, and to their deaths and births. For women, that life story may include the births that they commit themselves to, or refuse to commit themselves to, that is to childbirths or abortions. Like any other outcome of human action (in Arendt's rich sense), the child who is born because of the mother's decision to carry to term will be unique, with its own life story and distinctive character, not merely a continuation of that of any parental agent. Action typically results in new possibilities for action, but not so typically in new actors. Only when nations, religions, or other collective agents are intentionally brought into being do we get any other human action that is at all like intentionally giving birth to a new human person.

Yet, as Arendt emphasised when discussing the traditional place of women in the private sphere, giving birth is often not free action, but coerced 'labour' for others. As long as there is no individual control and no individual choice, then labour and childbirth is for the species' survival, not for any labourer's or labour-owner's survival or satisfaction. As long as the initiative, the control, and the choice rests with men rather than with the woman, then the labour and birth will be less than the mother's action. Arendt gives a central role to the idea of natality, and sees it to have a closer connection with action than with that of labour, or with the work that must 'provide and preserve the world for ... the constant influx of newcomers who are born into the world as strangers' (p. 9). This is because 'the new beginning inherent in birth can make itself felt in the world only because the newcomer possesses the capacity of beginning something anew, that is of acting' (p. 9) Of course, as she later notes when discussing Marx's concept of labour power (p. 88), the newcomer can also be seen merely as replacement of labour power, rather than as one capable of acting. If the child is consigned to factory labour, or (if she is a female) simply to reproducing her mother's unchosen procreative labour, then nothing new will have been begun, merely the old cycle continued. Birth will be paired with unchosen death, as correlative happenings that preserve a sort of species status quo not only at the biological level, but also at the socio economic level. It sustains a more or less steady labour force for the creation and procreation of saleable goods and labour. Despite these all too often actualised possibilities for birth, it still retains its power to symbolise the new start, the hope of new and better directions. Hence Arendt can write 'since action is the political activity *par excellence*, natality, and not mortality, may be the central category of political, as distinguished from metaphysical, thought' (p. 9). Heidegger had made mortality a central category of metaphysical thought. Arendt is balancing his act by a move that totally transforms it.[29] Natality for us today is a pretty central topic of political debate, if not so central a category of metaphysical[30] or political theory. The Hegelian 'truth' of Arendt's political thought may be found not in contemporary political theory so much as in the debate over *Roe v. Wade*, and in the confrontations outside abortion clinics.

[29] That, perhaps, was what he found unforgivable, once he got to read his ex-student/mistress's book, when in 1960 she forced it on him.
[30] See my presidential address, 'A Naturalist View of Persons', delivered before the Eighty-Seventh Annual Eastern Division Meeting of the American Philosophical Association in Boston, Massachusetts on 29 December 1990. *Proceedings* and *Addresses of the American Philosophical Association,* 65 (November 1991), pp. 5–17.

Arendt's prophetic powers, or should one say her thought initiatives, extend to the metaphysical as well as the political. The final section of *The Human Condition* is devoted *to* various reversals in 'the modern age' and one of these is 'the reversal of the hierarchical order between the *vita contemplativa* and the *vita activa*' (p. 289). She introduces this theme by a discussion of René Descartes' method of doubt, as well as of Copernicus' and Galileo's 'alienation' of the earth, their 'dislocation' of it, from their imaginary Archimedean point beyond it. She quotes Copernicus' words about 'the virile man standing in the sun … overlooking the planets', and seeing the earth move with them. Descartes' doubt and his thoughts about himself as a thinker, as much as his analytical–geometrical physics, are taken as expressions of this alienation of the familiar world, brought about by the new science. Whitehead is quoted as likening the new sciences' beginnings in the discovery of the telescope and in Galileo's use of it, to 'a babe born in a manger' (*Science in the Modern World*, p. 12,[31] quoted by Arendt at p. 257), a great thing happening with little stir. Arendt adds, 'Like the birth in a manger, which spelled not the end of antiquity but the beginning of something so unexpectedly and unpredictably new that neither hope nor fear could have anticipated it, these first tentative glances into the universe through an instrument, at once adjusted to human senses and destined to uncover what definitely and forever must lie beyond them, set the stage for an entirely new world' (pp. 257–8). The inquiring and imaginative mind too can give birth to inventions and ideas that break cycles and introduce new directions. It is not merely in social philosophy, but in physics and metaphysics, that the category of natality provides a favourite metaphor for what the innovative thinker aspires to. (David Hume mourned the apparent fate of his *Treatise of Human Nature*,[32] fallen 'deadborn from the press'.)

In the final part of *The Human Condition*, Arendt treats thinking, including the sort of earth-shifting thinking that Galileo and Descartes did, as activity, properly seen as part of the *vita activa*. (She continued her exploration of thinking in her Gifford Lectures of 1973, published as *The Life of the Mind*.) The Cartesian doubt,

---

[31] Alfred North Whitehead, *Science and the Modern World* (New York, 1960).
[32] David Hume, *A Treatise of Human Nature*, ed. L. A. Selby-Bigge and P. H. Nidditch (Oxford, 1978).

and exploration of subjectivity, as much as the telescope-using and technology-linked thinking of modern scientists, involved 'the removal of the Archimedean point into the mind of man' (p. 285). They involved mental labour, the making of books, and self-revealing or self-concealing action. Although Descartes called his metaphysical masterpiece *Meditations*, which may suggest contemplative stillness, and in the course of the *First Meditation* contrasted his thought with action in order to excuse the danger-ousness of his strategy of radical doubt, in his own language there was certainly the language of action. In the first paragraph he reports a resolve; he keeps making new resolves, and says he will stick 'stubbornly' to them; he complains of how arduous he finds his chosen path; he gives his mind a rest from its tough new sense-distrusting discipline for the duration of his discussion of the piece of wax; he celebrates the near-divine freedom of his will in the *First Meditation*; he takes himself to be made in the image of a self-expressive powerful creative God. Although earlier (after hearing of Galileo's fate) he had announced that he would go forth masked, his masks are mere veils, his writings acts of self-expression. His ethics, put forward in the *Passions of the Soul* under the thin mask of a gift of requested advice to the spiritually troubled and mentally sharp Princess Elizabeth of Bohemia, exalt that generosity of mind which disdains both jealousy of competi-tors and fear of human enemies, while indulging its own desire for truth and enjoying its love or willing union with the God-or-universe which it is trying better to understand.

A recent interesting philosophical phenomenon in this country is the number of women working on Descartes' writings, includ-ing his writings on ethics. Maybe this phenomenon is no more significant than that of the number of women Kant interpreters, but whereas the women Kantians prefer to stay off the topic of Kant's relations with women, women (such as Margaret Ather-ton,[33] Ruth Mattern,[34] and Eileen O'Neill[35]) who are working on

---

[33] Margaret Atherton, 'Cartesian Reason and Gendered Reason', in Louise B. Anthony and Charlotte Wit, eds., *A Mind of One's Own* (Boulder, San Francisco, and Oxford, 1992), pp. 19–34.

[34] Ruth Mattern, 'Descartes' Correspondence with Elizabeth: Concerning the Union and Distinction of Mind and Body', in *Descartes, Critical Interpretative Essays*, ed. Michael Hacker (Baltimore, 1978).

[35] Eileen O'Neill, 'Mind and Mechanism: An Examination of Some Mind–Body Problems in Descartes' Philosophy', Ph.D. dissertation, Princeton University, 1983, and subsequent publications.

Descartes' thought can turn without defensiveness to those (mostly royal and aristocratic) women who took up his ideas and carried them further, who engaged with him in his strenuous pseudo-meditative labour, work, and action. Perhaps Descartes appeals to women[36] not just because of the refreshing disdain of deontology in his ethics, and the engaging directness and apparent simplicity of his metaphysical moves, but also for his very doubleness – he is both solitary meditator and impassioned correspondent, both self-protective mask-wearer and reckless intellectual exhibitionist. His books ended on the index, but he led the church an entertaining dance for years before the full irony of his dedication of the *Meditations* became apparent to the professors of theology to whom they were offered.

As Naomi Scheman sees Ludwig Wittgenstein as a philosopher of the cultural margin,[37] and precisely for that reason having a special appeal to rebellious women, so one can see René Descartes as an inspiring rebel. He tried ways of subverting his culture from within, wearing the masks of orthodoxy while busy replacing the foundations and rebuilding the edifice of belief. His quite astonishing attempt, or pretended attempt, to persuade the church that he had an intellectually superior account of how, in the Eucharist, bread could become flesh, and wine blood, is, for its sheer effrontery, one of the high points of European intellectual and cultural history, a moment of supreme intellectual intoxication and divinely wilful *joie de vivre*. When a century later Hume offers the believers in religious miracles the thought that they have a continuing confirmation of the occurrence of miracles in their own ability to sustain belief in the miracles on which their religious faith is grounded,[38] when he ends his *Dialogues on Natural Religion* with Philo's switch to humble pietism, we get echoes of this philosophical playfulness, this daring dance

---

[36] Naomi Scheman, in 'Though this be Method yet there is Madness in it: Paranoia and Liberal Epistemology' (Anthony *et al.*, eds., *A Mind of One's Own*, pp. 145–70), allows that Descartes has had appeal for feminist women, despite his emphasis on the supposed need for control of the passions by a somewhat dictatorial reason. See p. 167, n. 15.

[37] Naomi Scheman, 'Closets, Margins, and Forms of Life' in Hans Sluga and David Stern, eds., *Cambridge Companion to Wittgenstein* (Cambridge, 1997).

[38] This Humean move repeats one which Cicero makes in *De Natura Deorum*, where Balbus suggests that the most providential thing of all is the human propensity to believe in providence.

on the edge of cultural abysses which may be typical of our greatest thinkers.[39]

In his *Discourse on the Method*[40] Descartes told us how he resolved to avoid making promises, which would have bound him to others and restricted his freedom, but how he had made and intended to keep this and other resolves. To get out of any forests he might seem lost in, he would walk as best he could in a straight line, pursuing his research strategy wherever it took him. It took him far, and he did, until near the end, avoid commitments to other people. He did not marry his daughter's mother, and he preferred to live as a resident alien in the relatively tolerant Netherlands to living as a presumptively loyal citizen in France. He showed devoted concern for the Princess Elizabeth of Bohemia, and was a faithful correspondent to her, but all without any formal promises. His commitment to serve Queen Christina of Sweden did restrict his freedom, and turned him from his straight scientific and philosophical path back towards the musical interests with which he had begun. His ties to her proved to be lethal, so he may have been wiser in his initial stubborn resolves than in his later capitulations to sociability and personal commitment. At any rate his life serves as a challenge to Arendt's thesis that, without promises to others, and without their recognition of our later promise-fulfilling selves as identical with the earlier promise-making selves, we would lose ourselves. In the privacy of his study, Descartes made resolves, including the resolve not to give promises, and then he published his resolves in the vernacular to the reading public. He did not seem to lose himself in the darkness of his doubtless lonely heart, and his actions of self-revelation

---

[39] I am grateful to Onora O'Neill for her suggestion that Kant's *Religion Within the Limits of Reason Alone*, especially given its reference to the Bible as 'das Buch, was einmal da ist' ('that book which happens to be there'), should be read as a conscious continuation of the sort of biblical interpretation which Spinoza gave in his *Theological Political Treatise*, an interpretation which offered the pious a way of accepting much of what their Holy Scriptures contained while at the same time effectively undermining any claim which might be made for the foundational nature of religious doctrines for moral or other knowledge. (Immanuel Kant, *Religion Within the Limits of Reason Alone*, trans. Louis Infield (New York, 1963), book III, div. ii, p. 123.)

[40] René Descartes, *Discourse on the Method of Rightly Conducting One's Reason and Seeking Truth in the Sciences*, ed. C. Adam and P. Tannery (Paris, 1964–76), vol. VI, pp. 24–5. Volume I, p. 123 in John Cottingham, Robert Stoothoff, and Dugald Murdoch, eds., *The Philosophical Writings of Descartes*, vol. I (New York and Cambridge, 1985).

(and also of sometimes judicious, sometimes playful self-conceal-ment) are a standing challenge to those of us who live less danger-ously. They are also a salutary challenge to those of us who criticise modern variants of individualism, since he is both an unparalleled individualist and also the philosopher who cel-ebrated love as the central ethical fact; both a despiser of tradition and the founder of a new tradition; both the solitary thinker and the energetic correspondent and dedicated friend.

I have in these ruminations exhibited two undeniable facts about women who write about ethics – that they often see fit to discuss the writings of non-feminists and of men, and that they are usually interested in more than ethics. For ethics refuses to stay neatly in the bounds of, say, the personal as contrasted with the political, or the practical as contrasted with the theoretical. Moral psychology spills over into metaphysics, as moral commit-ment does into political action. Descartes' philosophy of mind is scarcely separable from his ethics. In *The Human Condition*, Arendt merges philosophy of action, ethics, politics, and history of science, and that was one reason why I found her so stimulating, and why I chose to focus in this chapter on that book of hers. And a striking feature of that book is the way she takes up and trans-forms the ideas of male thinkers from Aristotle to Marx, from Augustine[41] to Heidegger. Feminists could well take up and emend her ideas.[42] We women whose voices are joining those of others in contemporary ethics will often choose to try to transfig-ure old ideas, to divest them of their anti-feminist or excessively masculinist aspects, to indulge in a bit of philosophical transvest-ism, as well as to try out androgyny, and to invent new styles. Ethics is a polyphonic art form, in which the echoes of the old voices contribute to the quality of the sound of all the new voices.

[41] Arendt's doctoral dissertation was on Augustine's views about love. It was published in Germany in 1929: *Der Liebesbegriffe bei Augustin: Versuch einer Philosophischen Interpretation* (Berlin, 1929). It was translated into English in 1966 by E. B. Ashton, entitled *Love and Saint Augustine: An Essay in Philosophical Translation* (unpublished).

[42] Seyla Benhabib seems to be doing just this. See her 'Judgment and the Moral Foundations of Politics in Arendt's Thought', *Political Theory*, 16 (February 1988), pp. 29–51, 'Hannah Arendt and the Redemptive Power of Narrative', *Social Research*, 57 (Spring 1990), pp. 167–96, and *The Reluctant Modernism of Hannah Arendt* (London, 1996).

12

❖❖

Common understanding
and individual voices

❖❖

RAIMOND GAITA

Some experiences are common to all human beings. They are responses to what R. F. Holland called the 'big facts' of human life – our mortality, our sexuality, our vulnerability to suffering, and so on. The commonness of these experiences is thought to transcend culture, even though different cultures make different things of them. Some people believe that acknowledgment of them includes a sense of common humanity that implies a sense of fellowship. It sometimes includes the thought, often voiced outside of philosophy, that human beings are at bottom the same, and that were we fully to acknowledge it, then that would of itself place certain ethical limits on our conduct. George Orwell expressed it when he said, in order to explain why he could not shoot an enemy soldier who was running holding up his trousers, 'I had come here to shoot at "Fascists", but a man who is holding up his trousers is not a "Fascist", he is visibly a fellow creature, similar to yourself, and you do not feel like shooting at him.'[1] Simone Weil expresses a similar, but stronger, thought when she says that if one recognises a person being as a perspective on the world, as one is oneself, then one could not treat that person unjustly.

This chapter explores what is involved in seeing others as

[1] George Orwell, 'Looking Back on the Spanish Civil War' in *Orwell, Collected Essays, Journalism and Letters*, ed S. Orwell and I. Angus (Harmondsworth, 1970), vol. II. Cora Diamond has a fine discussion of this and related matters in her 'Eating Meat and Eating People' in *The Realistic Spirit* (Cambridge, Mass., 1991). I am indebted to her discussion.

sharing with us experiences of a kind which might underpin our sense of what it means seriously to wrong them. Misunderstanding of this generates the wrong kinds of tensions between the full acknowledgment of the plurality of peoples and their cultures and the legitimate hopes for a universal ethics, and connected with that, between ethical truth and the cultural determination of ethical value. At fault is a particular conception of thought and its relation to feeling. My argument furnishes some reasons for believing that had philosophy been more attentive to the understanding of life offered by literature rather than by science or metaphysics, then we would be better able to cope with the tensions generated by the acknowledgment that thought about life and morality is inescapably *in medias res*, and the aspiration to a universal ethic based on a sense of the commonness of human experience. This argument implicitly speaks to concerns that are germane to contemporary theoretical movements including new historicism, post-colonialism and cultural studies.

I

Imagine a white woman who is grieving over her dead child. With apologies to Iris Murdoch, I shall call her 'M'. She is watching television where she sees a documentary on the Vietnam War which shows the grief of Vietnamese women whose children were killed in bombing raids. She responds as though acknowledging their shared suffering. She then says: 'But it is different for them. They can simply have more.' That remark could mean different things in different contexts. Coming from her it was a racist remark of a kind I trust is easily recognisable. She does not mean that whereas she was sterile they were not (or anything of that kind). Nor does she mean that as a matter of fact Vietnamese tend to have many children. She means that they could replace their dead children more or less as we replace dead pets.

We would misunderstand M's sense of the difference between herself and the Vietnamese women if we thought of it by analogy with the sensations and their relative degrees – if we thought, for example, that her response expressed a belief of the same kind as the belief that the Vietnamese could not have toothaches as painful as 'we' do. She need have no doubts that they do. Her sense of difference centres in how she conceives what suffering may *mean* to the Vietnamese; on how she conceives that it may go deep with them; indeed, on whether she finds it intelligible that it can go deep with 'them'.

We say that some individuals have rich inner lives and that others have poor ones. Sometimes we speak as though some people are irredeemably shallow. But we make such judgments, justly or unjustly, about individuals. M responded to the Vietnamese mothers as to a *kind* whose membership is (necessarily) indeterminate, but which is interdefining with a sense of herself and her kind.[2] She did not see in the Vietnamese mothers inner lives of any depth, but not because of anything she saw or failed to see in them as individuals. As I said, hers is a racist response. She might have gone on to say 'They breed like rabbits', meaning not that, as a matter of fact, they tend to have many children, but that children and all that is involved in having them and caring for them cannot mean to 'them' what it does to 'us'. She responds to the Vietnamese mothers as to a kind distinguished from 'us' because she finds it unintelligible that the meaning of anything they do and suffer could go deep.[3] 'Their' children are replaceable. 'Ours' are not. To be sure, she will admit that some of us – the shallow ones amongst us – act as though their children are replaceable. They may actually have more as though one could 'simply have more', but unlike the Vietnamese, they can be called upon to rise to the potentiality which they have for something deeper.[4] Indeed, that is the conceptual condition of their being judged to be shallow. *She does not judge the Vietnamese mothers to be shallow. She responds to them as being outside of the space of possibilities which gives sense to judgments of depth and shallowness.*

Between M and a Vietnamese mother whose child had been

---

[2] It is necessarily indeterminate because the determination of kind is, as the jargon now has it, 'response-dependent'.

[3] I do mean 'unintelligible'. It is unintelligible in the sense in which it is unintelligible that someone who looked to us like the Black and White Minstrel caricature of an African–American face could be cast to play Othello. That face could not express the depth of feeling attributed to Othello, any more than could faces that all look alike to us.

[4] Unless, of course, they are incapable of it because, they are, for example, mentally deficient. But then, they are one of us, contingently incapacitated, the victims of ill fortune. However, in M's eyes, the Vietnamese are not contingently unable to rise to the requirements internal to the inner life. That is a reason for saying that in 'them' it is not an incapacity in the same sense in which it is an incapacity in 'one of us' who is the victim of an illness or an accident or a genetic defect, etc.

killed, there could be no serious discussion about death, about sexuality, or about motherhood. Neither could call upon the other to make herself adequate to what she is trying to fathom in her grief. Dostoyevsky prayed that he would be deserving of his sufferings. If M could find it intelligible that Vietnamese mothers could do the same, then she would no longer say, 'It's different for them.' The examples I have given of what lies beyond discussion for M and the Vietnamese – motherhood, sexuality, death, grief – are obvious ones. As soon as one reflects on what they imply, it is evident that it includes virtually everything that we would discuss in response to the questions about life's meaning, or to the question, 'How should one live?'

II

The gulf that M perceives to exist between herself and the Vietnamese is as radical as the gulf she perceives to exist between them and animals. The reasons are similar. Animals are incapable of reflection and she responds to the Vietnamese as though they were incapable of reflection of the kind necessary for them to have inner lives such as she unhesitatingly attributes to 'us'. Nonetheless, M readily attributes to the Vietnamese all the capacities and properties on the basis of which many moral theorists construct their accounts of morality – of its content and, more importantly, of what it is for something to be of moral concern. She attributes to them all that we commonly find in lists of what are the necessary and sufficient conditions of being a person – first- and second-order desires, interests, self-consciousness, rationality, and such things. She attributes to them all that contract theorists usually invoke in theories about the rules of conduct that they claim would rationally be negotiated in a state of nature or under a veil of ignorance. And she attributes to them all that is invoked in reductive theories of the virtues that conceive the virtues as means to the achievement of ends that can be described independently of them.

If that is true, it shows what we take for granted when we accept such theories as serious candidates for an account of the moral life. It seems that we do not notice what sets the stage for their acceptance. The point, applied now to ethics, is one made many times in other contexts by Wittgenstein. Just as we do not notice what sets the stage for certain performances (standing in front of an object, pointing to it and uttering a sound, for example) to count as naming an object, so we do not notice what sets the stage for our taking a negotiated rule or principle, or a disposition of character, to be the kind we call 'moral' – for it to have the *kind* of significance in our lives to justify our calling it that.

The ethical theorists I have in mind as having failed to see what sets the stage for their pre-theoretical sense of the ethical phenomena they theorise are naturalists of a reductionist disposition. It has been objected against them – rightly in my opinion – that one cannot fully explain the nature of ethical seriousness by elaborating on our interest, desires, on human good and harm. The reason is that those interests, desires, and conceptions of human good and harm are themselves conditioned, at levels that count, by the ethical perspectives they are intended to explain. What we take to be our interests, or what we count as good and harm, is often determined by our ethical outlooks. We cannot – the claim continues – build from the characterisation of forms of human good and harm which can be characterised independently of any ethical perspectives, to the ethical perspectives that redescribe their significance for us. Thus, for example, it is argued that there is no way of moving from the acknowledgment of the importance of death that may be expected from any human being, irrespective of his or her ethical perspective, to the ethical perspective in whose light we attribute particular meanings to death. Or, to put the point in terms of my example: we cannot build from what M attributes to the Vietnamese to the ethical/spiritual perspective in whose light Dostoyevsky prayed to be worthy of his sufferings.

Officially, the reductionist theories grant – to rational negotiators in a state of nature, for example, or to a sceptic who is demanding an external justification of morality – only what M attributes to the Vietnamese. However, no theory can build from such materials a bridge to span the distance between the Vietnamese as M perceives them and her perception of 'us'. No theory can generate from such materials that sense[5] of what it means to wrong one another that M finds unintelligible to apply to what

---

[5] Strictly speaking, it is those 'senses' of what it means to wrong one another, which, though different, clearly belong to one side of a divide on whose other side fall the Vietnamese. Thus the ancient Greeks are on one side with the Christians and Jews, the Vietnamese are on the other.

'we' do to 'them' or to what 'they' do to one another. Her un-hesitating application of it to what they might do to us and to what we might do to one another is a critical part of what defines 'us' against 'them'. A certain fellowship is constituted by those who unhesitatingly find it intelligible that its members may be wronged in a sense that M cannot apply to what 'we' might do to the Vietnamese. That fellowship defines the constituency to which reductive naturalists apply their ethical theories, while not notic-ing all that has gone into making it *that* constituency. That consti-tuency and fellowship are assumed by all moral theories that take as the pre-theoretical phenomena those deeds, relationships, and experiences that M attributes to us but denies to the Vietnamese. Reductionists assume it no less than do non-reductionists, but their theories cannot account for it. That is the first of the philo-sophical implications of my example.

The second is still more interesting. M's finding it unintelligible that the Vietnamese could take an attitude to their sufferings of the kind Dostoyevsky expressed shows the gap between reduc-tive forms of naturalism and an adequate account of the ethical and its embeddedness in our unmoralised sense of the meaning of our lives. Her incredulity at the suggestion that grief could go deep with the Vietnamese is interdependent with her sense that 'we' cannot wrong 'them' as we wrong one another. If it is also true that she can attribute to them all that reductive naturalists believe is necessary to explain the nature of morality, then the trouble with reductive forms of ethical naturalism is not merely that they are reductive of the ethical. Another trouble, just as serious – and perhaps more surprising – is that they look to be reductive of our inner lives, insofar as we take them to be of the kind M thought to define herself and her kind, but found unintel-ligible to attribute to the Vietnamese.

One way of putting that point would be to say that we have reason to suspect that reductive forms of naturalism presuppose a reductive moral psychology. That means more than that they fail to see the ethically conditioned nature of many of the morally salient psychological concepts. To be sure, that is one way of being reductionist, but objections to it are, after all, just variations on the claim that such reductionism is attractive only to those who fail to see that the concepts of good and harm, interests and desires and so on, are ethically conditioned. The more interesting thought is that in addition to acknowledging the ethically conditioned character of many of our psychological concepts, an adequate account of morality – be it naturalist or otherwise – must avoid presupposing a reductionist sense of the psychological phenomena that are not explicitly morally conditioned, and which may even be in conflict with morality. Morality is *sui generis*. But so are many of the phenomena that make up our inner lives. Neither morality nor our inner life – the life of the soul – are reducible to what M attributes to the Vietnamese. An adequate moral psychology will, therefore, protect morality from reduction to the psychological. But just as importantly, it will also protect or inner lives from morality and from a reductive conception of the psychological. The threat from morality is a moralistic conception of it. The threat from psychology is a conception of morally salient psychological phenomena as intrinsically suited to investigation by forms of inquiry which, in the name of what is genuinely cognitive, strive always to separate cognitive content from emotive form. I shall concentrate on this threat from psychology to morality and to our inner life.

III

I said that M could not find it intelligible that the Vietnamese could be wronged as 'we' could be. That claim depends on two natural assumptions which people often express in responses to this example. The first is that our sense of what it means seriously to wrong someone depends on a sense of what human beings may mean to one another which is not wholly or explicitly moral. It is true and important that we show what human beings mean to us when we honour our obligations, or when we feel remorse for what we have done to them. But we also show it when we love them and grieve for them. The second is that what human beings mean to one another is crucially determined by the fact that we acknowledge them to be unique and irreplaceable in ways that cannot be captured by their individuating features, and in ways that determine our sense of what it means to wrong them.

Natural though those assumptions are, they are philosophically controversial. Kantians, for example, are unlikely to accept them. However, the plausibility of what I have thus far claimed to be the lessons of my example should make us suspicious of their reasons. Those reasons depend on the belief that our sense of the nature and authority of morality is independent of our sense of the meaning of our lives, as that meaning emerges, in crucial part, from reflection on our inner lives. Some of the appeal of Kant's contrast between categorical imperatives and imperatives resting on 'inclination', depends on it. Recall the rhetorical importance of his appeal to the person whose inner life was poisoned by grief and bitterness, but whose capacity to do deeds, motivated by the categorical imperative – deeds which would 'shine like a jewel' – was in no way diminished. If all of what Kant called 'inclinations' were states and dispositions no different from those M could recognise in the Vietnamese, it would not affect his account of the nature of morality. Yet, in my example we see immediately that M's denigratory sense of the possibilities of grief in the lives of the Vietnamese women is the reason we know that she could not find it intelligible that they could be wronged as she and her kind can be. It is because 'they can have more' whereas we cannot, and all that that implies.

What kind of 'cannot' does M mean when she says, 'we cannot simply have more'? Some of its nature and its relation to her 'we' will emerge if we note the fact that it would not be undermined if she were 'simply to have more'. The scope of that 'we' is unaffected by the fact that some of 'us' do what she says we cannot do. Those who do will betray their superficiality, but as I have already noted, for M the Vietnamese are not within the conceptual space of such a judgment. That will raise the suspicion that I should have said that M really thinks 'we' *can* have more, just as 'they' can, but 'we' *ought* not to. I think that suspicion is ill-founded. The 'cannot' here functions much as it does in moral contexts ('Here I stand; I can do no other') where we have reason to believe that it expresses something different from anything that 'ought' can express.

When M protests that she cannot (just) have more, she does not merely report an incapacity. She protests against the radically demeaning suggestion that she is like the Vietnamese (as she sees them). That 'cannot' defines an essential dimension of her identity. The suggestion that she could, but ought not to have more children, separates from her inner life the judgment of what it would mean if she did, in ways that are false to the significance of that judgment for her identity.

Her sense of the difference between herself and the Vietnamese defines her identity in ways that do not allow for its separation from her responses to the 'big facts' of human life. Those responses define much of her inner life. Their nature is partly determined by the application to them of the distinction between their real and counterfeit forms. That enables us to speak of joy or grief or love 'going deep'. The fact that we distinguish the real from the counterfeit forms of our response to the big facts of life is internal to the character of the conceptual space from which M excludes the Vietnamese when she finds it unintelligible to attribute to them depth or shallowness of response as she unhesitatingly does to 'us'. But now – and this is one of the main points of this part of my argument – the impossibility she gives voice to when she says, 'We cannot (just) have more', is internal to those standards in whose light we judge the real from the counterfeit in our responses, feelings, and actions. If you really grieve, if your grief is fully informed by an understanding of what it means to lose a child, then you 'cannot just have more', in a sense of 'cannot' that implies that you will not. This would not be true if we substituted 'ought not' for 'cannot'. 'If you truly grieve then you will recognise that you ought not to have more' does not entail 'If you truly grieve then you will not have more.'

Bernard Williams has made a similar point about practical necessity, and argues that if someone says that they cannot ϕ, but they then ϕ intentionally, then they should retract that they could not ϕ. I think that is mistaken about practical necessity generally, and more so in the case of the kind of impossibility I am now discussing. When M says that 'they' can simply have more but 'we' cannot, she marks out kinds of human beings, but of course not only that. She is not embarked on an exercise in anthropology. Reflecting out of her own grief, she implies that she cannot do what 'they' can. She is saying that she is the kind of person whose inner life – as revealed in this case by her grief – is constituted by standards whose requirements are expressed in those modalities; that were she fully responsive to those standards, were she fully to understand all that they imply, then it would literally be impossible for her to have or even to wish to have more (just like that). That impossibility would mark the purification of her grief and, in ways that are interdependent, her full understanding of what it means to have a child. But that does not mean that if she does 'just have more' children, then she was wrong to say that she could not.

I can now press the point more strongly against the Kantians. It is plausible that the concept of practical necessity and of a value that is *sui generis* are what is retrievable from the idea of the categorical imperative once its conceptual difficulties have been fully appreciated. We have both in a non-reductionist account of the inner life as M denies it to the Vietnamese. I have already indicated how certain impossibilities and necessities are internal to our sense of what others mean to us. What M's child means to her is shown by the fact she cannot just have another one. I have also argued that what others mean to us is interdependent with the nature of many aspects of our inner life – the nature of our griefs, joys, sorrows, despairs, and so on. Our inner life as something *sui generis* is revealed in the fact that no elaboration on what she attributes to the Vietnamese can bridge the gulf between them and us. No such elaboration can of itself take M to the thought that grief can mean to them what it does to us. The point against the Kantians can now be put like this. The concepts that mark the inner life in which morality is embedded have modal features similar to those Kant reserved for morality. Yet whatever their relation may be to morality, love, grief, and joy are not themselves moral states. Nor are they 'merely psychological' phenomena, merely 'inclinations', insofar as the rhetorical force that 'merely' is achieved by contrasting these with the moral. That denigratory 'merely' depends either upon a sense of the inner life as adequately characterisable without reference to the kind of modality M expressed when she said 'we cannot have more', or on a sense of the strictly moral modalities as independent from them and from the inner life as structured by them.

IV

M thinks that grief cannot mean to them what it means to us. What do I mean here by 'meaning'? I intend to bring together the sense of meaning we invoke when we speak of the meaning of a word, and the sense of meaning we invoke when we mark the affective place of something in a person's life. To explain why, I must again turn to the important fact that the inner life is constituted by states whose nature requires us to distinguish between their real and their counterfeit forms.

I have already remarked that we would not call something love if it did not allow for the distinction between real and false forms of it. What this distinction between appearance and reality amounts to in its application to the inner life – how it differs from is application elsewhere, in, for example, science – is given in the critical vocabulary which tells us what it is to probe the appearances. That critical vocabulary tells us what it is to think well and badly about these matters, what objectivity and distorting forms of subjectivity, understanding, and truth come to here.

It also shows how and why we are required to be lucid about our inner lives under pain of superficiality. It is hard to imagine that anyone could be indifferent to whether what they feel is love or infatuation, grief or sentimental self-indulgence. Of course, for a variety of reasons we can imagine someone who does not want to think or talk about it. But it is of the nature of these states that they profess their authenticity, that they profess to be truthful and true. To grieve is to take oneself to be properly related to the reality of someone's death; to be related, that is, in a way that makes that grief true to ('correspond to' in 'tune with') that reality. When it is pure, grief is a form of relatedness to reality whose cognitive character is marked by the critical vocabulary that distinguishes real from false forms of it. Sentimental grief falsely professes what pure grief achieves. One can no more be indifferent to whether one's grief takes one to or away from reality than one can be indifferent whether one's beliefs are true or false. To believe something 'just' is to believe it to be true and oneself to be properly related to 'what makes it true'. And to grieve is to take oneself to grieve authentically, that is, in accord with the reality whose nature – and whose status as genuinely a form of reality – is revealed in the grammar of the critical concepts to which grief is answerable. However, unlike beliefs about whether the person actually is dead, which may innocently be false, the sentimental distortion of the meaning of death is always both false and untruthful in the sense that implies the lack of authenticity. That connection between truth and truthfulness is recorded in certain uses of concepts such as 'authenticity', 'authority', 'integrity' and 'sincerity'.

Reflection on the epistemic and critical use of those concepts reveals, I believe, that the requirement to be lucid about the reality of one's inner life is internal to the grammar of the critical concepts which mark good and bad thinking about it. Such reflection reveals how thinking here is necessarily engaged and necessarily personal. Those critical concepts mark the character of the thought once it is engaged; and also the need for engagement. The need for that engagement and its relation to the quality of the thought is, again, marked in the concepts authenticity, authority, integrity, and sincerity. These are not psychological or quasi-moral concepts that substitute for critical and epistemic ones. They are internal to the critical and epistemic concepts as they apply in thought about morality and the spirit. I think that is why Kierkegaard said (somewhat misleadingly, it must be acknowledged) that 'the subjective thinker' necessarily thinks passionately.

To see more clearly what is at issue here, consider the concept of sentimentality. A sentimental grief relates one falsely to the meaning of someone's death. To strive to avoid it is to strive to 'see things as they are', things which in this case are what and as they are only in a world of meanings which are partly constituted by our affective responses. In order properly to understand this we need to understand the two ways 'sentimentality' works as a critical concept.

The first is as a cause of failure in thought where that failure is measured on some other primary dimension of assessment that can be specified independently of sentimentality (the factually true or false, for example). I have elsewhere developed an example of a scientist whose colleagues say that his observations of the behaviour of animals are distorted by his sentimentality.[6] The case is such that it makes sense for one of his colleagues to say something like this: 'These claims have been made about the behaviour of dogs. They look to be false. Quite likely they are yet another expression of the old man's sentimentality. The language in which he presents his observations strongly suggests that. But that does not matter. I am not interested in whether he is sentimental. I am interested only in whether his claims are true or false. We can extract the cognitive substance of those claims from his emotive language and investigate them in a properly scientific manner.'

---

[6] See my *Good and Evil: An Absolute Conception* (London, 1991), ch. 15.

That makes sense. Here sentimentality is invoked as a causal explanation of why certain empirical claims are likely to be false and why such claims are characteristically entered. It functions in the same way as does appeal to tiredness or drunkenness, that is, as a cause external to the cognitive and epistemic grammar of the cognitive capacity it disables and to the thought it distorts. Such a conception often gives rise to (or may be the expression of) the idealisation of a thinker who would be unaffected by these failings, who would free himself or herself as much as is possible from the forms of life which generate such threats to the proper functioning of the mind. That yields one conception of objectivity; one conception of impersonal thinking; one model of the separation of form and content.

Consider now a quite different case which reveals the second way that 'sentimentality' functions as a critical concept. Suppose that someone is accused of being sentimental in her thoughts about what the death of a dog may mean. She believes that it is proper and (for her) obligatory to bury the dog in a dog cemetery, to erect a monument to it and each year to light a candle to its memory, and other things like that. Someone may judge that belief to be sentimental. Someone else who is unsure could hardly say, 'I don't care whether it is sentimental. I want to know whether it is true or false.' What could they be after? In this case sentimentality is not rightly thought of as the cause of thought's failure on a dimension that could be specified independently of sentimentality and similar afflictions. Its being sentimental is the primary form of its failure *as thought* . But that does not mean that only the first example yields a substantial conception of truth. It means that truth and falsehood amount to something different in these quite different cognitive domains. In a broad sense, both are examples of the bad effects of sentimentality on thought, but that broad sense accommodates a difference whose importance is of the first order. It is between those who believe that concepts like sentimentality are critical concepts that mark cognitive failures in their own right, and those who believe that they mark only emotional conditions external to thought, which sometimes hamper it and which sometimes facilitate it, but which are not themselves forms of it.

I said earlier that our understanding of the inner life was liable to distortion by a reductive moral psychology. I identified that impulse to reductionism as being a conception of psychological phenomena as intrinsically suited to forms of inquiry which separated the cognitive from the emotive content (as reductionists tend to see these). That impulse is often called *scientistic*. It can be that. But we may now see that scientism is the expression of a more general disposition which goes very deep in philosophy. It is the disposition to see thought about the inner life as answerable to an idealisation of thinking that treats sentimentality, pathos, et cetera, as merely the contingently disabling conditions of a cognitive function whose character can be specified independently of our vulnerability to them.

The being who occupies the Archimedean point, who sees the world as from no place within it, from God's eye-view, is an exemplary form of such idealisation. This being is, *ex hypothesis*, a being whose thought is not answerable to critical categories which are essentially conditioned by a particular way of living. Such idealised knowers cannot be sentimental, not because they are invulnerable to sentimentality, but because it makes no sense to attribute either sentimentality or its overcoming to them. This is evident when God stands in for the idealised thinker. But whether one speaks here of God's eye-view, or merely of the view from nowhere, the grammar of the conception is the same. The thoughts of such idealised thinkers are, so to speak, expressions of thinking as such, thinking as it is in its essence for any thinking thing that thinks perfectly. It is evident that insofar as this represents an idealisation of our cognitive and epistemic aspirations, it assumes that the content which is common to us and these idealised thinkers is one whose cognitive character can be extracted from those forms of expression that mark particular forms of life – in our case, the natural languages shaped by, and which give shape to, our lives as human beings.

V

There are, then, many ways of seeing things as they are, many forms of objectivity. The differences show in the critical vocabularies which give substance to those differences – substance both to the fact that these are real differences, and substance to their being really forms of understanding, of seeing things as they are. It is an interesting fact about the critical vocabulary that applies to the meaning of what we do and suffer that it is predominantly negative. I have mentioned some of its terms: sentimentality, banality, jadedness, pathos, naïveté and so on. Misunderstanding of the significance of that fact sustains the common misrepresentation of the nature of those critical concepts as causes external to understanding and which interfere with its proper workings. The same misunderstanding leads to the denial that these critical concepts really mark forms of thought, and it therefore leads also to the denial that they are interdependent with a substantial conception of truth. In that case, emotivism will seem to give a plausible account of them.

The tendency to take what I have been saying as a form of emotivism that will not declare itself is strengthened by the fact that the concepts which mark the overcoming of sentimentality, pathos, jadedness, and so on are, as I have put it elsewhere, essentially personal; they are, as Charles Taylor puts it, 'personally indexed'. We speak here of finding one's own voice, or of having something to say, or of the need to speak for oneself; and we speak of these in ways that suggest that form and content cannot be separated. I have already canvassed reasons that support that suggestion. I shall now try to explore more deeply how this connects to the necessarily personal nature of thought about the appearances and realities of the inner life. I want to make clearer how it connects with M's finding it unintelligible that the Vietnamese could be wronged as we wrong one another.

The personal character of thought about morality and about the inner life is reflected in the fact that there can be no expertise about these matters. If we are accused of being sentimental in our grief, and if we are unsure whether the accusation is justified, we cannot delegate thought about it to an expert, asking him or her to deliver a conclusion, or even the main options, no later than Monday morning. We can no more do this than we can delegate thought about our moral dilemmas to an expert ethicist, with the same request, that he or she have a range of options, no later than first thing Monday morning. These scenarios are parodies of what it is to think seriously about such matters.[7]

The point, however, is not that we must *decide* these matters for

---

[7] For further discussion see ibid., ch. 14, and 'The Personal in Ethics' in D. Z. Phillips and Peter Winch, eds., *Wittgenstein: Attention to Particulars* (London, 1989).

ourselves. That is true of all practical matters, but it is not true of all practical matters that we cannot delegate thinking about them to experts. On the contrary, we can and do, and when we do it legitimately, we *can* say that we want solutions or at least a range of options by Monday morning. Of course we must decide whether to accept the recommendations. And it is a truism that no on can make our decisions for us. But the lesson of my parodies is not that practical problems are personal because decisions are necessarily personal. It is that we must think them through for ourselves, and that means more than reviewing for ourselves the deliverances of the experts and deciding amongst them. None of this means that we cannot seek advice, and that we cannot rightly judge some advice to be wise and some to be foolish, true or false. It means only that the epistemic grammar of the concepts of wisdom and foolishness is quite different from that of the concepts of expertise and inexpertness, competence and incompetence, and that is reflected in the grammar of 'true' and 'false' as they apply here. I think that this is what Kierkegaard meant when he said (again misleadingly) that for the 'ethical thinker', 'truth is subjectivity'.

Kierkegaard was mistaken, however, in thinking that an acknowledgment of the personal nature of moral thought, and of thought about the inner life, should lead to an idealisation of the solitary thinker. Indeed, such idealisation distorts the personal character of moral and spiritual thought. It also distorts our understanding of one of the most important facts about the epistemic character of thought about our inner lives and about morality – that we often learn by being moved by what others say and do.

We learn from what moves us because its epistemic authority is inseparable from the fact that it moves us. That means that we cannot always extract from its form the cognitive content of what moves us. I hope that it is now clear why. Reflection on the authority of what moves us reveals the dependence of our sense of that authority on concepts like authenticity, integrity, sincerity, and so on, as they apply to those who move us and to ourselves as critically responsive to them. And, as I argued, that same reflection reveals that we cannot assess whether we have been rightly moved by appeal to a conception of reason whose constitutive categories may be specified independently of our vulnerability to being wrongly moved (because we are sentimental, or tone deaf to banality and so on).

To be critically true to what moves us is to be properly responsive to the disciplined individuality of the Other as he or she is present in the speech or actions that move us. To speak here of the Other as present to us in ways that are internal to the authoritative force of what he or she has said or done, is to say that that authority and our critical acceptance of it is necessarily personal. It is a way of expressing the truism that something moves us to the extent that it 'speaks to us'. Something speaks to us insofar as we hear in it the disciplined individuality of its speaker. But of course, in rising to that, in responding to what moves me, I must acknowledge and submit to those same individualising disciplines which made the Other authoritatively present in his or her words or deeds and which gave them their 'voice'. There is only one way to do that. It is by submitting to the disciplines marked in the critical categories that determine what it is to be rightly moved. This is true whether we think in the presence of what moves us or in remembrance of it. No serious thought about the ethical can escape this kind of embeddedness *in medias res*. If I am right, then the public character of that thought is best conceived as an engagement between the first and second person, rather than between the first and third. To put the point in the idiom of a philosopher who was one of the first to see this and who has been much misunderstood: in responding properly to what moves me, I must make myself I to someone's Thou. That is an essential part of what determines the common-ness of the conceptual space from which M excluded the Vietnamese.

VI

Peter Winch, commenting on an argument of Stanley Cavell, said that 'treating a person justly involves treating with seriousness his own conception of himself, his own commitments and cares, his own understanding of his situation and of what the situation demands of him'. I have tried to show what is necessary for someone to be an intelligible object of such serious attention. I have argued that it is to be seen – as M cannot see the Vietnamese – as someone who is capable of an increasingly deepened under-

standing of his or her inner life, that is, of his or her 'own conception of [his or her] own commitments and cares . . .' et cetera.

We are now better placed to understand what Orwell meant
when he said, 'I had come here to shoot at "Fascists", but a man
who is holding up his trousers is not a "Fascist", he is visibly a
fellow creature, similar to yourself, and you do not feel like
shooting at him', and to understand Simone Weil's remark that if
we see someone as a unique perspective on the world just as we
are, then we could not treat that person unjustly. Clearly when
Weil speaks of a unique perspective on the world she does not
mean a distinct centre of consciousness in any sense that M will
acknowledge the Vietnamese to be. To be 'a unique perspective of
the world' is to be a form of subjectivity whose character is
determined by its being a perspective on the world of meanings.
The nature of that perspective and its kind of uniqueness is
revealed by the requirement of individuality as we find it in the
critical grammar that tells us what it is to think well or badly about
that world, and which is interdependent with the concepts with
which we mark its reality. World and subject are mutually con-
stituting under the individualising critical and epistemic disciplines which determine both the nature of that subjectivity which
is a 'unique perspective on the world', and the kind of intersubjectivity which makes it a common world. That being so, there is no
flat answer to the question, 'Is the common world of meanings
discovered, or is it invented?'

It has been the burden of much of my argument that one form of
the ambition to construct a universal ethic on the basis of experiences that all human beings have in common rests upon an
unreflective and impoverished conception of experience. It takes
for granted the conditions that make possible the distinction between the real and the apparent as that distinction partially defines the experiences which would make that ambition plausible,
while officially giving no place to those conditions and the kind of
thinking required to distinguish reality from appearance.

Nonetheless it is true that our common response to 'the big
facts' of human life is central to ethics. Much reflection which is in
a broad sense ethical or spiritual and much of our art and literature centres on the ways our responses to those facts enter our
sense of common humanity – a commonness that is marked by the
'we of fellowship'. That sense of a common humanity conditions

the conceptual space within which we converse with one another about what it means to live a human life. The relation of M to the Vietnamese helps us to see what is right and what is wrong here. On the one hand, the gap between them shows the inadequacy of any universalism that rests on what I previously called a reductive naturalism, that is on an ethical theory which thinks that it can get by with no more than M attributes to the Vietnamese. On the other hand, the dependence of that very gap on a sense of the commonness that defines her sense of 'us' against 'them' shows what is right. The sense of commonness that underlies Orwell's response, or Simone Weil's remark, is the one through which M defined herself and others of 'us' as fully moral beings. However, nothing in the nature of that opposition requires that there should always be some human beings who are treated as 'them'. We appear to acknowledge this when we say, colloquially but not as naïvely as many philosophers would suggest, that M fails fully to see the Vietnamese as human beings.

This lies behind some of what we mean when we speak of human beings and mean more than that they belong to the species *Homo sapiens*, but less than is implied in its morally driven uses ('What a human being!'). It lies behind what we mean when we speak of a shared humanity against whose background we understand one another. The ancient Greeks marked it when they spoke of human beings as The Mortals. They made death our common destiny rather than merely our common destination by speaking of it, in many ways, in the accents of pity. Something similar is expressed in the beautiful words of the prayer for the dead in *The Book of Common Prayer*: 'Man that is born of woman hath but a short time to live and is full of misery. He cometh up and is cut down like a flower. He fleeth as it were a shadow and never continueth in one stay.' The phrase 'the human condition', when it marks a difference from 'human nature', carries similar resonances.

Countless other examples could be given. Their philosophical interest lies in the distinction they implicitly express between a sense of common humanity defined by a sense of fellowship, but which is not morally driven, and the merely classificatory acknowledgment that we are all members of the species *Homo sapiens*, or all members of the species *Homo sapiens* who have what it takes to be moral agents. A critical difference lies in the role acorded to sympathy. One view takes sympathy as a motive for action, either directly, or as mediated by a sense of fellow feeling, and it sees sympathy as an affective state external to the characterisation of what it responds to – our mortality, our vulnerability, for example. The other view, which I have been trying to characterise, takes sympathy to be internal both to the concepts which characterise what we share, our common world, and those concepts through which we explore that common world in ever-deepening ways.

Index

Index

forgiveness, 253–8 *passim*
Foucault, Michel, 202
Fowler, Roger, 202
Frank, Arthur, 181n
Freadman, Richard, 16
Freud, Sigmund, 178
Frye, Northrop, 54n

Gadamer, Hans-Georg, 11, 36
Gaita, Raimond, 22, 29, 30, 35, 36
Galileo, 264
Gaugin, Paul, 154–5
Geertz, Clifford, 28
Glover, Jonathan, 64n
Goffman, Erving, 167, 168
Gold, Joseph, 53n
Goldberg, S. L., 12
grief, 270, 271–1, 276, 277, 278, 279

Habermas, Jürgen, 16, 36
Haines, Simon, 88
Hampshire, Stuart, 22, 27–8
Hardy, Barbara, 53n
Hardy, Thomas, 90, 97
Hare, R. M., 21, 26, 27, 59–60, 62, 63
   and fiction, 40–2, 46, 57
Harpham, Geoffrey G., 8
Hass, Robert
   Human Wishes, 118–23, 124
Hawkins, Anne Hunsaker, 181n
Hazlitt, William, 37, 38
Heaney, Seamus, 99, 101–2
Hegel, G. W. F., 68, 77, 78
Heidegger, Martin, 2, 36, 37, 71, 254,
   257n, 263
Hejinian, Lyn, 119, 127
Held, Virginia, 252
Hemingway, Ernest
   A Farewell to Arms, 145, 152
   For Whom the Bell Tolls, 145
   Islands in the Stream, 154–5
   A Movable Feast, 134, 136, 138–56,
      158–60
   The Old Man and the Sea, 137
   The Sun Also Rises, 148
Higgs, Roger, 182n
Hobbes, Thomas, 213n, 215
Holland, R. F., 269
Holquist, Michael, 15
humanism, 35, 36, 72
Hume, David, 27, 80n, 195, 260, 266
Hynes, Samuel, 50n

idealism, 37, 81
identity, 16, 68, 82, 101, 107, 121, 129,

161, 167, 171, 260, 261–2, 277
   relational, 169, 171, 173–4, 175, 176,
      179, 180, 196
   social, 79, 81
Ignatieff, Michael, 196
illness narrative, 181–3, 184–5, 189
   and ethical/moral issues, 185, 188,
      190–7
imagination, 41, 44, 45, 52, 53, 54, 55,
   66, 80–1, 90, 99, 104, 106, 108, 109,
   114, 115, 223, 224, 225, 234–5, 239,
   240, 246
inner life, 74, 271, 275, 276, 277, 278,
   279, 280, 283, 284, 286
institutions, 206, 207, 208, 209, 210–11
intuition, 10–11, 186

James, Henry, 50, 51, 86, 93–6, 116, 117,
   142, 179
   The Ambassadors, 53, 97, 117
   The Europeans, 52n
   Golden Bowl 41, 43–4, 54, 188
   The Portrait of a Lady, 97, 98
   What Maisie Knew, 96
James, William, 81
Jameson, Frederic, 1, 5–6
Jaspers, Karl, 254, 257n
Johnson, Barbara, 8, 13
Johnson, Samuel, 37, 104, 107, 189

Kant, Immanuel, 11, 31, 57, 136, 207,
   267n, 275–7, 278
Keats, John, 99–101, 102, 103, 104, 105,
   106–7
Kermode, Frank, 34
Kierkegaard, Søren, 68, 69, 71, 280, 284
Kleinman, Arthur, 181n
knowingness, 51–2, 100, 101
Krieger, Murray, 14
Kristeva, Julia, 8

language, 7, 8, 9, 26, 60–1, 64, 90, 204,
   206, 208, 238
   of literature, 29–30, 240–1
   moral language, 26, 27, 28–9, 30, 94,
      116
   philosophy of, 22, 62
   and self, 21, 22, 30
Lawrence, D. H., 104–5
Leavis, F. R., 53n
Leder, Drew, 197–8
Lejeune, Philippe, 170, 179
Lerner, Gerda, 190–1
Levinas, Emmanuel, 9, 68–9, 80
literary canon, 5

Index

literary theory, 2–3, 4–5, 7, 29–30, 33, 201, 203, 205, 212, 213–14
literature, 2, 6–7, 8, 12–13, 15, 30, 35, 84, 86–8, 90, 92, 98, 103, 105, 205, 206–7, 208, 211, 212, 224, 287
   see also moral philosophy; novels; poetry
loss, 60, 63, 91, 159
love, 117, 122, 142–8, 153, 160, 268
Lukacs, John, 165

Machiavelli, Niccolò, 213n
MacIntyre, Alasdair, 12, 13, 14, 16, 22, 23, 36, 194–5
Mackie, J. L., 11
Macklin, Ruth, 182n
Marshall, David, 80n
Marx, Karl, 263
Marxism, 5
Mattern, Ruth, 265
meaning, 8, 10–11, 36, 279, 286, 272, 274, 275
Meyers, Jeffrey, 148
Middleton, Thomas, 91
Miller, J. Hillis, 8, 13
Minter, David, 117n
Modernism, 50n
Moore, G. E., 21, 27
moral attention, 92–3, 95, 97–101 *passim*
moral consciousness, 114, 189
moral judgment, 28, 43–4, 45, 46, 48, 79, 115, 129, 133, 157, 221
moral luck, 135–6, 140–1, 142–4, 149, 154, 156–9, 160
moral perception, 93, 94–6, 97
moral philosophy, 9, 11, 12, 13, 21–3, 24, 31, 34, 36, 38, 62, 213
   and literary texts, 24, 39–64, 84–110, 113–18, 121, 186–7, 188, 270
   women in, 248
moral psychology, 52, 79, 274
moral thinking, 34, 57, 63, 213, 284
   and literary texts, 41, 44, 46–8, 50, 54, 55, 56, 59, 66, 87–8, 92, 100–1, 103–4, 105–6, 113–18, 129–33
moralism, 6–7, 213, 214
morality, 9, 23, 31, 33, 34, 36, , 5472, 92, 96, 108, 272, 274–7, 278, 280, 283, 284
   political, 213, 216, 221
   see also moral philosophy
muddle(ment)
   and literature, 94–7, 103, 109

Murdoch, Iris, 22–3, 24, 26, 27, 28–9, 30, 31, 35, 36, 40–1, 59, 84, 85, 86, 88, 93, 104, 108
Murphy, Robert F., 166

Nagel, Thomas, 2, 136, 137–8, 156–7
negative capability, 101, 103
Nietzsche, Friedrich, 2, 65, 67, 80, 83
novels, 41–2, 86–7, 105, 233–4, 236, 241–2
   individuals and types in, 40–1
   see also literature, particularity
Nussbaum, Martha, 12, 14, 16, 22, 30, 32, 33, 35, 39–64 *passim*, 84, 85n, 87, 92, 93–5, 99n, 102, 103, 105n, 113n, 116–17, 135, 145, 150, 186, 188, 197

objectivity, 37, 48, 282–3
Okin, Susan Moller, 16, 249, 250
Olafson, Frederick, 14
Onassis, Jacqueline Kennedy, 163, 165
O'Neill, Eileen, 265
Orwell, George, 269, 286
Other, the, 3, 5, 6, 77, 80, 81, 82, 127, 128–9, 130, 132, 133, , 145, 146, 278, 285

particularity, 40–1, 52–3, 56, 57, 58–63, 64, 188, 228
pathography
   see illness narrative
Peacock, Thomas Love, 38
perception, 89, 90, 91, 93, 192, 197, 235, 236, 273
philosophy, 23–4, 32, 55–6, 114
   feminist, 248, 249–51, 256
   of language, 25
   and order 87–9, 108–9
   women in 247, 252–6
   see also ethics, moral philosophy
Plato, 35
poetry, 30, 32, 37, 38, 48, 109, 113–33 *passim*, 207
political economy, 226, 228–32 *passim*, 238, 243–4
positivism, 12, 14
Posner, Richard, 227n
Post, Robert C., 166–7, 169
Pound, Ezra, 139
practical necessity, 277, 278
Pritchard, H. A., 21
privacy, 162–9, 173, 176–7, 185
Prosser, William, 164
Proust, Marcel, 63
Pynchon, Thomas, 38

Index

quality of life, 243–4
Quine, W. V. O., 22

Rachels, James, 168–9
Rapaport, Herman, 129n
rationality, 16, 30, 52, 223, 226
Rawls, John, 2, 249
reader, the, 44, 52, 54n, 67, 87, 98,
    102–3, 104, 106, 107, 109, 117,
    125, 224, 225, 233, 234, 239, 242,
    246
  reading, 99–100, 101, 105
reason, 11, 31, 32, 33, 44, 114, 234, 236,
    240, 241
Reiman, Jeffrey H., 162, 166, 168, 169
Remarque, Erich Maria, 50n
Reynolds, Michael, 148
Rilke, Rainer Maria, 123
Rorty, Richard, 11, 14–15, 23, 25, 114,
    125
Rose, Gillian, 184
Ross, David, 21
Ross, W. D., 197
Roth, Philip, 162
  Patrimony, 176–80, 188
Ruddick, William, 168
Rudner, Richard S., 61n
Ruhle-Gerstel, Alice, 255
Rybczynski, Witold, 165
Ryle, Gilbert, 28

Sacks, Oliver, 181n, 184
Sartre, Jean-Paul, 150, 194, 195
satiation, 140, 150
Saussure, Ferdinand de, 26
Scheman, Naomi, 266
Scott, Walter, 38
Seabright, Paul, 14
self, 3, 7, 13, 30, 31, 33, 34–6, 68, 69, 70,
    74, 77, 82, 105, 118, 119, 123, 125,
    126, 130, 131, 133, 140, 146, 150,
    151–3, 158, 162, 165, 169–70, 189,
    215, 230, 267
Shakespeare, 89, 91, 101, 106, 110
  Coriolanus, 86, 88
  Hamlet, 103
  Henry IV, Part One, 86
  King Lear, 107
  Macbeth, 98
  A Midsummer Night's Dream, 90
  Measure for Measure, 88
  Much Ado About Nothing, 90, 91
  Troilus and Cressida, 88
  Twelfth Night, 90
  The Winter's Tale, 91

Shelley, P. B., 38
Sidgwick, Henry, 230
Sidney, Philip
  A Defence of Poetry, 91–2, 103
Siebers, Tobin, 7, 14, 30
Smith, Adam, 80n, 240n
Socrates, 33
Sontag, Susan, 107–8
Spender, Stephen, 135
Spiegelman, Art, 171–2, 175
Spinoza, Benedict de, 260, 267n
Stead, Christina, 97
Steedman, Carolyn Kay, 162, 169–70,
    171, 175
Stevens, Wallace, 125n
Stevenson, C. L., 21, 27
Stinson, Peggy, 184, 185
Stinson, Robert W., 184, 185
Stocker, Michael, 249
Swift, Jonathan, 92
sympathy, 66–83 passim, 116, 182, 234,
    236, 288

Taussig, Michael, 183n
Tavernier-Courbin, Jacqueline, 139n,
    144n
Taylor, Charles, 9–10, 11–12, 13, 16, 22,
    23, 26, 28, 31, 86, 165, 283
Thompson, J. J., 248, 252, 253
Toker, Leonie, 14
Twain, Mark, 150

utilitarianism, 41, 72, 225–32 passim,
    237, 246
  utility, 244
universalism, 16, 49, 57, 67, 116, 287

Veach, Robert M., 182n
virtues, the, 11, 249, 272
Vonnegut, Kurt
  Slaughterhouse Five, 49–50

Warnock, Mary, 23, 195
Warren, Samuel D., 164, 165, 166, 167,
    168, 170
Weber, Ronald, 139n
Webster, John, 91
Wideman, John Edgar, 172–3, 175
Weil, Simone, 93, 94, 269, 286
Westin, Alan, 166
Whitehead, A. N., 264
Whitman, Walt, 54 f.n, 239
Williams, Bernard, 2, 12, 13, 22, 27, 28,
    31, 33, 34, 114, 116n, 118, 136, 154,
    156–7, 187, 277

Index

Winch, Peter, 285
Wittgenstein, Ludwig, 36, 38, 132, 266, 272
Wolf, Susan, 249
Wollheim, Richard, 43, 116n
Woozley, A. D., 58

Wordsworth, William, 58, 101, 102
  The Prelude, 42, 44–7, 49–54 *passim*, 105

Yeats, W. B., 38
Young, Robert, 162n